Praise for Marge Piercy and *Three Women*:

'Here is somebody with the guts to go into the deepest core of herself, her time, her history, and risk more than anybody else has so far, just out of a love for the truth and a need to tell it'
Thomas Pynchon

'Piercy writes with high intelligence, love for the world, ethical passion and innate feminism'
Adrienne Rich

'Marge Piercy can seat 15 strangers around a Thanksgiving table, and by the time dessert is served you'll know all of them'
New York Times Book Review

'If you enjoy a good character centred novel . . . then this book is definitely for you but be prepared and have a box of tissues on hand as it will tug on your heart strings remorselessly'
Irish News

'an insightful look at tangled emotional ties'
Red

'Marge Piercy's women leap off the pages and into the reader's imagination . . . A superbly written novel, thoughtfully told'
Choice

'. . . gripping . . . The various sub-plots are brilliantly interwoven in a nail-biting novel'
Jewish Telegraph

Marge PIERCY

Three Women

PIATKUS

Visit the Piatkus website!

Piatkus publishes a wide range of bestselling fiction and non-fiction, including books on health, mind, body & spirit, sex, self-help, cookery, biography and the paranormal.

If you want to:

- read descriptions of our popular titles
- buy our books over the internet
- take advantage of our special offers
- enter our monthly competition
- learn more about your favourite Piatkus authors

VISIT OUR WEBSITE AT: www.piatkus.co.uk

First published in Great Britain in 2000 by
Piatkus Books Ltd of
5 Windmill Street, London W1T 2JA
email: info@piatkus.co.uk

This edition published 2000

Reprinted 2001, 2003, 2004 (twice)

First published in the United States in 1999
by William Morrow and Company, Inc

The moral right of the author has been asserted

A catalogue record for this book is available from the British Library

ISBN 0 7499 3200 7

Printed and bound in Great Britain by
Mackays of Chatham Ltd, Chatham, Kent

For all those who are caught in the middle and pulled all ways
I dedicate this novel with love and respect

Three Women

1

Suzanne

Suzanne Blume finished up her day's lecture on the First Amendment in the cavernous auditorium and shook off the students who immediately surrounded her. She was the first woman ever to be permitted to teach constitutional law at the university, and she generally overprepared, as she overprepared everything from occasional holiday suppers with her daughters to every case she had ever taken on. But today she had no time for the students, as she had to get to her office and change from her university outfit of trim slacks, silk blouse, and blazer to her navy court suit, same blouse. Like every woman litigator she knew, she had a whole wardrobe of navy suits, gray suits, one daring one in charcoal. She took sheer panty hose from her middle drawer where she kept makeup for court, scarves for court, and dumped her dangling earrings. She kicked off her high-heeled boots and put on her pumps. At five foot three, she was too small for her role in the world. In spite of the backaches they gave her, she always wore heels in public.

Now she ran in them down the hall and to the parking lot. She had given the keys to her Toyota to her assistant, Jaime, and he had the car waiting at the door. He drove. She sat in the back reading her notes as he headed for downtown Boston. She would get there a little early for the afternoon session, but she would need time to run over her presentation. It was important never to appear to falter before the judges, but always to sound confident and a little diffident at once—especially as a woman.

She loved appellate work, because it was nice and tidy and controllable. It didn't offer the punch and zing of regular trial work, but she had started doing it when she still had the girls at home. It was scholarly, it was somehow soothing, points of law instead of Main Street at High Noon. It had its advantages and its drawbacks, but it wore less on her than trying cases. It demanded enormous meticulous preparation, which she customarily did in every case, but far less time in court: say, one morning as opposed to a month or several months. The power lines stood out quite clearly: she usually faced several white male judges from an upper-middle-class background in their archaic robes, operating from a view of the world she did not share but expected of them. The defendant was seldom present. Unless it was an exceptionally high-profile case, no reporters bothered.

"Can I come in to observe?" Jaime asked, breaking into her concentration.

"Park the car first." She thought for a moment. "Why not? It's good for you to observe. Just keep your mouth shut."

"Thanks, Suzanne. I'll never say a word."

He was a blend of American Black and Filipino, beautiful and wary, bright but overly sensitive. He was far from his family and had adopted Suzanne almost at once. She did not mind. She had only been teaching for the last twelve years, but in that time, she had acquired a hundred honorary offspring. Some fell in love with her, some were confrontational, some leaned, some whined, some flattered, but they all stayed in touch, and she remembered every one. Maybe she had done better with her academic children than with her blood children. Nowadays universities hired few lawyers with courtroom experience, but when she had been approached, she had already been involved with the university clinic—and the university was eager to hire a couple of women because of affirmative action.

She forgot Jaime as soon as she entered the courtroom. It was always that way: a case closed over her and she lived inside it. The appeal was on a murder conviction of a woman who had shot her ex-husband because she claimed he was abusing their daughter, of whom he had custody. He was a doctor. She was a laid-off librarian getting by on temporary office work. The question of the appeal of course was not whether she had shot her ex-husband, whether he had abused their daughter sexually, but rather if she had received adequate representation from the court-appointed counsel. Suzanne had amassed two good precedents and argument from the transcript. The prosecutor was the same one who had obtained the original conviction. She knew him well from her years of practicing: good but a little overaggressive. She began to review her brief in the half hour to forty-five minutes that would knock off the cases on the agenda before hers. At one point she noticed Jaime had slipped into a seat in the last row. What she remembered as she talked was the pale, drawn face of her client. She was taking this on pro bono. The woman had no money, and her family had exhausted its resources. She remembered too the girl Celia, terrified, placed in a foster home for the last year.

This was an appellate court and nowhere but in her mind would the faces of the convicted woman and her frightened daughter ever appear. Justice to Suzanne was about people, but here it was all about argument and precedent and the power of the judges. It was the law, questions of the law: these judges being male, like the lower court judge, should not be as much a problem as it had been in the original trial. It shouldn't bear so heavily upon the case that these judges would never willingly believe that a good professional man, a doctor of their own class, would discard his wife into poverty and make use of his own child sexually. No, she would only be arguing points of the law, but in her mind always she would know for whom she was fighting and why: the daughter, Celia; the mother, Phoebe, whom she had visited last Saturday at Framingham, the women's prison outside Boston. She could not make Phoebe understand that the judge would not hear arguments about whether her ex-husband had sexually abused her daughter, the act that had fractured Phoebe's world. Phoebe didn't understand, but it was not necessary that she should. Suzanne would win for her and get her back Celia. Ultimately Phoebe was right: that was the only thing that mattered. Suzanne was in her proper element, a legal fight, with the arguments marshaled in her memory like a row of soldiers ready to go into battle. The adrenaline sang in her muscles and in her mind. She remembered once taking her younger daughter Rachel to a presentation by a raptor specialist, when Rachel was eleven and impassioned by anything ecological. The woman had with her a hawk, hooded. As soon as everyone was settled, the lecturer removed the hood and the hawk gleamed into life, eyes glittering, looking for prey, eager for action. Fierce and utterly focused: that was what Suzanne felt like in court, that unhooded bird of prey. Finally it was her turn to rise and, in ten minutes, to present her case for appeal.

* * *

Suzanne was a morning person. Except when she was truly miserable, she snapped awake at six and viewed her day with determination and zest. She had a coffee maker on a timer, so that when she crossed the hall into the kitchen area of the enormous room on the east side of the house, she could already smell her morning cup. She loved things that took care of themselves automatically, like reminders on her computer. She took her coffee into the room that was now her study—it used to be her older daughter Elena's bedroom. There she turned on her computer, logged on to her provider, and began reading her messages.

She skimmed through them for a communication from Rachel. She had been having trouble getting Rachel on the phone. Her roommates in the Philadelphia apartment were always vague, and Rachel studied long hours with a group. It had taken a few messages back and forth for Suzanne to understand, for Rachel used Hebrew words for almost everything connected with rabbinical college. Thanks to Aunt Karla, Suzanne had been bat-mitzvahed, but she had long ago forgotten the Hebrew drummed into her. She wished she could follow her daughter farther down that road, wished she could understand half the time what Rachel was talking about. Suzanne was proud, for women had not been rabbis when she was a kid, but somehow becoming a rabbi was the last thing she had expected. Suzanne was modestly observant because her aunt Karla had raised her that way, for her childhood had been divided between her mother, Beverly, and Aunt Karla. Still, being a professional religious worker seemed to be overdoing it. At twenty-two she herself had given birth to Elena and nevertheless continued law school, so maybe Rachel was taking the better path. She would be a good rabbi, Suzanne was sure of it, understanding, committed, passionate, learned.

Rachel was as serious about rabbinical school as she was about everything, from rescuing frogs from science labs to protesting toxic waste dumping and being a vegetarian. Better that than the other way, Suzanne told herself, briefly thinking of her older daughter Elena. As far as Suzanne could figure out the message, Rachel was engaged in some obscure argument about halachah, Jewish law, having to do with caring for the bodies of the dead. So who was dead? The father Suzanne had never known had died out in California last year, but she had not even been informed in time to attend the funeral. She had received a letter from his widow two weeks after the cremation. Would she have gone anyhow? She had not even mourned for this man she could remember seeing only once face-to-face, awkwardly, when she was a skinny twelve-year-old with an attitude, and a year later on a platform giving a speech at a rally where Beverly, her mother—briefly his lover—was also speaking. It was perhaps the last Labor Day celebration she had ever attended. Labor Day belonged to her mother, Beverly. In her childhood it had meant that Mama was giving a speech and she was expected to march and sit and shut up, until later there would be a union picnic and lots of food, other kids, and maybe a swimming pool or a lake.

She wrote a vaguely encouraging note, unsure whether she should press Rachel to explain the debate or let it pass. She contented herself with worrying on the screen about Rachel's long hours studying. Was she sleeping enough? Was she eating regularly? When would she come home next?

An invitation to give a lecture on International Women's Day in Albany. She cited her fee and asked what they had in mind. Her legal listserv was full of discussion of a recent Supreme Court ruling on evidence. A university press requested she read a manuscript submitted to them on the changing law on domestic violence. She printed it out without replying. Interesting, but did she have the time? Maybe Marta would want to, as she had better credentials on domestic abuse, having helped write the current Massachusetts law.

She read quickly through her other messages, her friend Karen undergoing chemotherapy, her friend Alexa fighting for tenure, Celeste enduring a terrible divorce, Georgia just returned from Bali. She made herself answer everyone else before she opened Jake's morning message. They communicated almost daily, although they had never met. Jake lived in California, in the Oakland hills, a situation similar to hers: a house he co-owned with a couple, as Suzanne owned hers with her colleague Marta who lived upstairs with her husband, Jim.

Suzanne, Earthworks is thinking of opening a Boston office. We see a need to get involved in issues of water, land policies, and eroding protection of wetlands in the Northeast. I expect to be out there as soon as I can set up meetings with people who might work with us. Maybe two, three weeks. If we decide to open up an office in Massachusetts, I'd be running it—a big IF. Anyhow, here's a chance to get together finally and put faces on each other. I know I want to meet you in reality, and I hope you feel the same way. It could be fun.

That message she could not reply to. She felt as if she had started to sit down in a comfortable chair but someone had moved it as a joke.

She did not want to meet Jake in the flesh. A romance on the computer screen was one thing; a tête-à-tête with a forty-nine-year-old Suzanne was something else. She had not had an affair in twelve years, not since Elena's tragic mess. She had sworn off men then, meaning it to be a temporary measure so she could give all her personal attention to her daughters, but it had become easier and easier to stay uninvolved, until now it was terribly simple. Who chased a middle-aged woman? Not middle-aged men, certainly. So how had she gotten into this electronic flirtation? Because it was easy; because she liked the way he sounded; because it felt safe and yet frisky. She had checked him out when they first began electronic chatting, and mutual acquaintances gave him social clearance: not a weirdo, a sex offender, a stalker. Shit, she had told him things about herself she would never say to a real man, because Jake had been a fantasy, a figment of her imagination and her computer screen. Only a couple weeks ago, she had told him about an erotic dream involving her cat, Sherlock. Why had she done that? Because he was fictitious and yet self-animated. Not a man but a data stream.

She found herself pacing around her study and then the kitchen. From the counter where she fed them so she would not step on their tails while they ate, her two orange cats watched her, picking up her fear. Tamar flattened her ears and backed farther under the cabinet. Sherlock jumped down and rushed off suddenly as if remembering an appointment on the bay window ledge. She clutched herself muttering. She must stop this, for she was acting like an idiot!

One thing she worried about now that she lived alone was getting weird. One of the few advantages she could recognize of being in a relationship was that there was someone always there to act as a check, a balance, a counterweight. If she was paranoid or unobservant or projecting, the other would knock her back on course. After all, what law said she had to see Jake when he came to Boston? If he did invade her territory, she could say she was in Europe. In Australia. Sick with the flu. In New York visiting her mother, Beverly. She was not obligated to begin an affair just because she had been flirting with him for two years on the Internet. For all he knew, she had flirtations going with seventeen other men.

It had felt so very safe. She had told him things about her life and her feelings that she could not imagine sharing with a man sitting in the same room. She had male colleagues in the law school where she taught, on committees, in court. She had a decent relationship with Rachel's father, Sam, as long as they weren't in the same place for too long a time: they could handle about an hour safely. But she would never, never have started this long friendly flirtation if she had ever considered he might appear in front of her. It had felt totally disembodied, a meeting of two minds, an affair made of words alone. She began to remember some of those words. They had shared a fantasy that they were in Paris together, walking streets familiar to both of them. Climbing up among the strange stone houses of the dead in Père Lachaise, kicking up the autumn leaves. Eating crêpes at a pink restaurant way up on Montmartre with Paris stretching to the horizon. Competing in their knowledge and building up a map of their fantasy. He had taken her on a hike high into the Sierra Nevada. She had taken him into court with her, sharing the excitement of confrontation and victory, the desolation and guilt of loss. He had sent her diary entries from a trip to Greenland, on the ice field. She had watched condors take clumsy flight off a cliff in northern Arizona, released into new life in the wild.

The house she shared in Brookline was a large turn-of-the-century wooden structure painted pale blue with cobalt trim on the gingerbread and railings and window frames. She had the downstairs with spacious rooms and deep closets. Marta had the upstairs and the tiny third floor, under the sloping roof. When they had bought the house together twelve years before, it had been lived in forever by two sisters and a brother, strange wizened spinsters and bachelor who had collected salt and pepper shakers, model trains that ran all over the top floor, matchboxes, postcards, and a great deal of junk. She remembered Jim finding a box labeled *string too short to use*. The last sister had died and the heirs—distant cousins—put the house on the market as it was, full of dust and old clothes and worn rugs and battered furniture, candle ends, and mismatched crockery. It reeked of sad genteel survival. Marta, Jim, and she had put a great deal of money into the house, dividing it into two apartments with modern kitchens, inviting bathrooms, air-conditioning, up-to-date wiring, while keeping the fine old woodwork, the fireplaces, the stained-glass windows, and the encircling porch. Their house sat upon a high hill, on the curve of Addington Road, a street of occasional brick apartment houses, a few Victorians, some modern houses, and many frame structures about the same age as their own, usually on lots too small for the houses—like their own small backyard sloping downhill to the garage. She had moved to Brookline from the South End of Boston after Elena's disaster.

Jim, Marta's husband, was off at a therapists' convention. When Suzanne ran upstairs to Marta, her friend was sitting at the table in her old plaid flannel bathrobe reading an article in the *Yale Law Journal.* Marta waved her hand at the plate of muffins and the pot of coffee. "I haven't had breakfast," she realized. "His E-mail has really thrown me off course."

"Look, so he told you he might be coming. He may feel that's only polite. Maybe he's just as nervous as you are."

At night Marta always braided her gray blond hair, now hanging in two long plaits over the shoulders of her bathrobe. Suzanne liked the way Marta looked before she was dressed up for court, for meeting clients. Marta was far more elegant than Suzanne, taller, with prominent cheekbones. They had been friends since law school. They had worked out of the same Women's Law Commune in the late seventies and then gone into practice with their friend Miles. When they had bought the house together, Jim had still been teaching at Simmons. Now their children were out of the house—although Marta's son, Adam, and Suzanne's younger daughter Rachel still came home for school vacations.

"You think maybe Jake doesn't really care if we get together?"

"He may have doubts too. Why wouldn't he?"

"So maybe he won't press me."

"So maybe he won't." Marta grinned. "Will you be disappointed?" Marta was enjoying this conversation. In their long friendship, Marta had always been the volatile one; Suzanne was the more practical, the one who smoothed things over, the negotiator. Marta was deriving pleasure from seeing Suzanne discombobulated over a man, of all things. "Have you considered maybe you're just an excuse to stay over Saturday night so he can get a cheaper airfare?"

As they lingered over muffins and coffee, Suzanne regretted that she had not done her morning exercise routine. She would feel a little off her pace all day. Maybe if she got home at a reasonable time, she could make it up tonight. "I had one of those messages from Rachel that she knows I can't relate to. It's like she's rubbing my nose in it."

"You thought she'd go to law school."

"Well, why not?" Suzanne ran her fingers through her thick short hair, setting it on end. "She's bright, she has a good memory, and she's picked up a certain amount just by osmosis. Looks like we both failed to breed lawyers." Adam was studying film at NYU.

"Well, Suzanne honey, don't despair. Studying to be a rabbi is not quite like becoming a stripper. It's an honorable profession."

"Or a maître d'." Suzanne shook her head. "Don't get me started on Elena. In and out of four different colleges and now she seats people in a restaurant."

"Kids do what they can," Marta said. "The carpenter who's carrying out the renovations at Rackham, Klein and Forbes has a degree from Harvard. He was in computers. Now he makes cabinets." That was Marta's firm: she was the Klein.

"Time to hit the road. Classes, and then I meet my policewoman. Do you want to sit in?"

"Let me see how my day goes," Marta said. "I looked over what you gave me, and I think you can make a strong sexual harassment case— provided you get a decent judge. You don't know yet who you're going to pull?"

"Not yet."

"Knock 'em dead." Marta rose, and they went their separate ways into their separate days. Usually they touched base mornings and evenings. They were part of each other's support system. At times they had been the only support for each other. When Suzanne thought of getting old, of some dim future when she was emeritus at the university, she did not assume her kids would be around, but she always assumed Marta would be.

She decided she would reply to Jake tonight. She would just acknowledge his mention of a trip east and go on at some length about how busy she was now. That was a nice safe response and committed her to absolutely nothing—which was what she supposed she most desired.

2

Suzanne

Suzanne had just got back from court Thursday and was running a bath when Elena walked in, yelling from the living room, "Mother? Mother!"

"You startled me!" Suzanne cried, hastily pulling on her terry robe. She shut off the water. "Why didn't you call?"

"You know you're never here, Mother."

"Here I am right now. Besides, what are answering machines for?"

"I always thought it was so you could stand and listen and decide if somebody was worth your attention, before you'd pick up."

Suzanne drew a deep breath. Be calm, be calm. She felt rising in herself the particular sharp anxiety tinged with fear she always felt when she had not seen her elder daughter for a while. "I'll be right with you." She rushed into her bedroom to throw on slacks and a sweater. Suzanne was systematic, orderly. She made a joke of it. "I'm the only daughter of an organizer, and wow, am I organized." She called before going to a friend's house (except for Marta upstairs), made appointments with everybody including her daughters. She had a daily calendar of activities, appointments, and projects from the mundane (take suit to cleaners; put recycled goods at curb) to the important (work on speech for Harvard women's law alumnae meeting). She reminded herself in advance to buy presents for her children and her friends, all of whose sizes were kept up-to-date on her computer. Six months in advance, she made appointments with the dentist to have her teeth cleaned, and every November she arranged for Marta and herself to go and have their annual mammograms in January. Marta's mother had died of breast cancer, so Marta could never bring herself to make the phone call.

Suzanne realized this habit of meticulously planned days must irritate her older daughter, for Elena had certainly chosen to go to the other extreme, exalting spontaneity. Elena would never say, "I am coming to dinner next Friday," but would always hedge her bets. "I think I can make it, but I'll let you know." It was the adolescent hope that something more exciting than dinner with Mama would turn up, a belief that there were always other possibilities that might unfold before Friday. She understood, but nonetheless, it hurt her feelings.

Suzanne rushed into the living room. "You're looking good. Is everything okay, sweetheart?" It was impossible to tell from Elena's appearance if she were doing well or poorly, for she always looked lovely. Often it startled Suzanne that she had given birth to such a beauty. Elena had her father Victor's coloring, black hair and instead of Suzanne's nearsighted green eyes, she had large, large dark brown eyes, doe eyes, dramatic and appealing. She was a good five inches taller than Suzanne (Victor, the Guatemalan politico, had been six feet two). Her skin was olive like her father's, and her mouth was full and sensual. Nobody ever missed Elena in a crowd. She had a dramatic voice too, in a lower register; Suzanne herself was an alto rather than a soprano. She had often been told her voice led people to expect a bigger woman. Petite Suzanne and her statuesque daughter stood in the living room a bit squared off as always. Suzanne could not help the nails of worry that pounded into her.

"So how's the good daughter?"

"I assume you mean your sister."

"Who else would I mean?"

"She's working hard at school."

"She's always working hard. Even when she's asleep, she's working hard. That's how good daughters are."

"Elena, did you come all the way over here to pick a fight with me about your sister? Please tell me what's up. Please."

Elena threw herself down on the couch. She was wearing a tight short leather skirt that rode up. Suzanne had to control herself not to point that out. She had learned a few things over the years, one of which was never, never to comment on Elena's clothing or any new body piercings or tattoos she noticed. Various earrings in both ears and her nose stud, but she didn't observe any new mutilations. She was relieved. Her daughter's body was so beautiful, and she was always devising what seemed to Suzanne new punishments for it.

"Do you have a beer? Cold?"

"Maybe, I'm not sure." Beer was not something she regularly stocked in the winter. "Wouldn't you like something to eat? I haven't eaten yet myself."

"I'd rather have beer on an empty stomach. Then I'll eat a big meal and go swimming."

"Elena, is something wrong?"

"Of course not. What could be wrong with me, except for my existence? I'm sure you're going to say I told you so." Elena grimaced and turned away.

"Told you so about what?"

"That it wouldn't work out living with Jennifer. So now she's moved out on me and I'm getting evicted."

"Evicted, why? Do you need money for rent?" She was ready to write a check.

"What use is that? It's too late. They're throwing me out."

"But why didn't you pay your rent?" Suzanne had the familiar sense of being drawn deeper and deeper into a bottomless bog. "Don't you make enough at that restaurant?"

"That bitch fired me, that's why."

"Ah. Why?"

"You think she does anything that makes sense? She felt like it."

"If you've been fired without cause, I think you have a case." Suzanne had a hopeful moment: she could be useful to her daughter. She even imagined Elena's gratitude if she won a case for her.

"Oh, Mother, don't be such a lawyer prick. I slapped a customer."

"Oh . . . I'm sure you had good reason."

"So I'm going to be out on the street next Friday."

Suzanne was silent for a moment. Then she said what she had to. "Of course you can move back in. We can rearrange the rooms—"

"Don't act so martyred. I promise I won't stay long. I wouldn't move back here if everything wasn't so fucked up right now." Elena unfolded herself from the couch and paced to the fireplace and back. "Could we have a fire?"

"Let's have supper first. I'll check about the beer." Her evening was coming to pieces. She thawed a soup in the microwave. She would pull a couple of baguettes from the freezer and stick them in the oven. While the lamb barley soup heated, she washed greens and put together a salad. With a lot of work sketched out in her head, she had looked forward to collapsing on her comfortable leather couch, her feet in furry slippers up on the padded armrest and her papers for Sherry, the sexually harassed policewoman, on her lap.

Far from suffering from the empty-nest syndrome her friends had warned her about in tones usually reserved for commiserating about a root canal, Suzanne had flourished. She had expanded deliberately and joyously to fill the apartment, to fill her life. She even had a little time to play now and then on the Internet, to read a novel, to listen to music. She loved living alone, absolutely loved it. She felt so marvelously irresponsible in small details, not judged, not tested, not pushed or resented. She had become used to doing as she pleased with her own space and her free time, such as it was. Now Elena would expect to be taken care of and resent every single thing her mother did for her.

She had raised her daughters pretty much on her own since Elena was twelve and Rachel was seven, and before that, for Elena's first five years. She had not been a particularly good mother, too busy, too interested in her own work, too demanding. She could hear Elena talking to Sherlock in the living room. "Sherlock, you're so sleepy. What a sleeping Sherlock. That's right, blink. Roll on your back and I'll rub your wonderful striped tiger tummy . . ."

Why couldn't Elena ever address her with half that affection? Suzanne wondered—putting it on the agenda to bring up with Marta—if she was not a deeply irritating person, infuriating. Suzanne had always had good tight women friends, but she had also frequently annoyed many other women. They seemed to find her hard, uppity, lacking in the middle class kissy-face social graces. She never made much small talk or gave polite compliments. She was a good litigator, a good hired or pro bono gun, but a crappy hostess. Unfortunately, one of the women she most annoyed was her own daughter. Calm down, she said to herself, at least this time the problem is just money and a job. No drugs, no unsuitable men, Elena isn't pregnant or in trouble with the law. She should be relieved, but her anxiety remained. When Elena was fifteen, Suzanne discovered how well her daughter could lie to her, and she had never quite recovered from that shock. The doubt always quivered there, was she being fooled, was she fooling herself about Elena?

Over supper, she thought aloud. "So you need to move in probably over this weekend?"

"I'm not working, so one day is like another."

"Not to me," Suzanne said, then softened her voice. "So we should get my gym equipment out of the old playroom."

"I am not going to sleep in that room off the kitchen. You'd wake me every damned morning at six. No thank you."

"All right, you can use Rachel's room. She isn't about to come home until spring break at the earliest."

"I don't want Rachel's room. I want mine."

Suzanne took a deep breath. "Elena, that's fixed up as my office. It has been for six years. I have no place else to put my files, my computer—"

"You have an office at school."

"I don't keep my case work there. It isn't secure and the university doesn't approve of law school faculty conducting private practice on the premises. I have to work at home and I can't move six years of accumulation out of my office."

"It was supposed to be my room."

"Elena, you moved out with great fanfare six years ago. Did you want me to keep it as a shrine?"

Elena laughed. "With candles burning day and night and incense and flowers."

"Incense makes me sneeze," Suzanne said reasonably. "I can go buy some flowers."

"It's only for a month or so till I get another job. Rachel can stay in that stupid room off the kitchen. I'm sure she gets up at six every morning and thanks God he didn't make her me."

"In some ways, your sister has always admired you. Sometimes she envied you."

Elena grimaced. "Because she has no idea how to talk to men."

Because Rachel looked like Suzanne except for lighter hair. She remembered Rachel crying in high school, *My life would be so different if I were beautiful like her, my life would be much better*. Suzanne had a brief impulse to tell Elena about Jake and his plan to appear in the flesh. Once she had almost told Rachel when they were chatting about the Internet, but on reflection, she had not considered it becoming to inform her daughters that she had a long and intense flirtation going with a man she had never met, and was now terrified to meet: an environmental activist dogged by the FBI who wrote her an ecstatic two-page E-mail about butterflies in Costa Rica. This man who had lain down in front of bulldozers had sent her a perfect little carved seal from the Inuit and another time a salmon smoked till it resembled a piece of wood. This man had taken a ship into a nuclear test zone, and now was threatening to invade her own territorial waters.

Elena rose, stretched gracefully as a panther, and sauntered to Rachel's room. She stood in the doorway, shaking her head. "I'm going to have to change things around. I can't sleep in here, the way it is."

There was no use in her arguing that the arrangement was supposed to be temporary. If Elena announced she could not sleep, she would not sleep. Rachel was going to get a lot of practice being forgiving. Elena was back, and maybe they could learn to talk to each other instead of always fencing, and heal some of their old scars. Maybe. Suzanne the top-notch negotiator always seemed to falter when she went head-to-head with her older daughter; Suzanne the litigator always lost her case when she was arguing points with Elena. Somehow she had to find a mode of communication between them that actually communicated. Once, years and years ago when Elena was a child, they had had intense intimacy. Elena had been her precious miracle, with her father who had disappeared into mythology leaving her a child beautiful as an orchid and strong as a tiger cub. Elena's childish paintings had been lush, vivid, unlike the scrawls of other more ordinary kindergarten finger-painters. Elena had danced as early as she walked. How affectionate she had been then, flinging herself into her mother's arms when Suzanne walked into a room. And how radically it all changed when Elena passed puberty.

"Elena, if we try, maybe we can make this work. Get along better with each other," she said softly, trying not to put too much force into the words lest they seem a demand.

"It's just for a while, like a month, six weeks," Elena said. "We don't have to get in each other's way."

"I want us to do better than that."

"Whatever."

Rather than intense preparation for her sexual harassment case, most of Suzanne's weekend was spent moving Rachel's things into temporary storage along one wall of the room she was still using as her gym and helping Elena move into Rachel's room. A lot of Elena's possessions and off-season clothes went into the basement, crowded before Elena's stuff was shoved in.

On Saturday they had the help of a gangling orange-haired young man Elena knew from her former restaurant job. He was a sous-chef there, making salads and arranging food on plates. He was clearly smitten, but Elena was uninterested. "A big baby," she said. "Sex appeal of a cooked shrimp."

Sunday's help came in the form of a man perhaps fifteen years older than Elena. He was of distinctly less use than the boy had been, puffing on the stairs. He complained of his back and wanted to argue about where things should be put. Elena and he disappeared into her room for an hour in the middle of the afternoon. What could Suzanne possibly say? It made her uncomfortable to think of her daughter in bed with that oily creep, but she knew she had to keep her reaction to herself. Elena had been sexually active since puberty, and there never had been anything Suzanne could do about it. It did not help her mood that she had not made love to anyone in twelve years. She turned on the stereo and did her laundry in the basement.

"Is he your current . . ." Suzanne fumbled for the word. *Boyfriend* seemed absurd for a forty-plus-year-old man, but she could think of nothing else. ". . . your current boyfriend?"

"I see him."

I see him too, Suzanne thought, and I don't much like what I see. "What does he do?"

"That's all you ever ask about someone, isn't it? Peg them. The next question is, where did they go to school?"

Suzanne waited. She was better at silence than her daughter. Finally Elena burst out, "He sells swimming pools. As if that defined who he is!"

"Divorced?"

"Twice. Satisfied?"

Suzanne shrugged.

Elena relented slightly. "Anyhow, he's on his way out," she said. "Doesn't he complain all the time, a drone like Muzak in elevators? He's boring. Like most of your generation, he whines." Elena shook out her hair, weighing it in her hands. "Want a swimming pool? I can get you a deal."

"Swimming is not my exercise. Nor his, I imagine."

Elena snorted. "The only exercise he likes requires a partner."

Suzanne was grateful to the outgoing pool salesman nonetheless, because when Elena was displeased with somebody else, she was friendlier to her mother.

They settled in gingerly. Elena was wooing the cats. Sherlock had succumbed to her at once, but Tamar belonged only to Suzanne and would not let Elena touch her. She had found them on the street, abandoned kittens of no more than seven weeks, flea-bitten, with worms of three kinds and a respiratory infection. Now they were huge and beautiful, Sherlock lean and muscular, with clearly Oriental head shape, a long nose (like hers). She considered his profile aristocratic. If she held him up extended across the doorway, his body stretched from doorjamb to doorjamb. Tamar was apricot rather than reddish and fluffier. Her eyes were huge and round, giving her a perennially astonished expression. She was as big as her brother but softer bodied. She had an enormous purr only for Suzanne. She slept pressed against Suzanne's side and would have liked to keep her mistress on a leash. Both cats shared tiny squeaky voices, a remnant of their starving kittenhood and ludicrous in such large gorgeous cats.

Elena could not help being seductive with the cats, as with half the world. It was her way of wanting to be liked, Suzanne told herself. Jake and she had been chatting again about everything in their lives. She had told Jake all about Elena—well, a little about Elena would be more accurate.

Elena got into a mess with two boys when she was fifteen. Fortunately this whole tragedy happened around the time that law schools were briefly searching for "qualified" women to hire, to keep their governmental funds. I had been serving as adjunct faculty with the university law clinic. So finally I was offered a full tenure-track faculty position, and I took it so that I would have more time home.

Understand, being a law professor is kind of cushy. The way the tenured faculty complain about the students and facilities, you'd never know it, but actually it's far more relaxing. You don't make the huge bucks, but it's prestigious and you have plenty of time to take cases you want to take on the side, increasing your visibility, reputation, and sometimes making lots of money if it's that kind of case. Since I was absolutely riddled with guilt about Elena, the offer no matter how crassly motivated came at a time I needed to regroup. And I've been teaching there ever since.

I appreciate that you haven't asked me exactly what happened to Elena. I think that even today, I couldn't write it down. I've never been able to come to terms with it, I know that. Someday I will, and then I'll tell you the whole story.

I envy you knowing your daughter so well. I lost custody years and years ago, and so I rarely see Leaf, and never alone. She's twenty-five and married already. She works in an insurance office in Boise. My last photo of her is from her wedding. I haven't lived with her since she was five and my wife left me. I was a quintessential hippie then. I worked in a head shop, I was an orderly in a hospital, I sold hot dogs at the beach, I was a messenger. My wife just got sick of a life on the edge of nothing in particular and went home to her parents in Idaho. She got a divorce with a judge who considered me a menace to society because my hair was shoulder length and I smoked dope. I think off the record he also considered me a dirty Jew who had no business with a blond and lovely daughter of Idaho. He kept calling me a New Yorker, although I grew up in Worcester.

Even after I cleaned up and finished school, she—my ex-wife Patsy—had no use for me. She never believed I'd changed. Whatever I said to her, she had this Oh Yeah look in her eyes, sort of squinted, letting me talk but never listening.

Patsy was crazy about me when we were first together, but after our daughter, Leaf, was born, she began to judge me and our life. I should have caught on but I was so comfortable doing whatever I felt like when I felt like it, a perennial adolescent all through my twenties, that I just never saw what was happening. I was so used to Patsy adoring me, so used to being adored, that I never noticed how pissed off she was until she took off and left me.

Suzanne read the message that night in her office while Elena was moving stuff around in the next room. Suzanne was exhausted and would normally get into bed by ten-thirty on a Sunday night and read for fifteen to twenty minutes, something soothing like catalogs or a travel book about the Greek Islands or New Zealand. It was not that she intended to take an expensive or extensive vacation anytime soon, but someday surely she and Marta and Jim too would go off and see some of these places together. She had abandoned her earlier dreams of traveling with her daughters. Elena would not willingly go down to the corner deli with her, and Rachel was keeping kosher now, which made cooking for her less than fun. Kosher vegetarian: one of the world's lumpier cuisines. Rachel never talked about going anyplace abroad now except Israel.

Tonight Suzanne was overexcited. She was yeasty with hope she labeled irrational that perhaps she and Elena could actually get along, could reach some breakthrough in communication, in affection. It was a new chance. She had never expected Elena to live under her roof again. Yet now Elena's sounds seeped through the wall. Moving furniture? Pounding nails? The sound of salsa through the wall. She had overcome her earlier stupid sense of being invaded. Wouldn't Jake be jealous of her, not only in contact with her daughter but once again living with her? She should appreciate what she had, instead of sulking about her privacy and her routine. She was lucky to have her daughter with her, and she should dedicate some of her energy to making things better between them. Still she had her policewoman to worry about, the sexual harassment case against the Dedham Police Department. She wanted very badly to win this case, for her client Sherry, and because if she won, it would set a precedent in the area, letting many other women who had been treated just as badly come slowly out of their private hells and begin to demand justice and reparation. The Latino music came through the wall to her where she lay wide awake in her bed, and she found herself nodding to the beat.

She suddenly thought of Victor, his lean body, his olive face with the sculptured cheekbones and the sensual mouth, and even after all the troubles and all the years, something moved deep down in her. How she had been mad for him. Besotted. When he touched her, her bones liquefied. Her brain turned off like a computer whose plug had been pulled. They made love mostly in Spanish, besides the universal language of their bodies. How could she have loved him so strongly? But she had. He was not her first lover, but he was the most potent male force that had ever entered her life. He had left her pregnant, shaken, and mistrustful of the power and danger passion held for her. He had taught her how easily she could be rendered foolish, passive, all the things she despised; how easily she could be hurt. That was twenty-seven years ago, and still she shuddered. She had learned after that adventure how to protect herself from the possibility of subjection, her defenselessness before her own body's desire. If only Elena could learn the same at a smaller cost. She had bequeathed to her daughter her terrible vulnerability, but not the lacquered shell she had grown to protect it.

3

Beverly

Beverly climbed the steep stairway from the 103rd Street subway station. "May, hello." She greeted the homeless woman who always sat on the landing, where Beverly paused to catch her breath. Stairs took her breath away lately.

"Hello, Beverly. Is the world treating you all right today?"

"Not bad. I just hope the snow holds off."

"As do I, dear."

She knew all the street people in her neighborhood and made it a point to speak to them, the ones who weren't too far gone. Half of them were mental. Fucking budget cuts. Save the state money and dump patients on the street. The other half had just lost too much. Flo Kennedy had said many years ago that every woman was just one man away from welfare. Of course that hadn't applied to her, since she had never relied on the support of any man since her poor father. Well, every old person was just one lost check away from the streets. Who said that? Beverly Blume.

She had been out to Brooklyn to see her sister Karla, as superstitious as ever. They had been fighting about Rachel. Beverly simply could not accept that such a bright able girl should do something so useless as becoming a rabbi. Karla was thrilled and defended her grandniece—as well she might, since she was the one who had infected the whole family. Beverly would never forgive her for that. It was one of the worst mistakes she had ever made, leaving her daughter, Suzanne, with her younger sister while she was down south organizing textile workers. Oh, she was as proud of being a Jew as Karla was, but it was the cultural heritage that meant something to her, not the religious mumbo jumbo. Why seek out irrationality when it leapt at you from the TV, from the tabloids?

But at least she had to give Karla credit for overcoming racism. After Suzanne had gone off to law school at Harvard, Karla had adopted first one mixed-race child and then another. She often said she would have adopted ten more if she'd had the money to support them. So after helping Beverly raise Suzanne, Karla had spent her middle years raising two more girls, Suwanda—generally called Wanda—and Rosella, with whom Karla had moved in when her health began to fail. It was her weight that was doing her in, but Karla had always loved to cook and eat. Karla lived now with Rosella, her husband, Tyrone, and the twins. Karla was very involved with Rosella's children and Tyrone's family, the way she had always been involved with any available kind of family. Karla was in many ways a very traditional woman.

"Miller, how's the leg?" She greeted him at a table outside a Latino café on Broadway. It was cold to sit outside, but Miller had always smoked, and like her, he wasn't about to stop because people had got fussy about it. God, to imagine how he had made her blood race. Was it Dorothy Parker who compared love to a bus accident? You were just going along the street minding your business when bam, love fell on you and flattened you. Or picked you up by the nape of the neck like a huge eagle and bore you off, tore your heart and liver out, and then let you fall half a mile to earth. Certainly Miller had made her feel as if every bone in her body had been broken when he left her flat and took off with that Greek girl, Marina—who later became a follower of some guru and shaved her head like a bowling ball. Beverly stood patiently while he complained of his rheumatism and his heart before she could turn the subject to the governor and the mess he was making in Albany. He had promised to repeal that stupid mandatory sentencing law, and he had dropped it after election like a lump of dung. There were women in there for half their lives because of a purseful of marijuana, while gangstas who slit open their girlfriend's belly were out in eight years. Women were the mules, the bottom of the heap. Suzanne would understand about that, even if she didn't see much of the way the world worked.

Now here was Miller with his legs stuck out as if they could no longer bend, his complexion pickled, glasses thick enough to walk on like river ice. She could give him a big smile and a hello and not be able to imagine how once he had burnt her eyes like the sun itself. He had been a vigorous, charismatic man, full of stories and a line thick enough to tether an ocean liner. "Oh, Bev, you're the only woman who's ever understood me. You have the mind of a man and the body of a houri." For a year she had been crazy about him and then he had bounced out the door, gone. And always, always, even in bed she had called him by his last name, for he would tell no one his given name. She had seen it years later in the FBI records when she had got her seven-foot stack under the Freedom of Information Act. Hymie, his name was, and he was ashamed of it as too Jewish, a borscht belt joke.

He had never been a good speaker, but he was a solid man in a demonstration, and he had thrust his tough big body between her and danger more than once. How he had loved a good fight. He was a natural brawler, quick and effective with his fists. She had liked that. They had enough talkers. She knew it was silly to respond to physical strength and daring in a man, but she couldn't help it. It was after such a demonstration they had first gone home together and fallen into her bed. What an explosion. She could remember it yet. At first, one of the best lovers she had ever had, but he cooled down in a matter of months. He was the kind of man who was hot for novelty and tired fast of what he had. She turned on 105th and headed for Amsterdam.

"*Eh, Gutiérrez, ¿cómo va?*" She always spoke Spanish to the dry cleaner, to the fish peddler, to the super. She'd had to get her good suit dry-cleaned after her old friend Charlotte's funeral, it had been so muddy, and she'd need it Sunday when the neighborhood organization dedicated the pocket park she had helped lobby for, where the kids could play safe out of the streets. She wished she knew some Korean to speak to the greengrocer. She loved languages and had learned a bit of eight of them, just enough to get along and have a friendly conversation. She had friends who did crossword puzzles, but she had always learned languages for fun. It was a game you could play with people instead of alone—the best kind. You only had to be willing to take a chance, to make a fool of yourself and be a child in another language. Sometimes she felt desolate when she realized that at her age, she would never learn Chinese the way she had always intended. It was like realizing you were never going to meet that one person you wanted to spend the rest of your life with, that it just wasn't going to happen. Not that she truly minded living alone with her cat. She had only herself to please, and she was pleased with herself, as she always said when anybody asked her if she didn't get lonely.

People said New York was cold, but she had little conversations with twenty people between the subway and the door to her apartment. She knew hundreds of people in her neighborhood, from the group trying to preserve rent control, to the tenants union created to fight the landlords, to the reform party meetings and all the people she had known in fifty-five years of being politically active. She had lived in this apartment on 105th between Columbus and Manhattan for thirty-one years. She had seen the neighborhood change and change again. Friends died and new friends came into her life. She felt sorry for old people like Miller who could only relate to people they'd known back when. She was determined to remain curious and ready to learn new things from new people until the day she dropped dead, preferably on a picket line.

She stopped at her favorite resale shop on Columbus to scan the clothing racks. She was still a size six, and she kept her hair a warm light red. "Oh, Bev," Tina, the young Jamaican woman behind the counter, called to her, "I got a black number you would look great in. Asymmetrical, very stylish."

"Now where would I wear such a thing?" But she took it, gave Tina her suit to hold, and went behind the partition where a mirror stood.

Umm, she liked it. At her age, she couldn't wear décolletage any longer, and this dress covered her pretty well. The tag said thirty dollars, but Tina would usually bargain with her. "Such a dress, what would an old lady like me need with it?" But the tenants organizing group always had a Valentine's Day party.

She got the dress for twenty-two dollars. No bottle of wine for the next few weeks, but she would knock the old guys' eyes out at the party. She still enjoyed that, she couldn't help it. And maybe Hank would get a few ideas. She saw one of the kids from her building, Bobby Choi, hanging around outside P.S. 145 as she passed and waved to him.

The super greeted her warmly and gave her a package. A friend in England had sent her his new book on British miners. She collected her mail and took the creaky hesitant elevator up, muttering to itself as if it were senile. It was a narrow old building the landlord did not bother with. If you wanted the apartment painted, you painted it yourself. The kids daubed graffiti on the walls that stayed until other kids spray painted over with new graffiti. She opened both locks on her door, went in, and shoved the dead bolt to.

Her sleek black tomcat, Mao, came to greet her, twisting about her legs and making that Siamese cry of his. No man had ever greeted her more ecstatically in her entire life than her cat did whenever she went out, even if it was just to the corner to pick up the Sunday *Times*. She hated to admit it, but Karla's neighborhood had better kosher deli now than the Upper West Side. She had bought herself a good supply of pastrami and kishkes and knishes. What a supper she would have tonight, and she would share it with Mao. She could get good smoked fish in her neighborhood when she was willing to spend the money and good strudel still, bagels, rugola, but proper knishes and kishkes, no way.

Karla had also given her a plastic container full of chopped liver. Karla was a good cook, but then, she had always liked fussing around the house, the way Beverly could never be bothered. Most nights, she just opened a can of tuna to share with Mao or maybe a can of soup. Unlike most women her age, she had not gone to fat and she had not withered away. She was perhaps five pounds heavier than she had been at forty, and that was it. Weight was always visible on a small woman, but nobody would ever call her fat like Karla. Suzanne never gained weight either. That was one of the few ways they were alike, mother and daughter. She hung up the black dress on the rack over the tub to shake out the wrinkles and get rid of the musty smell.

Suzanne had bought her an answering machine ten years before, and after letting it sit under the bed for three years, finally she had given in and begun to use it. She played her messages now.

"This is Gordon from the Tenants for Rent Control. We've got an important meeting with our state rep tonight and I want everybody on the steering committee to show up. Seven-thirty my place. Beverly, are you listening?"

About half the messages were political and half were friends. Her poker group was meeting again after a hiatus when Bianca had her heart attack. Nat had called trying to get her to go to a movie with him. He'd like to start up again, the old reprobate, but once fooled is smart afterward. She did not return his call. Let him stew. He had been so taken with that widow with the condo in Vero Beach. Now he thought he could just pick up where they had left off two years ago. She grinned. She was more interested in Hank, who was on the steering committee with her. His wife had died last year, and he was coming out of his mourning. He was a retired academic who had written a couple of books that had impressed her. She usually wasn't that taken with writers, but he was good-looking with abundant snowy white hair and blue eyes the color of those weeds that grew in vacant lots in Brooklyn, chicory. Kept in shape. Yes, she would sit next to him tonight. If she had time, she'd flirt with him, but she had a proposal to push. It required research on the landlords, but she knew how to do that, and she'd teach the younger folks. It was important to pass on skills.

She sat down to her copyediting, putting on her reading glasses. She hated them, forgot them on every table and surface in the three-room apartment. She had never worn glasses until she'd turned fifty. But she could no longer do copyediting without them, and that was her livelihood. She freelanced for several journals and magazines and the occasional small- to middle-size publisher. She had a reputation for knowing many languages and jargons and being fast and careful. She operated mostly through messengers, because she had been dropped by a couple of large publishers when they realized how old she was. On the phone, no one could tell, for she still had a fine clear speaking voice. As if being seventy-two made any difference to her accuracy. Snobby little pipsqueaks out of Ivy League schools ran publishing now, and their knowledge of the world was as narrow as a shoelace.

She lit a cigarette and drew heavily on it as she began proofing the biography of a civil war naval captain. Karla would not let her smoke in Rosella's apartment. They acted as if a puff of smoke would give the twins TB. Beverly had to ration her cigarettes, no more than half a pack a day, not because she gave a damn what the scare mongers said, but because that was all she could afford. She got by, she got by just fine on Social Security and her copyediting and the check Suzanne sent every month. That covered some extras, like a pack of cigarettes every other day and the deli from Brooklyn. An occasional bottle of wine. Scrupulously she used the check from Suzanne only for extras, so that no one could say she was not supporting herself, as she had since she was eighteen. It was absolutely essential to stay independent.

She had never gotten used to being old. When she would walk down Broadway she would half expect men to stare at her the way they always had, something about her walk, the way she carried herself, the sense of style she had been born with. She would catch sight of herself in the mirror and think, who is that old bat? Because inside seventy-two-year-old Beverly Blume was Beverly Blume, the same woman she had been since eighteen, full of energy and opinions and ready to laugh and ready to take a chance and clear-eyed about what was going on in the world.

She remembered the first time she had a cigarette. She was eighteen, still living at home with her parents, on Twelfth Street near Second. They called it the East Village now, but it had been simply the Lower East Side then, the ghetto, and they lived all seven of them in a four-room cold-water flat next to an old-age home for the indigent. She had taken a job in a box factory on Third over near Avenue B. After she got her first week's paycheck, she was walking out when that gorgeous Irishman Jimmy fell into step beside her. He asked her to supper. Now, she knew if she didn't show up for Shabbat dinner, her mother would kill her, so she only took a walk with him and had a soda, a chocolate egg cream. As they walked, he offered her a cigarette and lit it for her like a gentleman. Then he kissed her. She could still remember how sweet and sultry that kiss was, tasting of the tobacco and chocolate on both their breath. Nothing had ever come of it—she had been a virgin and living at home—but she still relished that first cigarette and that kiss in the doorway of a dry cleaners. Ah, she had had some fine times, no doubt about it. Life was mean and hard, but it handed you something sweet now and then, something really sweet.

4 Thirteen Years Earlier

Elena

Elena was furious when Sam moved out. She knew it was her mother's fault. If Suzanne had been nicer to him, if she had played up to him, he would not have left them. She knew he had had an affair with a client. She had listened with a glass at the wall to her parents' fighting. Not that Sam was her father, but he was better than most fathers. Suzanne should have fought for him, got dressed up, had her hair done over, sat in his lap and told him how wonderful he was. Instead she stupidly blamed him for being unethical, as if ethics had anything to do with sex. Even Elena knew that was garbage, and she was still a stupid virgin at fourteen.

Even her cat Big Boy missed Sam, whose lap he liked to sit in. Everything was falling apart in her life. Her two best girlfriends, Genette and Helen, were no longer hers. Ever since they'd moved to the South End when she was just entering the first grade, Helen had been her other self. Helen was Black, but they had the same name in different forms, and Helen's mama was a lawyer too. Genette transferred in at the beginning of third grade. Helen was closer to Genette than Elena was, but they all hung together, inseparable in and after school. She learned all her jump rope chants from them. Then around the time they were all going to take their exams to go to Boston Latin School, Helen's family moved to Lexington. Elena saw her a couple of times after that, and they called and wrote, but their closeness gradually died. Genette had gotten interested in boys, and her grades were suffering. She didn't make the cut. Elena went on to Boston Latin alone, and Genette got into a crowd in her middle school.

Even though Elena was in seventh grade, at Boston Latin she was called a sixie, and they were the bottom of the heap. The school went through twelfth grade, and the older kids were so sophisticated and knowing, they were always picking on the sixies. Elena had begun to grow tall, so she wasn't towered over like most of her class, but that didn't keep her from being a target. The first year, she tried hanging with the Latina girls, but she was studying for her bat mitzvah, and that set her apart. She wasn't about to pretend she wasn't Jewish.

So far, she had done it all right, the way she was supposed to. Her mother kept telling her that Boston Latin was the place she had to be, like a private school except it didn't cost anything. That was a big help after the divorce, since her mother had to buy Sam out of the row house they lived in on Rutland Street. She had gotten As in everything but math. Like her grandma, she liked languages. She was taking Latin because she had to and Spanish because she wanted to. She got through algebra only because the guy sitting next to her let her cheat off his papers. That was Evan, who lived in the South End too on West Newton, although he'd gone to a different grade school. Evan was almost as dark as she was and Jewish too. He was great at math, and in ninth grade, he took a science prize. He was skinny and wore glasses and refused not only to go out for sports but to take football or basketball seriously. Boston Latin was big on sports in spite of being an elite school: their traditional rivalry was the Thanksgiving football game with Boston English. Evan and Elena decided not to attend. It was like going on strike. They went to a slash movie instead and sat there laughing, making bets on who would get cut up next.

The first time they had sex, they were stoned and kept giggling. It didn't hurt, but it didn't feel like much. They didn't date like the straight kids. Both his parents worked, and her mother was always at the law office or in court, so they just fucked whenever they felt like it. When Rachel was home from grade school, Elena and Evan just went in Elena's room and shut the door. They played music loud. She had Rachel cowed. She knew even if Rachel suspected anything, she wouldn't tell Suzanne: she'd be scared to. Evan put on his father's overcoat and went into an adult bookstore. He bought two books about sex and several videos. After that, he spent an hour looking for her clitoris till he found it.

If other girls asked her about him, she said he was like her brother. They were alike, intense and dark and singular: more than her brother or her lover, Evan was her twin. They liked the same thrash bands that drove adults frothing insane. They also liked some alternative groups. They liked dark violent movies that felt real. They liked taking their clothes off and trying different things. They always did their homework together and they always had sex, using a condom. They went through a couple of packs every week. Neither of them could drive a car, for they were both fourteen. They had to use their bikes or the MBTA to go anywhere. They bought their dope in the neighborhood, at a spot outside a drugstore where guys she knew from grade school were selling. Evan lived in a brick row house a story shorter than hers, but his family had the whole place except for the basement apartment. Both of them loved their neighborhood, with its blocks that matched, each block a particular type of row house, but every one of them individual too, all red brick and some with funky little strip gardens in the middle of the street.

Evan and she didn't talk garbage like love and families. They talked about peace and death and hypocrisy and lies. They did his next science project together, and then they let the mice go in the basement of the school. She hoped they could make it on their own.

She listened to the other girls talking about their boyfriends, and it wasn't like that with her. She wasn't crazy about Evan. She didn't dote on him. It was as if they were each other's shadow. He called them E squared or E to the second power. There was no hand holding, no smooching, no rings or pins or flowers. They fought sometimes and called each other names, but it never lasted. They would start laughing, as if for them to be anything but one being, one conspiracy, one gang of two was a joke. She could not even have said if she loved Evan. It was like loving her arm. They were a unit. His parents and her mother asked questions, but they had no idea how much time the two of them spent together. Their grades stayed high. She thought sometimes that if she robbed banks, it would be okay with Suzanne, just so long as she maintained her grade point average and stayed in Boston Latin. Suzanne was always telling her how lucky she was to be there, but she didn't fit in. She was too weird for the other girls. She was always an outsider, and if she stood with a group of girls, conversation slowed down or even stopped. She got her breasts and she was tall, so guys were always trying to feel her up, poking at her, making noises, but they were scared of her too and never bugged her about dating.

Evan and she could talk about everything. They talked about being Jewish. He told her, "My grandma made it something important, beautiful. My parents, it's like something they stepped in and if only they scrape hard enough, they can get rid of it. Last year they had me get bar-mitzvahed, but it was like this meaningless thing. My grandma had just died and I felt shitty, and all they could think about was how much the party was costing and who was the right caterer and who to invite and who to leave out and who gave the best presents. It was gross. They're gross. Don't take it seriously if it doesn't make money."

"I'm not into the religion. I want to have both my heritages. Sometimes I wish I knew more about Sephardic Jews. My aunt Karla, she told me that's what I look like, and she told me something about them. They speak Ladino instead of Yiddish. She's got this adopted daughter, Rosella, who I think looks a little like me. When people see us together when they're visiting or we go to Brooklyn, they think we're sisters." Sephardic Jews seemed to Elena much more romantic than Ashkenazi like her family. She read a historical novel about the Spanish Inquisition and conversos, and it was cool and frightening and epic. Elena did not bother to explain to Evan that Rosella was really Puerto Rican, because that was less interesting.

The next year there was a new student who transferred in from Kansas. They both had history with him. He wasn't a jock, a club kid, one of the super students who ran the school, or a burnout who would be tossed, but like them, one of the weird kids. He was between them in height and had pale sleek blond hair he wore to his shoulders. His eyes were a dark haunting blue. He had a scar through one light brown eyebrow. His cheekbones were high and sharp, and his profile looked to her as if it should be carved on the prow of a sailing vessel. He always had shadows of stubble on his cheeks that made him seem older, more experienced. Half the guys had just started shaving. Evan had a darkish beard but not much of it. He only had to shave every other day, and it took him about a minute, although she did like to watch, 'cause it was such a male thing to do. She was almost hairless on her body and never even shaved her legs. To each other, they called the new kid the Decadent Viking. "I want him," Evan said.

"So do I," she said. "We'll share him."

They made up stories of capturing him, tying him up and doing things to him. His name was Chad. It seemed a silly name for such a fascinating-looking guy. He was broody. He sat at the back, and even when he knew the answers, he sounded as if he resented being right. She sat down next to him in assembly one day. His wrists stuck out below his shirt. There was a scar on each of them. He caught her looking at his wrists. They stared at each other. He did not hide his wrists. Then he smiled.

For two months they didn't do anything more than make up stories about Chad the Decadent Viking. Then Evan asked him one day, "Want to study for finals in history with Elena and me?"

"Is she your girl?"

"I don't even know what that means. . . ."

They went over to Evan's house. He didn't have a pesky kid sister, only an older brother, at William and Mary. For the first hour they studied together up in Evan's room, smoking cigarettes and dope and studying really hard, but she knew Evan was planning something. It made her feel tense and high. She trusted Evan and she didn't care what he did, as long as Chad didn't laugh at them. She got excited just sitting there, knowing that Evan was about to make his move.

He stood up suddenly and came over to her, drawing her to her feet. He began unbuttoning her blouse. "Get undressed, Elena, and lie on the bed."

Chad remained in his chair. "Hey. What's going on?"

"Watch," was all Evan said. He waited till she had stripped and lay on the bed, feeling exposed but also high from the way that Chad was staring at her. She knew that she looked good and that he couldn't turn his eyes away. In the meantime, Evan quickly undressed and put on a condom. Then he lay down on top of her. He could tell she was excited already and simply pushed in and began to fuck her. She glanced over at Chad. He was staring at them, but he hadn't moved. She loved the feeling of him watching them, as if he was in their power and couldn't break away. She came quickly. So did Evan.

He stood up, not covering himself, and came to stand in front of Chad. He motioned for Elena to come over. Slowly, loose and wet after coming, she obeyed. She almost felt sorry for Chad. Instead of looking cool and in command the way he always did, he looked lost, almost scared, but he stood his ground. She had no idea what Evan was about to do, and in a way she was scared too, but she trusted him. It would be something wild. She thought Evan was enjoying the upper hand and the power to shock Chad.

"Do you want us?"

Chad was so startled he couldn't reply for a moment. Then he repeated, "Us?"

"We come as a set. We don't separate. Or are you scared?"

"I never did it with a guy."

She knew Evan hadn't either, but he wasn't going to say so, and she wouldn't betray him. "Have you ever done it with a girl?"

"Once . . ." Chad said reluctantly. His gaze returned to her body. His eyes excited her. Evan never looked at her that way. They were so used to each other's bodies, they took their nakedness as a matter of course. Anyhow in the year they had been fucking, her body had changed. She had real breasts now, and her behind was curvier. She liked Chad staring at her. Chad raised his gaze to look into her eyes. "Don't you have a will of your own?"

"We're together," Elena said indignantly. "He doesn't make me do what I don't want to. We're honest with each other."

"Do you love Evan?"

Elena took a step backward away from Chad, shaking back her hair. "I don't know what that means."

Chad grinned narrowly, as if she had given him back a measure of initiative. "But I do."

"If you don't want to, nobody's making you." Elena made as if to reach for her T-shirt from a Twisted Sister concert.

He caught her wrist. He gave her a push so she sat down hard on the edge of the bed. Then slowly and deliberately he undid his belt buckle and then his shirt and then his jeans. Evan watched him with his head cocked, smiling slightly. Chad was erect, so he couldn't be that put off. She stared at his cock, because it was only the second one she had ever seen. He looked different from Evan, sort of bigger and looser around the top. "I'm not circumcised," he said. "My father doesn't believe in it."

Evan straddled his desk chair, keeping out of the way. Elena waited until Chad had undressed completely and sat on the bed's edge next to her. Then without waiting for him to make a move, she slid toward him and, taking his face in her hands, gave him a sensuous tongue kiss. She moved her thigh against his. She wanted him so bad she ached. She did not think she had ever wanted Evan this strongly, but she would never let him know that. It would hurt his feelings, and he was her own. Her flesh. Her more than brother.

Chad's hand was on her breast now, a little awkwardly, squeezing hard. With Evan she would have instructed him, but she could not take a chance on discouraging Chad. They had wanted him and now they were going to have him, both of them. Now he was lying on top of her, kissing her almost frantically. She put her hand on his prick and guided him in. Normally she would have liked fooling around with him longer, but she did not want anything to go wrong. He thrust hard and came almost at once, long before she could. Then he lay spent on the bed, while she eased out from under him.

Evan let him lie like that for several minutes. Then he motioned for her to get up. She took the desk chair, which Evan had dragged to just beside the bed to watch more closely. Evan lay down beside Chad. At first he just caressed him from the back, making spoons. Evan's chest and pubic hair were dark, almost black, and Chad's body hair was the palest brown. Chad was tanned over his arms and chest. Evan was milky pale. Evan patiently caressed Chad, reaching around to his cock. Then he rolled Chad onto his stomach, used the surgical jelly and slowly, caressing his way, put himself into Chad's ass. Chad winced and bit at the pillow, but once Evan was in, he seemed to mind it far less. She liked watching. She loved watching. She was possessing Chad through Evan's cock. She was fucking him through Evan. She wanted Evan to thrust harder, but he was careful, gentle. She could almost feel his come. Then he rested for a moment, turned Chad over and began to suck his cock. She came just watching them.

Afterward Chad lay as if dazed. "Do you do this a lot?" he asked finally, trying to recover himself.

"We fuck all the time," Evan said. "We study and we fuck. But it's the first time we've ever taken anybody else with us. You should consider it an honor." He was grinning widely.

"Did you like being with us?" Elena asked almost shyly. He was so beautiful, Chad with the blue blue eyes and the carved face.

"I've spent worse afternoons." He reached out and pulled her down on the bed with him. He was staring into her eyes. "I don't understand you."

"Sometimes I don't understand myself."

With a light caress now his hand moved over her breast. "You're like something I made up lying in bed at night."

She jerked away. "I'm no fantasy."

Evan said, "You know, we could all have a lot of fun."

Chad looked at him, his hand coming to rest on Elena's bare thigh. "I think you're right."

| 5

Suzanne

Rachel was silent for an entire week. Suzanne tried to call her twice at the apartment she shared with two other rabbinical students. Suzanne left pleas on the answering machine, but Rachel did not return her calls. Finally a reply came in her E-mail.

Mother:

I really can't imagine what you were thinking of, to give my room to Elena. I just can't believe you did that to me. I think it was incredibly selfish of you not to give up your gym or your office, but to make me the sacrificial lamb. I am certainly not coming home until I have my room back. You are always expecting me to put up with anything to satisfy Elena, who can never be satisfied anyhow!

It seemed to Suzanne that Elena somehow occupied seventy percent of the apartment. Her jacket lay on the back of the couch. Her CDs were scattered about as if flung. She left the television on and wandered away. Her flame red brassieres and bikini panties hung on the rod in the bathroom. She was on the telephone as much as in high school, when Suzanne had gotten Elena her own phone in self-defense. Furthermore Suzanne had to deal with Sam, who dropped in on his adopted daughter a little too frequently for Suzanne's comfort.

Sam was ensconced on her couch at the moment. "I pulled Judge Fogarty. That man must be a hundred years old. Why don't they have mandatory retirement for judges? It would help if they had to leave the bench before senility overcomes them."

Sam was big—broad shoulders, big bones, and curly sandy hair. He had been a good-looking man when she had married him, twenty-three years ago, but he had spread out considerably since then. She had never been madly in love with him the way she had with Elena's father, Victor. She had not wanted to be. She had seen herself going down the same road as her mother, rendered idiotic by blind passion for a series of ill-chosen men. Sam had been a rational choice. She had made that choice as much for Elena as for herself. She had loved him, certainly, but with clarity, with her mind as well as her body.

Their careers had got in the way, so that in an average week, most of the time they spent together was in bed and almost all of that, asleep. They were both young political lawyers very much on the make and far more passionate about their cases than about each other. Their marriage had disintegrated under the pressure. But Sam had always been a good father, to his three children with his current wife (who did not work); to his own daughter Rachel and to Elena, whom he had adopted shortly after the marriage. She had chosen well in that regard, and as much trouble as Elena had got into, it might have gone far worse if Sam had not been there for her. Elena's own father had disappeared before she was born. Suzanne heard about him very occasionally. He was in the mountains in Nicaragua. He had been shot down on the streets of Guatemala City. He turned up again in Chile. He was in jail in Panama. She wondered. His family had money, and she would not be surprised if he were running one of their corporations instead. He did Elena no good, except to excite her imagination. Suzanne still remembered seeing a composition Elena had written in her second college: "I am a bastard out of Brookline, Massachusetts. I am a bastard, the daughter of a bastard. My father was a hero and a guerrilla leader." Suzanne sighed. Sam was looking at his watch.

"Sometimes I wonder if we shouldn't have been more truthful with Elena about her father. Then maybe she wouldn't romanticize him so ridiculously."

Sam shrugged. "Compared to us, he was a romantic figure. You were crazy about him."

"For a while. For a while. Until he took to abusing me. I did not find that romantic."

"I bet you didn't." Sam grinned. "Besides, what harm does it do to give her a sense of a colorful background? It isn't as if she's about to go off to the jungle to look for him. Or as if she's ever taken a serious interest in anything political." Sam looked at his watch for the third time.

Sam was waiting for Elena. Doing anything with Elena usually involved a great deal of waiting. Elena had only begun to dress when Sam arrived. They were going to a concert by a Chilean group. If Elena did not appear soon, they would be late. But Suzanne was determined not to hurry Elena. She was constantly telling herself to treat her daughter as if she were a houseguest rather than a child of hers. Of course, she rarely entertained houseguests. She was too busy. Aunt Karla came to see her and the girls every year, yes, sometimes with Rosella and the twins, and Beverly visited maybe once every five years. That was about it. But what she tried to keep in mind was that a hostess was far more polite to a guest than a mother to her daughter, and she needed to muster all her tact and resources to handle having Elena back home. She felt an intense usually subliminal fear for Elena, always, that she would get into some desperate trouble, that something violent would happen to her. For Rachel, her fears had always been more mundane. Don't catch cold. Don't strain your eyes. Are you sure you can handle six classes? But there was no limit to her anxiety for Elena.

The redwood protest case has been postponed again, this time by the prosecution, so I am free to fly out. I have appointments with the people I have to see Monday and Tuesday. It sounds as if having an office there might happen, but I won't know till I talk to supporters face-to-face and see if I can be effective in the Northeast. I'll be flying in Friday night, hoping that we can spend Sunday together. Let me know if that's possible. How are your schedule and other commitments?

Suzanne hit "return" on her E-mail program and sat there, trying to figure out what to say. Panic told her to type that she was going to be out of town, out of state, out of the country. She was planning to drop dead on Friday night. The memorial service had already been arranged. Jake was not invited.

What does it matter, she told herself, if he's disappointed in me. So what? So we will or will not continue corresponding. Maybe I'll be disappointed in him. Of course I'll be disappointed in him; how could I not be? What good can come of this? She could not think what to say and she ended up getting off the computer altogether, as if even being on a potential link with Jake was too dangerous to handle.

Elena was still in bed. Suzanne ran upstairs to Marta. "He does want to see me! He wants to spend Sunday with me. What am I going to do?"

"I guess you're going to spend at least part of Sunday with him." Marta smirked. "So what could be so bad? Even if it's a disaster, you can eat out for a month on the story. It's romantic, Suzanne. Meeting a man on the Internet is so trendy and fin de siècle. I'm rotten with envy."

"If you truly are, dearest one, you can meet him in my place. He doesn't know what I look like."

"Hmm." Marta pretended to consider, head cocked. "But Jim and I have to go to New York this weekend." Her son, Adam, was at NYU. "He's showing the film he made. I have to go see it. I was thinking of asking Beverly if we could sleep on her couch. I don't want to drop a thousand for a stupid weekend. If we have a free place to stay, we can fly instead of driving and worrying myself sick about the car." Marta had a new Jeep Cherokee she did not look forward to parking in Manhattan.

"Ask her. Beverly likes you. In fact I think she likes you better than me."

"Well, my mother always liked you better than me. We should have traded mothers twenty-five years ago and made everybody happy."

"What a wonderful idea." Suzanne sat up. "Elena could get into that. Suppose when you went away to college, you exchanged parents. Everybody by lot draws somebody else's. Or a computer could make matches. So much less angst. I think I'm onto a great piece of social engineering."

"You've changed the subject from Jake. Jacob Kallen, eco-terrorist."

"He is not, counsel. He is an eco-activist."

"Jacob, who wrestled an angel, or god, or whatever." Marta played with her long braid the color of weathered shingles. "Think he might want to wrestle you?"

"Don't be obscene, Marta. This is an absurd tête-à-tête I backed into. The truth is, I never thought of him as a real man. He was a figment of my computer. And I liked it that way."

Suzanne did nothing about Jake that day. The next morning she did not even turn on the computer but spent an extra fifteen minutes on the treadmill, then took a long hot shower. By the time she had breakfast and dried her hair, it was time to rush off to the university.

The gender equity committee of the law school met every Thursday at seven-thirty, so she had supper with Alexa, a friend from women's studies, and then went to her committee meeting. When she got home just after ten, Elena was watching a gangster movie on TV. At the next commercial she strolled into the kitchen, where Suzanne was setting up her coffee for the next morning. "Oh, some guy called. From California. He wanted the address and directions."

"Is he going to call back?"

"He goes, 'Well, is she going to be around?' Anyhow, I looked at your schedule and I told him that Sunday looked clear all day. Is he some kind of friend of yours?"

"You told him I'm going to be around? On Sunday?" She spilled ground coffee all over the counter. "You said I was going to be here?"

"Well, aren't you?"

"I hadn't decided."

"Whatever," Elena said, losing interest. She strolled back into the living room, where her movie had resumed.

6

Suzanne

Suzanne spent an hour dressing for lunch. Jake had called her from the Inn at Harvard Square. She felt like a bloated adolescent about to go on a date: ridiculous and pitiful. To spend all this time worrying about her appearance was humiliating. No matter what she did to herself, she would still look forty-nine and she had never been beautiful. She was simply pleasant-looking and small, and that summed up the best she had to offer to the gaze of any man.

The truth was, most of her clothing that could be called dressy was selected for class or for court. She had a bunch of suits in gray or navy and some silk dresses, conservative and careful. She had two party dresses she wore at holiday time. She had a couple of caftans, comfortable and interesting-looking, in which she entertained, on the occasions she had time and energy to do that. She had exercise gear. Almost everything was ordered out of catalogs, because she found shopping tedious. It was always too hot in department stores. It took hours to find anything, and then they would be out of size eight. Finally she dressed as if for class (rather than court): nice pants, a chenille top, and a silk blazer. Earrings and pendant. She avoided looking in the mirror and marched out of her bedroom.

"Where are you going?" Elena asked suspiciously.

"I might be back for supper, I might not." She paused. "I almost certainly will be back. But I'm not sure."

"I'm going out with this guy, Roy, so I won't be here for supper anyhow. But where are you going?"

"To meet a friend."

"What kind of a friend? This is that guy who called from California, isn't it, and you're dressed up for him. Who is he?"

Suzanne shrugged, a little flustered. "I hardly know him." She yanked on her coat and ran for the door.

"So who is he," Elena called after her, stimulated into curiosity by Suzanne's reticence. "How do you know him?"

All right, all right, she would meet Jake and blow their silly thing out of the water and she would save ten minutes every morning. Get it over with.

The two elevators in the atrium of the Inn were side by side. She was sitting, as she told him on the house phone, on a couch facing them. Two men got out, arguing. A woman and a child. Then the doors opened and a small man emerged, looking around. Of course he was not small compared to her, but still he struck her as small. She realized that both the fathers of her children had been a foot taller than she was. She had never thought about that. Did she have a preference for tall men? Had she had a preference for tall men when she was younger? In years, she had not exercised a preference for men of any sort. He was perhaps five feet seven and wiry, small boned. He had piercing brown eyes in a sharp face. His brows were arched in surprise (what had he expected?) and he was smiling tentatively. He stuck out his hand. "Suzanne, I presume?"

"Jake?" They shook hands, rather shyly. She asked, "How was your trip?" Then forgot to listen to his answer. His handshake had been firm, his hand warm, almost hot.

Afterward she could not remember anything they said on the way to the restaurant. When they sat down at a table, he said, "You shouldn't be nervous with me. I haven't bitten anyone in several years. And I have been tested for rabies."

That cut through her mental fog. She was beginning to feel desperate. They had not had a real conversation yet and she felt herself frozen into mechanical jabber. She was an experienced and competent litigator, seldom at a loss on her feet. She had pulled more than one case out of the fire with a brilliant closing, but here she was unable to make coherent contact. She had somehow expected him to be a vegetarian, but he said he ate just about anything. "Except ham and anchovies. I don't know why. A childhood antipathy."

She pulled herself together. "Have you ever spent time in the Boston area?"

"Is that like doing time? Sure, I went to Brandeis as an undergraduate. I was born on Long Island and then my family moved to Worcester. But it's been close to twenty-five years."

"It's a big leap from the Bay Area. Climate, culture, how people relate. Different ocean, different orientation. You face west, we face east."

"I thought if you had time, you might take me on a tour and let me look around. Not the tourist things. But neighborhoods. The kind of places I might live and shop and eat and hang out."

"I'm free," she said, although she had planned to work on her brief. "We'll improvise."

The food was good, and he had an appetite. As she began to relax, she began to eat. There was something about his voice, deep and resonant and quirky, that moved her. She liked hearing him talk. She asked him about his recent trip to Antarctica. He told her about acres of penguins. The breath of a whale—fishy, warm, that touched his face when she breached beside the small boat. Sterile mountains beautiful and grim. It was summer there in January, and the sun barely set, glittering blindingly off the ice. But often it was overcast and the wind cut through his clothes. He kept getting windburn. His eyes had a steadiness and intensity that made her keep catching on his gaze as if it were barbed. His hands were large for his size but finely shaped. He had presence. Of course: he was an organizer, a macher, a leader. Why should she be surprised that in the flesh, he radiated strength, energy like radiant heat? As they were leaving, he said, "Let's take a walk around here, if you're willing."

They walked along the Charles together. The sun was out, the snow had melted the week before, and the temperature was above freezing. It was not yet spring, but it promised spring. The Charles was free of ice. Families of mallards paddled along. There was even a rower pushing the season.

"It'll be a shock for you to go through winter again."

"I lived up in the mountains for a couple of years. We had fierce winters. We were snowed in sometimes for a week." He made a gesture up over his head. "That was my mountain man phase."

"But for the last fifteen years, you've been living in Oakland, and you haven't seen a snowflake or an icicle or a sleet storm."

"Actually, in Antarctica," he said mildly, "I saw quite a lot of ice. Besides, even at home, I did go through a couple of earthquakes and a fire that just missed my house by three blocks. . . . Are you trying to talk me out of this move?" He sat down on a bench in the sun and motioned her beside him. He turned to her then, taking her by the shoulder. "What are you afraid of?"

"In general? Death, accidents, disease, something happening to my daughters—"

"All right, let's go at this another way. What do you want, Suzanne?"

"I want things to continue. I like my work. I like my house. I like my friends."

"Everything just the way it is. No changes."

"Well, life is never like that, is it? I'd like Elena to find her own place to live. I'd like my mother to make an effort to see me as I am, I'd like my dean to stop patronizing me—"

"And what do you want from me? Anything?"

"I don't know," she said in a much softer voice, almost choked. "What do you want?"

"I'll show you." He took her hand and stood. He kept her hand as they walked. "For two years we've been talking, we've been flirting, we've been sharing our minds. I don't want it to be less real now. I want it to be more real."

"I'm not . . . perhaps who I've seemed to be . . . I don't . . . have affairs, go out with men, that sort of thing." She was deeply, poignantly confused. She knew him and she didn't know him at all. He was a close friend, an intimate confidant, a stranger.

"Obviously you've been with men in the past. Your daughters weren't the result of virgin birth. You told me about their fathers."

"I can't believe how much I told you."

"Believe it. Why not? You have some idea who I am." With her arm tucked securely in his, he walked briskly back in the direction of the Square.

"It was easy in my office, alone there in the mornings, typing messages on a screen. I'm sure I came across as far more at ease, far more . . . sophisticated, far more interesting than the woman you see. I'm dynamite in a courtroom but so awkward right now I feel like a twelve-year-old."

"You're out of practice. But I'm not a set of skills to be mastered, not a brief to be prepared. I'm just a man who's interested in you."

Heat slammed up her body. She could think of absolutely nothing to say. Yes, she had entertained fantasies about Jake, but the best thing about them had been that they were fantasies. They cost her nothing. They did not make her vulnerable, being as easily put away as Rachel's paper dolls had been, into a box covered with gold foil that had held chocolates. But this fantasy was out of its box.

"When you listed the things you want, you never mentioned love. Most people would. I would. Why not?"

"I suppose because I'm a realist."

"And you don't let yourself want what you don't think you can have?"

"Something like that. Or something I think might harm me."

"I won't harm you. Intentionally. We all step on each other's toes now and then."

The heat of his hand on her arm made her imagine the heat of his body. He had remarked at lunch that he had a high metabolism and burned up food. His body felt like a little furnace glowing in the chilly air.

She felt giddy. This was all unreal. It was intoxicating and flattering and outside of her real life. He would go back to California and she would go home and it would be sealed into itself, whatever happened, whatever. For some reason, she felt safe now. She relaxed. He put his arm around her as they approached his hotel and she did not draw away. She felt like laughing aloud. Nobody would believe this was Suzanne the Sensible being led along to his hotel room, which was obviously where they were headed. This man had emerged from her computer and he would vanish back into it. Lately she had been having occasional hot flashes and she had missed a couple of periods last year, including one in December. Her gynecologist told her it was the onset of menopause. Change of life. Perhaps one aspect of that change was hallucinating this man whose arm was around her waist, whose hip occasionally bumped hers as they walked, as they crossed Mass. Ave., as they entered the lobby of the Inn.

She felt ridiculously pleased and excited, even aroused as they went up in the elevator and walked along the corridor open on one side to the central atrium, then around a corner to his room. It was neat. He had his laptop set up and several folders on the desk. No clothes lay around, no wet towels.

He put his hands on her hips. "We've both been moving toward this for two years. Don't be coy with me now, Suzanne. Don't you want to know how we are together? Haven't you imagined this time and again?"

"Of course," she said honestly. She did not add that imagining was all she had expected.

He kissed her then, his mouth strange and invasive and exciting. As she kissed him back, as she loosened his shirt even as he undid her blouse, this molten Suzanne was familiar. She felt twenty again, back in late adolescence and early adulthood when sex had been an adventure, when she did not yet fear her own body and the consequences of passion. Here, she thought, there were none. It was all happening in cyberspace. He was a visitor in every sense of the word. A Suzanne she had thought dead, stirred, blossomed, grabbed control. Things moved quickly. She had always liked leisurely lovemaking, but her hunger wanted satisfying now, fast. He was slender but tight, the body of an active man, not buff like a young athlete, for he had a soft belly, but fit, stronger than his size would indicate. Easily he picked her up and spread her on the queen-size bed.

It had been so many years since she had put anything in her mouth besides food and a toothbrush, she was surprised how quickly her old skill at giving head came back to her. She ran her tongue around the head of his prick, then took him in her mouth. She still felt giddy. He was going down on her before she suddenly thought of contraception. She hadn't been on the pill in over a decade. Lectures she had given her daughters about unprotected sex came back to her with a sudden rush. "Uh . . . do you have a condom?"

He showed her the packet and she helped him put it on. He hurt her a little, although he entered slowly and she was wet. It was hard to separate the pleasure from the pain, the sharpness from the urgency. He settled into a steady rhythm and she bounded up to meet him, thrust for thrust. He was waiting for her and she concentrated. As excited as she was, she did not think she could come. She was too nervous with him. After several minutes, she faked an orgasm, as she had remembered doing with Sam. He moved then into a harder rhythm, building toward his own climax, and as he pounded into her, the almost forgotten rush of warmth and power and pleasure began building in her until she exploded just before he did. Afterward she felt like laughing, because she had made much less noise during her real orgasm than she had when she mimicked pleasure.

They lay for a while loosely holding each other. Then they showered and she began his tour of neighborhoods. It was clear they would make love again later. Have sex, at any rate. Although she felt close to him, she did not trust the intimacy. Nor did she fear it. Some women went on spa vacations to feel better. She was having a one-day affair.

7

Beverly

Beverly got Elena when she called. "So how come the only beauty in the whole family is answering the phone? How come I'm so lucky?"

"Only you'd say so, Grandma. It's my good luck to get you. So how are you doing? Did you get it on with that writer guy you were interested in?"

"I'm bumping along, what else can I do? I haven't had any luck with him yet, but I haven't given him up for dead. So how's the restaurant?"

"I was fired."

"Those kind of jobs, they'd just as soon get rid of you as exploit you. Hang around too long and they figure maybe you'll get something on them. The fish is rotten. The kitchen is full of roaches."

"All of that!" Elena laughed. "I got evicted and so I moved home. I'm looking for work. You know, Mother doesn't really like having me around. I'm always in the way. I always was."

"Elena, nobody can not love you! You and your mother, you just never understand each other. You're more like me, you're spontaneous and you get into trouble and you have a big mouth and men are always wanting things from you. She never does anything off-the-cuff. She'd have liked you to make a reservation six months ago. Mother, I plan to be fired next February and then I plan to be evicted, so you can expect me around the first of March."

"Grandma, you have the wickedest tongue. So how come you called?"

"I'm raising money for some tenants fighting eviction—"

"Ah, you want to put the bite on Mother."

"Well, she can afford it. She makes more money than the rest of the family combined. Look, I'll call back tomorrow evening. Where is she?"

"Taking some guy to the airport. I don't know where she met him, maybe at some conference?"

"Suzanne has got herself a boyfriend?"

"I been trying to figure that one. He didn't sleep here. Frankly I think he's just a friend of a friend, whatever. But she got decked out to see him."

"Let me know. How about yourself, my beauty girl?"

"Nobody I give a shit about, frankly. Just guys."

"Wait till you get to my age to be disillusioned. By now either I already did a thing with every old geezer I meet, or I might as well have, because I know his whole story from his ex-wives and ex-girlfriends. Or I had one just like him in 'fifty-five."

"I want something more special, something purer, something more intense. Something that matters, Grandma. Not a guy like a Diet Coke, not a guy like a hamburger. I want to be moved. I want to be forced to care. I want to love, really love, again. Do you think I'm too burned out?"

"No, precious. You're full of fire. You just need someone strong and right for you."

The next afternoon, Beverly went up to the Bronx to walk the picket line with her friends in the union. They were good kids. They worked so hard and they got so little. Her heart went out to them. She talked with dozens of them, some in Spanish, some in French as best she could, the Haitians, the brothers from Mozambique. It was a cold raw day with a wind that felt like it was peeling the skin off her face. They had bitter coffee in a plastic container, and one of the women went off for sandwiches and chips. After she had marched the line for a couple of hours, her knee began to give her trouble. After two guys from the American Nazi party had beat her up in Central Park years ago at an antiwar rally, her knee had never been the same. They liked to target the women, especially to gang up on women they guessed were Jewish.

She had to stand on the subway going home as it was already rush hour, and she just stayed on the express to Ninety-sixth. When she got to the top of the steps, she felt dizzy. She dragged herself along the twelve long blocks to her apartment past the unisex beauty parlors, the theater that showed Spanish-language films, the shoe shops, the hardware store, the nail salons, the gym, the travel agencies. She was too tired even to stop and pick up something to eat. She thought about chicken from the take-out place but she didn't have the energy. Maybe she had something she could defrost. She was beat. If that Chino-Cuban place that had been on the corner still existed, they would have delivered. She was struck by how as she went through the streets of her neighborhood, she marked distances by landmarks that no longer existed. Oh, that's a block from where the New Yorker bookstore used to be. Yeah, she's upstairs from where Murray's Sturgeon was before he moved. Turn left at where the Thalia was. A map of ghosts.

She let herself drop on the couch in her apartment. Mao came and lay on her chest. He felt heavy, but she was too tired to push him off. In a way it had been nice to have Marta and Jim here. She enjoyed the gossip about Suzanne, things Suzanne would never tell her. She enjoyed having an independent relationship with Suzanne's best friend, and she enjoyed having a good-looking man like Jim around. Still, the apartment was small. Although the couch opened into a double bed, there was only one bathroom. She was not much of a hostess, but she did run out for bagels and lox and cream cheese, and make them coffee. It turned out Jim was no longer drinking coffee. Beverly sighed. People increasingly seemed to define themselves by what they didn't do: didn't smoke, didn't eat fat, didn't eat meat or anything palatable. Didn't wear leather. Didn't drink. Didn't. If you ever said you loved something, they would say you were addicted to it. What a boring bunch of people the next generation had turned out to be. Jim was a handsome man, a little younger than Marta, but he kept himself up. Since he'd lost his teaching job and become a therapist, he spent a lot of time at the gym. She had never known anybody who worked out the way people did now. Guys were never hesitant in the old days to take off their shirts. Everybody felt as if showing some skin was a treat to the other sex. Women didn't feel they had to look like bone thin models to turn on a guy, and guys didn't think they had to be built like Charles Atlas. After all, a lot of them did heavy labor. In fact her friends used to laugh at the muscle guys. Oh, they liked some strength in a man, but not those carved muscles that were all the rage now, like pet snakes, she thought, exotic, useless, and time-consuming to keep up.

Two boys in the neighborhood had drowned last September, jumping into the river to swim in their clothes. Men did that more often these days, because they were getting to be as vain and ashamed of their bodies as women. They were embarrassed to strip to their underwear. They might not look like an underwear ad from the subway, Calvin Klein and his ghouls. So they went swimming in their clothes to cool off, and the waterlogged oversize pants dragged them to their deaths.

But Jim was proud of his body. He liked to show it off. For a while he had practiced distance running, but then he had taken up weights instead. She really liked him, but she didn't see the point in wasting all that time heaving and grunting around a gym, paying out good money to pretend to be a teenager. He was some kind of therapist, she had never gotten it straight. The truth was, she thought all therapists did was persuade people that problems were theirs, not the system's. Why blame General Motors or Coors or General Dynamic, if you could blame Mommy? Jim had been a college teacher, but in a budget crunch, he had been laid off. Like so many. She'd never had a profession beyond being an organizer, although she had worked at a great many jobs. But none of them had meant a thing besides a paycheck and a chance to do some political work. Sometimes, just a paycheck.

Beverly sighed. When she looked back over her life and thought about all the good changes she had hoped for, she could get into the dumps. But what the hell. You just had to keep slugging and have fun along the way. Mao was kneading her chest with his paws. She knew he was hungry, and she felt guilty. Finally she hoisted herself up. Felt dizzy again. Now what? High blood pressure? She rarely went to the doctor—just a waste of time and more money for the drug companies. Dr. Moss had given her those ghastly pills that had made her feel like her head was disconnected from her body. She had stopped taking them two months ago. She wasn't going to poison herself to profit some drug conglomerate. She undressed and put on her nightgown. She sure wasn't going back out, as wiped as she was.

She dragged herself into the kitchen, ashamed of her fatigue. She opened a can of salmon and split it with Mao, toasting a bagel left over from Marta and Jim's visit. Marta shouldn't have let herself go gray. She made more money than Jim. That didn't shock Beverly the way it would have a lot of women. After all, her own mother, working as a button maker, had made more than their father. Papa got what work he could on the Lower East Side, but Mama had always been the real breadwinner.

Many political women had been able to get work when their husbands were blacklisted or worse, so it was no big deal to her that Marta earned twice what Jim did, but she could tell it was an issue to him. He had not expected to have to go back to school at thirty-six and begin a new career. Eight years later, he was always looking back over his shoulder at the life he should have been leading. She suspected him of getting it off sometimes with his women patients, but she had never said a word to Marta or certainly not to Suzanne, who'd make a federal case of it. She wouldn't just see that a little of that on the side probably kept him from seriously straying. After all, a guy in a position of authority and sympathy with a woman patient, why wouldn't they both be tempted? She just observed the signs and kept her mouth shut. Beverly had known Marta as long as she'd been tight friends with Suzanne. As husbands went, Jim wasn't half bad.

She had wondered how it would go with the three of them sharing that big old rambling house, wondered if Suzanne wouldn't be tempted by Jim, wondered if she could bottle up her jealousy at living with a couple. But Suzanne had always been controlled, except for that early fling with the Latino guy. Beverly had not liked Sam. His politics were okay, but he was a cold fish, superrational, the kind of guy who would rather argue all night than have a good time. He had married again, a woman who had a trust fund and no ambition but to please him and keep him, and she did. Too bad Victor wouldn't marry Suzanne. She would have liked him for a son-in-law, but Victor wasn't the marrying kind. Apparently Suzanne could live in the same house with Jim for years and never give him the eye. Admirable, sure, but a little inhuman. Suzanne had set out to make herself over into a flawless woman, one without weaknesses. A perfect professional who consumed herself in her work. So much of what Suzanne did seemed a silent reproach to herself about the way she lived her life.

Beverly lay on the couch watching her old TV because her eyes were too tired to read. Before she'd gone up to the picket line, she'd knocked herself out, finishing that manuscript she was copyediting. Now she couldn't see straight. Her vision felt blurry. She turned on a PBS program on cybernetics, but she just couldn't focus.

When she woke, the TV showed nothing but snow. It must be the middle of the night. She couldn't see the clock well, which was unusual. When her eyes got tired, she couldn't read, but she could usually see distant things just fine. She didn't feel . . . right. She sat up slowly and her dizziness increased. Her head hurt, sharply. She lurched to her right and almost fell to the floor, realizing she could not put weight on her right arm. Her right hand would not close. She had a feeling of something in her head, something pushing, something pressing. She grabbed the phone clumsily in her left hand, the hand that still worked, put down the receiver and poked at the numbers. She was calling her friend Lucy, who answered after four rings. Once again Beverly clutched the phone in her functional left hand. She was ready to cry with joy when she heard Lucy's voice. Lucy would come over and help her into bed and maybe call a doctor or persuade her that nothing was really wrong. Maybe she was just dizzy or had a virus. Some middle-ear virus that made her dizzy. But why couldn't she move her hand? It didn't feel like pins and needles. It didn't feel like anything. Why was her hand paralyzed?

"Who the hell is this at four A.M.?"

She meant to say, "Lucy, something's wrong with me," but what came out sounded like slow and slurred babble.

"Some stupid drunk!" Lucy snorted, and hung up.

She stumbled across the floor, hanging on to the sofa and then the bookcase and then the door. Her right leg was dragging. Something was terribly, terribly wrong. Was this what dying felt like? Her life was not flashing before her, but her heart was pounding fiercely and her head felt as if it were split open. It was as if some dentist had injected Novocain into half her body. Her right side was not only numb but uncontrollable, as if she had been cut in two.

She put it together as she finally got the door open. She was having a stroke. Utter panic seized her. She leaned on the doorpost, frozen with terror. Calm, calm, calm, she told herself. You've had concussions. In antiwar demonstrations, she had been clubbed. On picket lines, she had been knocked down and kicked. *Stroke* was just a word. She was still alive. Her mind was functioning. If she could recognize what was wrong with her, it could not be so bad. Several of her acquaintances had suffered strokes. One had never walked again. The other recovered his abilities, but afterward moved more slowly, more hesitantly. But at least he could move. In the hall, her leg gave way under her and she fell. Then she crawled forward until she could knock on Madeline's door. They were not friends, but they helped each other out. Madeline fed Mao when Beverly went out of town—which seldom happened nowadays. Beverly walked Madeline's poodle when Madeline had the flu or visited her son. They accepted packages for each other and shared leftover goodies.

She lay on the floor banging on Madeline's door, but Madeline did not come. However, the Korean woman across the hall looked out. "Mrs. Blume, my God, what happened?" She turned and shouted to her husband in Korean.

Now Madeline finally came to the door, opening it an inch on its chain. "Beverly, what are you doing on the floor? Did you hit her? What's going on?"

"She's been mugged in her apartment, I bet. Look, she's in her nightgown. We have to call the police. It's like that poor woman on 108th."

Beverly tried to tell them that she was having a stroke. Madeline bent close to her. "Look at her face. It's all twisted."

Mrs. Kim called 911. Mao came creeping out, but Madeline saw him and shut him in her own apartment. Madeline and Mrs. Kim ventured into Beverly's apartment, Madeline holding her cane and Mrs. Kim brandishing a kitchen knife. "There's nobody in here. No windows open."

It was as if she were already dead and a ghost. She could hear them, she could understand them, she could think clearly what she wanted to say, but she could not make her tongue speak the words. She had become far more mute than Mao, who was pretty good at making his needs known. She was a piece of furniture, a sack of flesh lying on the floor. She began to weep quietly with frustration. The tears ran over her face and onto the floor.

The police figured out she was having a stroke and called an ambulance. She was only half conscious, but she was relieved when finally she was carried into the rickety elevator to be taken downstairs. She was terrified, but at last she was off the floor. Doctors dealt with strokes all the time. Lots of people her age had strokes. They would fix her up at the hospital.

8

Suzanne

Suzanne had been in court all day. Her client's suit against the Dedham Police Department was in its second week, while colleagues were covering her classes. She was planning to wind up today. When the secretary from the law school appeared in the courtroom, Suzanne was startled. The woman passed a note to the court officer, who glanced at it and passed it to Suzanne.

> *Your mother has had a stroke and is in a hospital in New York. This is the phone number. The dr's name is Weinstein.*

She stared at the note. "Are you sure?" she mouthed.

The secretary nodded. Suzanne asked to approach the bench. She showed the judge the note. He frowned. "How old is your mother?"

"She's seventy . . . two."

"Can anyone take over for you?"

"Yes , Your Honor." She motioned to the defense table, where Marta was sitting. "I'm finishing in perhaps half an hour. Let me do that and then I can try to find out what's happened."

"It sounds as if what has happened is perfectly clear."

"If we could adjourn until Monday, I would be able to fly down and see my mother."

The judge motioned the police department's counsel forward. "I don't have any objection to the delay. Do you, Counsel?"

She called the hospital from her car phone. "Mrs. Blume is in intensive care. Are you a family member?"

"I'm her daughter."

"I thought her daughter was in today. . . . No, I see that was her granddaughter. She has had a stroke, but she's conscious now."

She packed in fifteen minutes, left instructions with Elena, and ran upstairs. Jim was sitting at his computer. He saw clients three days a week and the rest of the time he worked on his book *Shafted and Beyond: A Manual for Those Rendered Superfluous in Middle Age*. He had a book contract with a small publisher of self-help books and had been working on the manuscript for two years. She told him the situation and asked him to keep an eye on things downstairs. "But don't you think Elena will manage?" He swung around in his swivel chair and faced her, leaning back, every bit of his posture indicating a willingness to be interrupted, to talk about her situation.

"Just in case." She did not take the seat he beckoned her to. Her time was tight.

Jim was a tall, rangy man with an intense smile and the capacity to brood for weeks. His hair was light brown and his eyes such a pale blue they looked silver. She liked him, although she considered him vain, but her real relationship was with Marta. Jim was an appendage. They rarely had a private conversation. They got on, but they did not truly know each other in spite of having lived in the same house for twelve years. It was amazing, Suzanne thought, how much time you could spend with someone and never actually get personal with them. "You and Beverly have a rather fraught relationship, as I recall."

Recall? He had visited Beverly last week. He was getting into therapist mode. She began to feel a time panic. "Listen, Jim, I really have to get out of here." She was never comfortable when Jim switched into his therapist role, and right now she could not deal with it.

"I care about Beverly," he said, leaning forward to indicate a change of focus. "She's a strong, vibrant woman. Let us know how she is, please. If you need help down there, I could juggle my schedule and drive down."

She thanked him and tore downstairs. Her supper consisted of a yogurt eaten standing and a tangerine she peeled while waiting for the shuttle. Her stomach was clenched on itself, sore, knotted. All those years of smoking. How many times had she begged Beverly to quit? How many articles had she sent her? Books on the tobacco conspiracy, hoping that politics might succeed where health facts failed. Beverly ate fatty foods, fast foods, processed meats, fruit, yes, but almost no vegetables.

Yet Beverly was such a vital woman, opinionated, energetic, stubborn, independent, and feisty, an elegant woman, still attractive. She caught colds every winter that sometimes went into her lungs, but she had never had a serious illness. Beverly always said, "I'm too busy to get sick." Suzanne could not imagine what she would find. Was her mother dying? She knew nothing about strokes, imagining lightning striking the brain. A charred smell. Fire and devastation within.

She went straight from La Guardia to the hospital. At first they would not let her see Beverly. She did find out that the stroke had occurred the night before and that a neighbor had called the ambulance. She sat in the small lounge with its air of general tackiness and anxiety soaked into the worn upholstery and the wan carpeting, crowded with other individuals and family groups waiting for word, for a little time with their people in intensive care. It was as if each person or little group was inside a glass box of their own fear, unable to see each other or speak a word across the room.

Rachel walked in. They hugged each other fiercely. Suzanne kept herself from crying by making faces into Rachel's shoulder. Rachel too was taller than Suzanne, but not as tall as Elena, with a mane of curly light brown hair. Rachel drew away to call her attention to a young man. "Mother, this is Michael."

Shifting gears abruptly, Suzanne looked him over. A slight, almost wispy man, he had a firm handshake. Probably worked on that. "Do you know each other from school?"

Rachel nodded. "We've been seeing each other since late September."

So why didn't you mention him? Usually Rachel told her more details of her life than Suzanne could absorb, so why had Rachel held back? Michael seemed to be Jewish, he seemed intact and functional, so what did her silence mean? Suzanne filed away that query for later. "You've seen Beverly?"

Rachel nodded. "It's awful. She can't talk. Her right side is partly paralyzed."

Rachel knew exactly what had happened, including the names of the two neighbors who had found and helped Beverly. Finally the nurse told Suzanne that she might go in to see her mother for fifteen minutes. She felt like shouting a protest that she had not come all the way from Boston to see her mother for fifteen minutes.

In the hospital bed, Beverly looked like a broken doll. Her right arm lay on top of the covers as if discarded there. Her face drooped. Her mouth twitched but no words came out. Yet Suzanne could tell that her mother recognized her. Beverly attempted to speak but produced only muddy gurgles. Suzanne felt her chest tearing open with grief and pity. She took Beverly's limp right hand. The left hand moved over to stroke her arm. Suzanne fought back tears, bit down on her cheeks to keep from losing control. She was terrified for Beverly, who looked half dead. Were the doctors doing enough? She was just lying there with tubes in her. She must ask them if there wasn't some sort of operation, something that could be done.

Her mother was definitely there, conscious. She could feel the intellect behind her mother's green eyes. "Mother," Suzanne said. "If I could only find out if there's anything you need me to do for you."

Her mother was stroking her arm. No, not stroking. Suzanne looked at the finger. M. Beverly was sketching an M. Suzanne scrabbled in her bag for a pen and a bit of paper and put them in her mother's still functioning left hand. However, Beverly was right-handed. Still Beverly dug at the piece of paper with the pen. M again.

"M, Mother? What's M?"

A jagged A. A crooked O. "Mao. Your cat. You want me to find out what's happened to your cat?"

Beverly nodded.

"Ah, you can move your head yes and no. That's great." She felt an enormous flood of relief. At least there was some communication possible. "You can understand what I say?"

There was familiar irritation in that vehement nod.

"When they kick me out, I'll go to your apartment. How will I get in? Will the super let me in?"

Beverly traced a P on her arm.

"P? Postman? Pills?"

Beverly groaned. She traced a U, then an R.

"Purse? Your purse?" Suzanne felt absurd. They were playing twenty questions, a children's game she had played with Aunt Karla many times. She could see from Beverly's furious expression on the side of her face still expressive that her mother was aware of the absurdity and hated it. Beverly had always been a formidable presence to Suzanne, judgmental, opinionated, and always in her own way, elegant. A small woman like Suzanne, but not a woman who felt small in her manner, her impact, her bearing. Suzanne had always felt she was a disappointment to her mother, who combined militancy with style. Even at seventy-two, Beverly remained a flirt, a charmer. Nobody in their right mind would ever call Suzanne flirtatious or charming. She was capable. She was organized. Her intellect was far more honed than her mother's. She was successful. But in her mother's presence, she felt awkward, lumpy, unadorned. Plain but serviceable. The woman in the bed was a parody of her mother, but Beverly was present, trapped behind that ghastly grimace, that twisted face and limp body. Suzanne felt guilty she had not returned her mother's call. When Elena had told her that Beverly needed a check for some tenants' strike, Suzanne had been miffed. She had plenty of expenses and causes without needing her mother to put the bite on her. She should have called back anyhow.

She searched the room and the purse turned up. Indeed, the keys to Beverly's apartment were inside. "I'll stay in your apartment tonight."

Beverly nodded.

"Is there anything else you need?"

Beverly threw up her left hand in a helpless gesture. A tear rolled down her cheek from her left eye. The nurse appeared. "Now, time for our little patient to get some rest."

Suzanne could not endure hearing Beverly referred to in such a condescending way. "Please. My mother is a very able, highly intelligent woman. I want her to have the best care. I want her to have intensive rehabilitation."

"I'm sure Dr. Weinstein is doing everything that can be done." The nurse ushered her firmly out.

She had supper in the hospital cafeteria with Rachel and Michael, who were returning to Philadelphia that night. "But I'll come back. It's easy. We can even study on the train." Rachel fussed over Michael as he ate. She did everything but cut his meat for him, and she probably would have done that if he had eaten any. They both seemed to subsist on salads and juice. Of course, the food here wasn't kosher. Michael seemed to take being fussed over for granted. He liked it, obviously. She would never approve of the way her daughters behaved with men. Rachel had been involved with a few boyfriends previously, but this seemed different. She could not remember Rachel acting so possessive. In some ways they behaved more like an old married couple than like people who were just falling in love. She wondered sharply if they were living together, for they had a strikingly domestic air. Maybe that's why she'd had so much trouble getting Rachel on the phone in the last few months.

"Rachel, I didn't mean to offend you with Elena using your room. She's been evicted. She won't use the room off the kitchen. But her old room has been my law office for six years now. I can't move my stuff out. It's set up with the office equipment I need, my law library, my files. You know she isn't going to stay long. She doesn't like living with me one bit."

"It's just so like her to take my room. What's wrong with the room off the kitchen? It even has its own bathroom."

"She says I make too much noise in the mornings."

"Ah, the princess Elena sleeps till noon. . . ." Rachel grinned suddenly. "It's fine, Mother, really. I overreacted. Michael said I was being a baby. It isn't as if it's really my room any longer." Rachel had the habit of suddenly breaking her own pouts and snapping to with a luminous smile. She had done that since she was eight or nine. It was a charming habit that always melted Suzanne. It was an enormous relief to focus on Rachel and her boyfriend for a few moments, to block out the condition of her mother's battered mind and body.

"It's your room whenever you want it, Rachel."

"I mean, next year I won't even be in the country." Rachel turned to beam at Michael.

Suzanne clenched her hands in her lap. She found the notion of her daughter in Israel a little too dangerous to enjoy contemplating. "The college is still planning to send you to Israel, in the middle of this crisis?"

"Mother, Israel is always in the middle of some crisis."

Both future rabbis laughed. Suzanne did not.

After Rachel had left with Michael, Suzanne went back upstairs. She was permitted another fifteen minutes with her mother. It was even more frightening than before, for Beverly kept sinking into unconsciousness.

Then Suzanne took a taxi to the apartment where she had spent a night on the couch maybe fifty times over the past ten years. Mao greeted her hysterically. She supposed he remembered her and she also supposed he was frightened and lonely. The apartment smelled musty. She threw her overnight bag on the table and went to investigate. She took the trash and garbage to the incinerator and began to deal with dirty dishes in the sink. Someone had been feeding Mao but had not bothered washing his saucers.

She fed him again, fussed him up, and then went to talk to the neighbors. "You've got to do something about that cat," Madeline, the neighbor who had been feeding him, said. "I'll call Animal Rescue for you."

"Are you tired of feeding him?"

"He cries all the time. And he can't stay in that apartment alone. I'm not going to empty his shit, believe me. Just call the Animal Rescue people and they'll take care of him."

"Execute him, you mean. I'll take him until she gets out of the hospital."

Madeline shook her head. "She had a stroke, honey. Don't you get it? She'll never be herself. She can't even talk. She can't work anymore. How's she going to pay the rent?"

"I'd better call the landlord. Give me his name. I'll pay the rent for the time being. My mother is a strong woman. People can make amazing recoveries from strokes with good rehabilitation and the will to work at it."

She sat in her mother's small apartment, feeling a weight as substantial as a ton of rock on her head. It was all too much. What was going to happen to Beverly? What was going to happen to all of them? Her mother had gone in a few short minutes the night before from being an independent working woman to being perhaps an invalid, perhaps what? Her responsibility? Or would Beverly recover? Suzanne felt guilty even asking herself these questions, but as she sat in the chair usually occupied by her mother, some book on British labor organizing in the mines still open where Beverly had left off reading it, Mao in her lap with his claws dug into her sleeve as if she too might vanish, she could not turn off her mind. She could not vanquish the fear and the questions. If Beverly needed care, there was no one else to provide it. Karla lived on her teacher's pension and with her adopted daughter, Rosella, and family.

Her laptop was in her briefcase. She set it up on the coffee table, went on line, and began to access the various websites on stroke. She sat up until after midnight reading whatever she could and getting more and more depressed and more and more frightened. She could not believe what had happened to Beverly, so quickly, so unjustly—although as soon as she thought that, she mocked herself. What illness was just? What calamity was earned?

She wished she had possessed more energy to draw Michael out. Obviously Rachel was far more interested in him than she had been in any young man before. Rachel was not as glib and seductive with men as Elena—in fact, Rachel probably did not have it in her to be truly seductive. She had fallen in love before, but always she had been more serious than the boy. Rachel had recovered quickly from these small romances for her gaze was fixed on academic achievement. For several years she'd had a passion for tennis and played in local tournaments. She had been involved with ecological organizations since ninth grade. Whatever Rachel did, she did wholeheartedly, and now she seemed to have seriously formed a couple.

Thinking about Rachel gave her a little rest from studying stroke, but she could not focus long on her younger daughter. She kept feeling as if a wall had fallen on her as well as on Beverly. She had no idea how to proceed, but she could not endure that feeling of total loss of control and total helplessness. She would have to have an earnest conversation with Dr. Weinstein about her mother's condition and the options for treatment. She must make the doctors and nurses understand that she was actively monitoring what happened to Beverly. It would not do any harm to let them know she was a litigator. Doctors grew marvelously thorough when dealing with a lawyer. She felt a thrill of protectiveness: she would show her mother how useful she could be. She could master the medical jargon. She had already picked up a fair amount of the vocabulary on-line tonight. Tomorrow she would attack. Whatever Beverly needed in the way of therapy, medical intervention, Suzanne would make them understand was to be provided for her.

*   *   *

Suzanne sat in the back of the shuttle with her mother's cat in his carrier whimpering under her. Occasionally he gave a sharp cry of despair just for emphasis. It was Sunday evening, and she was exhausted. It felt wrong to leave Beverly in the hospital where Suzanne was not at all sure she was getting the kind of attention she needed. But obviously given Beverly's condition, the hospital was the only place for her.

There were elaborate instructions available for introducing one cat to another in a household, but all these rules involved much more time and energy than she had. She hauled the carrier into the kitchen and opened it. Mao bounded out, hissed at everything around him, and ran out of the room before she could feed him. She chased after him, but she had no idea where he had gone. "Elena," she called. Half the lights in the flat were on and in fact the TV was turned to music videos, but Elena was nowhere. How could she leave the house with the television running? Suzanne tried to gain control of herself. It had been a bad weekend, and it was shaping up to be a bad year. No reason to take that out on Elena. She sat on the couch feeling flattened. The image of Beverly in the hospital bed threaded by tubes, her face twisted, unable to speak, haunted her. A fat tear leaked from her eye. She rubbed both eyes hard and sniffed her nose clear. No point weeping now.

Everything had happened so quickly, a big wind, a storm out of nowhere. She turned on her computer. Ninety-seven messages awaited her, many from her law and feminist listservs, but a number were personal. Those she would read. Jake had sent two messages:

I hope you enjoyed the weekend as much as I did. Meeting you at last was a delight. As I told you when you were kind enough to give me a lift to the airport, my meetings went well. I'll share my notes with my staff and directors. We should come to a decision soon about New England. I'm hoping it will be positive. I felt very positive about our time together.

This morning another message:

I haven't heard from you. I hope this means you're busy catching up on the time you lost with me last weekend, and not that you are

having regrets? Don't second-guess your emotions—what happened
was good.

Jake felt distant to her, irrelevant. She had no energy to spare.
Second-guess? He would be insulted if he knew that she had almost
forgotten about their time together in fretting about Beverly. Suzanne
sighed deeply, could think of nothing to write, and went upstairs to
check in with Marta. She found Jim and Elena at the kitchen table just
finishing dessert while Marta cleared. "Do you want some supper, Suzanne? There's leftover chicken cacciatore. Jim made more than
enough."

Suzanne cocked her head, considering. "I guess I am hungry. I've been
living on hospital cafeteria sandwiches for three days. I'd love some of
Jim's chicken."

Elena got up at once. "Thanks for supper."

"Hey," Jim said. "I never finished telling you my lab rat story."

"Later. I'll remind you."

"Elena, there's a black cat in the apartment. Remember your grandmother's cat?"

"Chairman Mao? What's he doing here?"

Suzanne explained briefly. "So don't let him out. Maybe you should
put some food down."

After Elena left, Suzanne said, "I hope she didn't invite herself to
supper. The way I just did."

Jim frowned. "She isn't an angry teenager any longer. She's her own
person now."

Marta asked, "So are you here for a while? I'm not quite up to speed
on your sexual harassment case. If there's a chance I might have to take
over, I'd better master it."

"I think I can confine my trips down there to weekends, unless there's
another crisis. I paid the rent on her apartment, cleaned out the refrigerator and brought her what she needs in the hospital. . . . As to what's
going to become of her, Marta, I have no damned idea. One day you're
healthy and making some money and living your life. The next day you're
in a hospital bed with tubes sticking into you, unable to walk or talk or
stand or take yourself to the toilet. I can't think of much that's scarier."

"How's your blood pressure?" Jim asked.

"Right now, probably off the scale. That's one of the reasons I exercise so passionately. It keeps my blood pressure down."

"I should get one of those handheld machines and start taking mine regularly," Jim said. "My father died of a heart attack when he was sixty-two."

"I don't know what my father died of. The widow never told me."

"Shouldn't you know?" Marta sat across the table, sipping decaf while Suzanne ate. "Suzanne, just because you never knew your father doesn't mean his genes aren't active in you. You didn't spring parthenogenetically from Beverly, no matter how much it may have felt that way."

"I don't even have his widow's address. . . . She didn't encourage contact. This chicken is great." She smiled at Jim, who looked pleased. He had taken up cooking in the past few years. He was the best cook in the house.

"Suzanne, Jim and I have been talking. Elena needs a job and Jim needs a receptionist. Why not?"

"Elena is not the world's most responsible citizen, you know," Suzanne said slowly. "I'd be really happy for her to go back to work, but have the two of you thought this through?"

Jim waved his hand airily. "You're too down on her. It's not a demanding job. It's three days a week. She might even like it. I don't have an elaborate history with her, like both of you, so she's more herself with me."

"Did you ask her?"

"Of course," Jim said. "Why wouldn't I ask her? She's an adult and it's a quieter environment than the restaurant. I don't expect it to be permanent, but my office is falling apart since my assistant got a full-time job."

"What do you think about it?" she asked Marta.

"It sounds worth trying. Jim's been complaining about getting behind in billing, his records incomplete, double-booking appointments. . . ."

Suzanne understood. When Jim complained, Marta felt obliged to solve his problems. Probably the idea of hiring Elena had been hers to begin with: since Marta had defended Elena in court, she had always felt a little responsible for her. Not that Elena usually appreciated that any more than what she saw as Suzanne's meddling.

When she came downstairs, she was able to locate Mao immediately by the sound of loud hissing—a den of snakes—and a harsh yowling she could not imagine issuing from her gentle Sherlock in spite of seeing him with his back arched and his fur on end. Tamar was up on the counter out of harm's way, but her fur too was erected in an attempt to look even bigger than she was. Both cats were bigger than Mao, but he was standing his ground. The confrontation had occurred over a dish of cat food that Elena had put down on the kitchen floor. She wished she could explain to her cats that Mao was a visitor and needed support, not hostility. She scooped up Sherlock who made terrible threats but allowed himself to be carried off to her bedroom, where she shut the door and fussed over him. Then she unpacked her carry-on bag and tried to figure out exactly what overdue piece of work she should tackle first. It promised to be a long night. She would answer Jake in the morning. At the moment, he felt like one more demand in an increasing list of them. When she tried to call up his face, she saw only Beverly, twisted and in despair.

Elena was sprawled on the sofa with Mao on her lap. "So I think I found a job."

"In Jim's office?" Suzanne asked cautiously.

"It doesn't pay great, but it's not exactly brain surgery."

"Elena, if you go to work for friends, it doesn't mean you don't have to work hard, get there on time, the whole ball of wax. Because they're friends, you can't just walk out."

"Do you think I'm a total flake? I've held all kinds of jobs, and it's no big deal for me to work for Jim and handle his little office."

"But, Elena, sitting up in a therapist's office making appointments isn't anything like as lively as working in the restaurant. The proprietor may have been oppressive, but you liked the scene. You told me you loved going to after-hours bars and hanging out with the kitchen crew and the waiters."

"Yeah, it's a scene, but I've had it. Nothing real comes of it, just surface excitement. Some waiter goes, Look who just walked in. The second-string sportscaster from Channel Four, big deal! Enough. . . ." Elena slowly scratched Mao under his chin and he leaned into her hand, safe in her lap from the big orange monsters her gentle sweet cats had become. "Mother, you're the one been telling me for years, think about your future. Think about what you want to do. Et cetera. Et cetera."

"But surely the future you crave isn't being a receptionist."

"I want to see what a therapist does. You're always making jokes about therapists, but when people hurt, that's where they go. Remember when you thought it was awfully important for me to spend months and months in therapy!" One of Elena's rare references to what had happened twelve years before. "Besides, I took a bunch of psychology courses."

In the course of her four colleges during years of on-and-off schooling, Elena had taken courses in almost everything. "Do you really think you might be interested in therapy? You could go back to school."

"How do I know if it's real? I need to watch a therapist in action. Then I can decide."

She would beg Jim not to blame her if it didn't work out, and urge him not to hesitate to end the situation if Elena was getting in his way. But, yes, it seemed to her a better situation than the restaurant. From her pre-academic years in the law collective, she had a pretty good idea how much cocaine and speed and heroin passed through the kitchens of restaurants. It would be much better for Elena to be out of there. She was always at risk. She thought that Elena had stayed clear of drugs since she was fifteen, but she could never be sure. Never. She supposed she just wanted to believe that.

I feel like a bad mother. I think on the whole I have been barely adequate—like Beverly, my own mother.

I'm also feeling guilty that one of my first reactions—silent, of course—to my mother's stroke is to worry about what impact it's going to have on me. What will happen to her? How much will all this cost? Is she going to move back into her apartment, ever?

I know I've presented myself to you as organized, capable, rational, in control. Most of the time that's how I think of myself. Yet sometimes I look at my life and I feel just the opposite is true, that everything outside of the law is a series of overreactions and careening blunders.

*Like my mother, I got pregnant at twenty-two. I had just entered law
school. The smart thing I did was not to drop out but to continue.
The other smart thing I did was not to marry Elena's father, although
I have to confess he didn't ask me.*

Victor had been five years older than Suzanne and dazzlingly handsome. When he began to pay special attention to her, she could not
believe it. She met him in the clinic their law school was running, where
she as a first-year student was involved in a work-study program. He was
in danger of being deported. She could still remember the moment he
had turned and suddenly stared into her eyes, when she felt the floor
dissolve under her soles. His eyes were large and luminous, a radiant
dark brown: Elena's eyes. Stories swirled about Victor, as they always
would, for he looked as if he should be a hero. Perhaps he was. He was
also a skillful liar, but then that might go with being a hero in danger.
She had never understood him. She had only experienced him.

She knew she should not become involved with him, and she was
unable to resist. His desire simply encompassed her and she burned. She
still could not imagine why he had selected her among all the women
who flirted with him, even after he and she were involved, even right
in her presence. But he found in her exactly what he was looking for.
She was not a virgin, but she might as well have been, for his touch
consumed her. She was besotted with him. She adored him, even as part
of her studied him more cautiously than he ever realized.

One thing she was not too besotted to figure out was that he was not,
as the rumors said, a peasant who had taken up arms. He was the son
of a family with considerable money. He had been educated in private
schools abroad, as was the custom in his family. Yes, he had become a
radical and yes, he had fought the government. She did not doubt he
had put himself in danger. But he was never short of money. What he
lacked was comfort. He had decided to move in with her almost immediately, and he expected to be taken care of. In spite of her feminism,
she did not doubt for a moment that she must cater to him. He was
semidivine. His skin was satin. His eyes were those of a proud predator.
His stance was that of a conqueror. She capitulated; she collapsed. She
brought him his coffee with sweetened warm milk in the mornings while
he lay in state in bed. She picked up his clothes where he tossed them

and did his laundry. She cooked only food he liked or purchased it ready made. He was surprised at first how poor she was, and that he had to give her money for his accustomed luxuries of cigars and wine and pastries. She saw all this clearly and with a wry grimace at the same time that she was melting under him and fluttering to fulfill his every whim. So it went until she was four months pregnant.

I married Sam because I already had Elena and was overwhelmed with raising her alone. I had Rachel because I felt I had to have a baby for Sam too, since he seemed to want one. I stayed with Sam long after everything between us was gone except arguments, because of the girls. Some personal life.

I feel guilty that I loved living alone. For the first time in years and years, I had quiet at the center of my life. Ultimately I think I am a failure at human relations, except for friendship. I have been a silly lover, a lackluster wife, a failure as a mother, and inept as a daughter. I do well with cats and friends. I should have married a tomcat.

She felt guilty, that was the one absolutely sure thing: guilty because of Beverly, guilty because of Elena, guilty because she had fallen in bed with Jake like a twenty-two-year-old. Actually she didn't feel particularly guilty about that, she just thought she ought to. She smiled at her computer screen. Secretly she was rather pleased at her adventure. The only person who knew was Marta. After all, when most people go to bed with a new lover, they have to tell SOMEONE. Her someone was Marta. Only little girls and adolescents were supposed to have best friends, but maybe unmarried women could have them too. She was sorry that Jim and Elena had been upstairs, because she wanted nothing more than to sit down with Marta and tell her about Beverly in great detail, to confess to Marta how frightened she was and how confused about what to do next. But since she could not tell Marta, once again she collapsed into telling Jake—her late at night and first thing in the morning confidant.

9

Beverly

Beverly was talking to a worker at a machine in the jeans factory in South Carolina. The machinery was all going, the air was heavy with dust, and the boss was threatening her. She had to get out. She would meet the workers outside. But she could not move. Her legs would not obey her. The thugs the bosses had hired were coming after her with billy clubs and wrenches, but she could not move. Her legs were too heavy. She was falling.

She was at Jones Beach lying on a blanket with Ralph Caputo. He was rubbing suntan oil into her back in sweet sensuous circles. Now he was putting something wet on her back. Maybe she was in the water. The water was warm as a tub. But the water dripped along her sides and then it was cold. "Please, Mrs. Blume, am I hurting you?" Why was Ralph calling her Mrs. Blume?

Beverly came out of the haze slowly as the pain in her head abated. She could remain conscious longer at a time. She figured out she was in the hospital and gradually she remembered the stroke. She thought Suzanne had been there and Rachel and Elena. She wasn't quite sure. Her dreams were vivid, making it hard to tell what had happened and what she had imagined as she kept sliding under. They had her on intravenous, but at least they had taken the disgusting tube out of her mouth and throat. Some of the time, she just lay in the bed and cried— cried on her good side. The left side remained loyal, but her right side had betrayed her. She finally got through to the nurse with the bushy perm that she wanted her purse. She could look at herself in her purse mirror. Her face was drooping as she had thought, but not as badly as she had feared.

She could hear and see perfectly well. The doctor who asked the same questions five times kept inquiring if there were blurry spots in her vision. No, no, no, she shook her head. On the right side, her head had a tendency to flop on her neck. She had become a rag doll. If only she were ambidextrous the way her friend Nell had been. Nell had had her arm broken in a demonstration back in the Vietnam years, but she had been able to write with her left hand. Well, she would just learn to print with her left hand.

She was still intact inside. She could think, she could understand what the patronizing nurses said to her as they addressed her as if she were feebleminded or a child of four. She wanted to scream. She tried once, but nothing came out of her mouth but a weird inchoate banshee moan. The effort made her drool. She clamped her lips tight. She would not drool. She would communicate, somehow, somehow. She was still herself, but she was stuck inside a body that no longer obeyed her. She had never made a mind/body split the way Christians and Platonists did, but here she was in a body that no longer seemed to fit. Her body had gone on a sit-down strike against her mind.

That guy, Ralph Caputo, they had beat him up when he was organizing women in a sweatshop in Brooklyn. The thugs bashed his head in. He was paralyzed afterward. He couldn't talk straight. That's why she'd been thinking of him, for she was like him now, broken, useless. Her friends would gradually forget her. Everyone would say, poor Beverly, she'll be missed; but not for long. Nobody was missed long. A new person filled the space. How often had she thought of Ralph in the past twenty years? She had gone to see him a few times out of remembrance of their good times in the sack and in the field together, but then she too had forgotten him—until she became him.

They lifted her on a gurney like a bag of trash and wheeled her to a machine and stuffed her into it. She felt as if she were about to be cooked. Nobody explained anything. They just treated her as if she were not conscious, alive, involved. She lay in the machine wanting to scream again, claustrophobia bringing her close to panic. By the time they let her out, she was convinced they had stored her in one of those sliding trays in a morgue, except for the noises the machine made. Her hearing was just fine.

Three doctors came in and chatted with the nurse around her bed, discussing her. They were talking about her the way a vet might talk about a dog's injury in his presence, without any sense that she could comprehend. She felt that any moment one of them would recommend she be put to sleep, which wouldn't be a bad idea. If life was to go on like this, death would be preferable. Of course that was a fantasy. They'd rather stick more tubes in her and do tests for the next ten years. They wouldn't suddenly say, Okay, old lady, do you want a way out? Yes, sir mister doctor, yes!

Rachel appeared suddenly, her light hair blown wild by the wind. "Bubeleh, can you understand me? It's Rachel, your granddaughter."

Beverly nodded wildly. At last someone was talking to her and not about or at her.

"But you can't speak yet? I was here last week, remember?"

Beverly nodded. She did sort of remember. She made a talking motion, like a turkey gobbler with her left hand and motioned toward herself. Rachel understood. "Well, I'm here with Michael, my boyfriend, but they won't let him come in to see you."

A boyfriend? If he came with her, he must be interested. No guy just casually dating a girl would go up to New York with her to hang around a hospital where her grandmother was stored. She made a gesture from charades at drawing Rachel out.

"Oh, you want to know about Michael. He's wonderful. We're going to get married, but that's a secret, I haven't told Mother. I know she'd carry on how I just met him. We have so much in common, Grandma. We haven't decided whether to get married before or after we go to Israel for our rabbinical studies next year."

Beverly pointed to the mirror and then made the motion of drawing out.

"What does he look like? He's tall and thin and very serious. He has marvelous hazel eyes. His family are Conservative, verging on Orthodox. His grandfather was a rabbi in Germany before the family escaped in the thirties, but his father was in the garment business. His father still wants him to come into the business."

Beverly snorted. After spending most of her life organizing in the garment business, she did not have a high regard for garmentos, men who subsisted off cheap labor here and now abroad. Always somewhere women and girls were sitting in a dim room full of dust sewing jeans and dresses, hour after hour, year after year for pennies and the profit of those men. Better he should be a rabbi.

The nurse came in and made Rachel leave just as things were getting interesting. She was dying to ask Rachel where he was from, were they sleeping together, everything. Rachel went back to Philadelphia, Suzanne appeared, and the tests went on. They prodded and poked every part of her body. They drew enough blood to make her anemic. "Your blood pressure is still dangerously high, Mrs. Blume." What got into that young doctor? He actually addressed her. Improperly trained. He didn't understand she had become a rag doll. She beamed at him as best she could and nodded wildly.

Finally they took her off the intravenous. Some kind of therapist came to teach her to eat, as if she had not been eating all her life. However, after they had been at it together for half an hour, she was willing to recognize that she had to learn to eat all over again. She could not use a knife properly with her left hand, and she had a tendency to spill the food over herself. She was a one-year-old, not even a toddler. She could not talk, she could not walk, and she was just learning to feed herself. Food had a tendency to accumulate on the numb side, where she couldn't tell there was anything tucked into her cheek and threatening to slide down and choke her. All she was taking now were liquids and very soft foods like Jell-O and cream soup. She imagined eating roast chicken. She imagined a steak, although she had never been a big meat-and-potatoes woman.

Suzanne appeared, talked, worried, fussed. Disappeared again. The nurses gave her pills, injections, more tests. The therapist who was teaching her to eat now made her try to stand. She promptly fell over like a toy horse with a broken leg. Thump. They caught her, but she banged her good arm. She did not look forward to the times they hauled her out of the room, no longer on a gurney but now in a wheelchair she was picked up and placed in. She hated to see the other stroke sufferers all waiting for X rays, for CAT scans, for yet more tests. She knew that she looked as bad as they did, and that made her want to weep and bang her head. They were all helpless, hauled about and pestered.

She lay in the bed, too weary to lift her hand. Her left hand. She was terrified when she had the energy to think of what would become of her. How could she do her work if she couldn't speak? How could she even buy food? What would her friends want with her? How could she do any political work?

Why me? Why me? She cried and then grew angry with herself. Really, she was sounding like one of those people who demanded the world make personal sense. If something happened, it was part of the divine plan. Accidents, catastrophes all had to mean something. Yeah, they meant pain. The days flowed into one another and the long gray nights. Suzanne had gone back to Boston with Mao in a carrier.

"That was two weeks ago, Mother," Suzanne said. "I took him to Brookline two weeks ago."

At least he would be all right. Poor boy. He would not understand what had happened. The janitor had found him in the rubbish starving and injured, and now he would think he had been deserted again. If she was to die, as they said she almost had that first night, would that be so bad? It was living on in a broken body, dumb and crippled, that terrified her. It was surviving this catastrophe, the betrayal of her mind and her body. It was enduring in the prison of her mind, unable to speak, unable to walk, like some poor animal run over in the street and lying in the gutter mangled beyond recognition, but still feeling, still in pain, caught hideously between living and dying.

10   Twelve Years Before

Elena

Elena was bored. She saw high school stretching on forever. Each day was infinite. Each class drained the blood from her. It was like eating dust all day. She did not know which class she hated more, algebra or biology. The only classes she liked were Latin, Spanish, English, and gym. She liked gym because they were dancing. She loved to dance. Languages were always fun, like playing dress up in words, and she was the best. In English she got to write about her feelings, and she had plenty of those to spare. Her teacher liked her. She wanted to pat his bald head and scratch behind his ears. He perked up so when he looked at her. She had been growing again. She was as tall as Chad now though still shorter than Evan. When she walked down Washington or Tremont, men were always calling to her out of cars, making rude noises, as if she were a dog that would come to a whistle.

Sam said that she should be flattered, but if some man twice his weight leaned out a car window to call him a sweet ass, he wouldn't think it was so cool. When she walked with Chad or Evan, they left her alone. It was always better to be with them. Her mother said to her, "I know these friendships seem all-important to you now, but high school friendships dissipate with time. You probably won't go to the same college. You'll develop different interests. You'll start going out with boys and you'll make new friends." Her mother was worrying that she was spending too much time with Evan and Chad. Brat Rachel had told Mother that one or both of them were always around, which simply wasn't true. They were at Evan's more than anyplace else, because nobody was ever home there.

"What do you think will happen to us?" she asked them. They were all lying on Evan's bed.

"Nothing," Chad said. "What happens to anybody? They get older and stupider."

"What do you want to be when you grow up?" Evan mocked in a fruity voice.

"Dead," Chad said. "Stone dead."

Chad had gradually filled them in on his situation. When his parents divorced, his father had won custody. He had persuaded the judge that he was more responsible and better able to provide for Chad and give him a strong male role model. "I suppose," Chad said, lying with his head propped on his arms, hands clasped on the back of his neck, "that I'm supposed to develop that strong role model from his rows of fancy shoes, or perhaps his suits, because I sure do see his clothes a lot more often than I see Dear Old Dad. Not that I'm bitching, you know. If I never saw him, so much the better."

Chad missed his mother, but he wasn't permitted to say so. He was in therapy with a guy he despised. His father had interviewed him first. Charles the elder—they had the same name, but Chad refused to be Junior and had called himself Chad since he was ten—worked as a financial consultant. "He gets people to let him play with their money. Things like rare coins and annuities and investments. He gets the world's most boring magazines. All he talks about are ways to make money."

Chad was only supposed to see his mother every other Sunday and sometimes on vacations. She lived in a tiny apartment in Medford with the dog he hadn't been allowed to keep. They made appointments to talk on the phone when Charles the elder was out. She was a secretary again, as she had been when Charles the elder married her. Chad insisted they come with him one day instead of going to school. It was his mother's birthday, and he wanted them to meet her. He said he'd take them to lunch. When they cut school, Evan wrote notes for them, because he could imitate all the handwritings, Charles the elder, Evan's mother, and Elena's mother, Suzanne. Suzanne had this terrible sloppy scrawl that Elena could never read, that Evan said was the easiest to fake.

They took the green line to Park Street and then walked to a restaurant where they were meeting Chad's mother. Elena picked her out at once, at a corner table. She was tall for a woman and fair, but she had a perennially worried look. She rose to meet them, flustered, her hands seeking each other on the table. "Chad, are you sure it's all right to do this? I don't want you to get in trouble with your father. I don't want the judge to find out and your father to drag me into court again and reduce our visitation. We have to be careful."

"He never knows where I am, Mom. And he never remembered your birthday, so there's no way he's going to know it's today and even ask."

"But what about school. You're supposed to be in school."

"It's all right, Mom. It's taken care of."

It was funny, Elena thought. With his father, Chad was a sullen little boy, just a kid. But with his mother, he spoke in a lower voice, reassuring, in command. He was the man. Elena wondered if she would feel less incompetent if her mother weren't so take-charge. He even ordered for his mother, telling her what she wanted. It was cute.

"Are you Chad's girlfriend?" she asked Elena.

"Just sort of," Elena said. "My mother thinks I'm too young to date."

"You look very mature for your age."

"Thanks."

"I'm so glad Chad has friends at his new school. Even before the divorce, we were always moving. Every time Chad and I would start to like a place and I'd get to know the neighbors and we'd make a few friends, Charlie would see someplace he liked better or he would take a job with another firm or he would get fired and we'd have to move."

Her hair was blond and very short. Elena thought she dressed better than most mothers. She had a nice blue wool dress, simple and long. Tall women could wear slim long things like that. She tried to imagine what she would look like in that blue dress, for she almost never wore dresses. She was surprised how attractive Chad's mother seemed. She knew the woman had little money, but she spent it well. Elena liked her better than she had expected to. She understood why Chad preferred her. She was soft and quiet to be with. She didn't butt in. She wished her own mother were more like that. Chad's mother was soothing and flattered them. She thought she understood better than Evan did why Chad was crazy about her. Evan just saw a sad middle-aged woman who couldn't even figure out what she wanted to eat for lunch. No, Evan didn't get it. But she did. The next day, she let Chad know, and he was grateful, she could tell.

Chad lived way over in Back Bay on Beacon Street on the side toward the Charles River. The buildings were taller there and they didn't match. Chad's father had the top floor of a six-story building that was supposed to look like some of the older row houses, but didn't really. Some days a housekeeper was there, Mrs. Garcia. They never went near the place when she was working. Besides, it was a longish walk. It was furnished with chairs and sofas and tables that all seemed too big, as if made for a giant, in dark woods and with carving on the chairs.

One Thursday Chad wanted them to come over. First he showed them his room. It looked out on the river. He had a Nintendo and his own TV and stereo. He put on Ozzy Osbourne. Suzanne would only have one TV in the whole house, and she acted as if watching it would produce instant brain rot in Elena and Rachel. Elena perched on the window ledge, admiring the view. It was early spring, but there were sailboats already. He took them into his father's bedroom and opened the top dresser drawer. "Look at this."

It was a revolver, with a black handle and a shiny body.

"Your father has a gun in his drawer?"

"He has lots of guns. But this is my favorite. It's a classic. Smith & Wesson .357 Magnum." Chad sighted along it and Elena ducked out of the way. "It's not loaded," he said. "He doesn't keep bullets in them."

He rummaged in the drawer and pulled out a heavy little box. "These are the cartridges. Want me to show you?"

"Put that down," Evan said. "This is stupid. Who wants to get shot playing with a gun?"

"I wouldn't mind it," Chad said with a big grin. "But I know what I'm doing."

"Famous last words," Evan said.

"Charles the not so great taught me how to shoot. It's one of the few things we can stand doing together."

"You mean he takes you hunting?" Evan made a face. "Like bravely blowing holes in bunny rabbits?"

"I won't do that anymore. No, we just go target shooting at a range."

"My mother has a gun," Elena said.

"How come you never showed it to us?" Chad asked.

Elena had never thought of it as anything to show. "She keeps it locked up. She's always been terrified I'd play with it when I was little, or Brat Rachel would get into it. She and this lawyer friend of hers go target shooting, like your dad. I don't even know where she keeps it. It goes out of the house in a green bag when she and this woman Marta go off, like on Saturday morning."

"How come your mother has a gun?" Evan asked. "I mean, I can't imagine my parents having a thing like that in the house."

"She and her friend at the firm they're in do a lot of domestic violence cases, and sometimes the husbands or the boyfriends come after them. Besides, they enjoy it, her and her girlfriend, going shooting. Like they're playing macho."

"I like guns." Chad leveled the gun at the wall. "When I'm shooting at targets or skeet shooting, I pretend it's his head. Pow!"

"You really hate your father." Evan sat down on the bed, caressing the black velvet spread. Evan didn't care about guns any more than she did. She knew the velvet bedspread made him think about sex.

"He's really hateful." Chad remained standing.

"I don't hate my parents. I'm not close enough to them to have any strong emotions. They're like, my landlords, you know. Nobody I feel much about, but they take care of repairs and keep things running."

"Look at this." Chad pulled open a drawer in the nightstand next to the bed and pulled out a pistol. "This is just a .22 Ruger, but he's had it for years and he's fond of it. He has a warm feeling for his guns he never had for my mother or for me." Chad put the Ruger back in its drawer. He flourished the Smith & Wesson and then put it away too.

Evan had always been in control, of her, of Chad. But today with the guns, Chad was taking control. He was running things his way. He opened the locked door of his father's study with a credit card. "Do you have your own credit card?" Elena asked, surprised.

"Sure. But it has a really low limit. Just eight hundred dollars. That's really a crock. Anyhow, I saw this in a movie. Isn't it cool? Come on. This is Charlie's office. See, that's his shotgun from when he used to go hunting. The last time he went was with a bunch of other investment sharks, to a game farm where like they have tame tigers you get to murder for fun. It's a Remington 12 gauge. Aren't you surprised how much I know about guns? That's his liquor cabinet. Want anything?"

"How about a scotch?" Evan said. "I'm going to ask my parents for a Visa card too. Great idea. I bet they'll give it to me."

"He drinks only single malt. You'll like it." Chad handed the bottle to Evan, who took a swig and almost choked. Sometimes when they could get it, they drank beer or wine, but they almost never had hard liquor. Chad however could swig it without blinking. He must have practiced, she thought. She took a careful sip. It made her eyes water. Chad then took a small sip. She was watching his throat to see how much he swallowed. Then he handed off the bottle to Evan. "You can hold on to it," he said. Evan was drinking more than both of them put together. After a while he lay down on the leather couch. Chad pointed at his father's big TV. "I'll show you what he watches in here." He loaded it with a tape.

"Is that pornography?" Elena asked. She had never seen any.

"What do you think it is, Roadrunner?" Chad laughed. "Sit on my lap."

Evan was out of it. It was as if they were alone. They had never been alone together. Chad was different with her this time, slower. He kissed every part of her body. After the first ten minutes, the tape ran on, but they didn't look at it. She was convinced he had got Evan drunk intentionally. Afterward she realized that afternoon, the afternoon of the guns, everything changed. That was when Evan lost control of the three of them, and Chad came out on top. That was the first time that Chad

had sex only with her and not with Evan too. It was the first time she had sex only with Chad. It felt almost as if she was being unfaithful to Evan, doing it with him passed out on the couch. That was when everything began to be different, the way it was until the end.

11

Suzanne

Suzanne and Elena were eating an early supper of Chinese takeout, before Suzanne took the shuttle to see Beverly in the hospital. "Why don't you come to New York with me? You've always been your grandmother's favorite. All you'd have to do is throw underwear in a backpack and we'll fly down together."

"She wouldn't want me to see her like that."

"I think she's glad for any company. She's bored to tears."

Elena threw down her chopsticks. "I can't do it!" she shrieked. "You know I can't stand to see death and dying!"

Suzanne cringed. "I'm sorry. I thought maybe you'd gotten over it—"

"I'll never get over it." Elena rose and stalked from the table.

Suzanne found the routine of taking the shuttle to La Guardia every weekend and back again Sunday night grueling and depressing, but her presence helped ensure a decent level of medical attention for Beverly. She hoped it cheered Beverly up, although it was difficult to tell. This weekend Beverly was furious. Suzanne could feel the waves of anger coming off her mother, making her feel like an inadequate ten-year-old.

"Mrs. Blume can use her vocal cords," said the speech therapist. "They are not paralyzed. Her stroke has affected her speech center. But she can relearn to speak, if she would only try."

"I'll have a conversation with her about trying," Suzanne promised. Beverly used to get angry when anyone called her "Mrs." Blume, for she was proud that she had never married, but here she could not protest.

At least the room was a little less grim. Beverly was installed with two other stroke patients. One was much older than Beverly, a white-haired woman whose skull had been partly shaven for some procedure. The other was a woman in her forties, who wept constantly. She talked and talked. Suzanne heard the nurse call her Tammy. Tammy rattled off an occasional coherent sentence in the middle of babble and obscenities. She could not seem to stop talking, but she also could not seem to understand a word anyone spoke. The tears seemed to have no connection with what came out of her mouth. "Lazy fucking son of a bitch eat shit!" she would say. "Rover wants a cracker. Done the dirty laundry. Wrong dishes."

Suzanne sat on an uncomfortable chair beside the bed and talked earnestly at Beverly. She tried to decide the best approach. Sympathy? I know how you're suffering, Mother. . . . Beverly hated pity. At least her mother's face had straightened out. The nurses combed her hair occasionally. Suzanne had brushed it for her an hour ago, but it was standing straight up as if indignant. She decided to be blunt and straightforward. Attack and insist. "Mother, you have to try. You must do what the therapists ask you to."

Beverly printed in that awkward crooked left hand, BAD DOG.

She stared at Beverly, clutched with fear. Was Beverly going crazy like the woman in the next bed. No. Her eyes were lucid. "You mean, they're trying to train you like a dog. Obedience training."

Beverly nodded wildly.

"But, Mother, if they don't get you to cooperate, you'll never speak again."

WANT DIE

"Mother, you aren't going to die. That isn't an option. You'll live for years and years, so you have to learn how to communicate again. You have to get better. You must take seriously what they're trying to teach you."

POTTY TRAINING

"Well, do you want to dirty yourself? You're practically an infant in what your body will let you do. Don't you want to take back control?"

Now Beverly was weeping, only from the left eye. The other just stared.

It felt so odd. Instead of feeling ten now, she was her mother's mother giving her childhood instructions: learn to dress yourself, learn to speak so that others can understand you, learn to feed yourself, learn to tie your shoes and wipe your behind. No wonder Beverly was humiliated and furious. It was unjust that a mature and intelligent woman should have to go through this forced childhood; it was not right that Suzanne should have to play this hectoring role. Sometimes when Beverly glared at her, she wanted to tell her mother, all right, don't learn a thing. Rot in your bed!

She pulled herself closer. "Look, you're in great shape compared to What's her name, Tammy over there. At least you aren't blathering."

Beverly actually made a noise that could have been a laugh. She printed, GET ME OUT

"I can't." Suzanne felt desperate. "You have to do what all the therapists show you. You have to cooperate, Mother. Or you'll end up in a nursing home. The occupational therapist, the physical therapist, the speech therapist . . ."

WANT GO HOME. The conversation was extremely slow because Beverly had to laboriously print the words with her left hand.

"You'd starve to death. You wouldn't be able to feed yourself, to dress yourself, to get food in. Mother, you have to learn to do these things. You have to. If you really mean to get out of here, you have to work at all the stupid things they try to make you do. You can't get into college until you finish grade school."

NEVER WENT COLLEGE

"Actually you went for two years, remember?" She was a little frightened that Beverly didn't seem to remember that.

NO COUNT NO DEGREE

Suddenly Beverly sat up in the bed and began to sing, "We Shall Overcome."

Suzanne ran for the nurse. "She can talk now! She can talk!"

The nurse stuck her head into the room and shook her head. "That's just singing. A lot of them can sing when they can't talk."

"But if she can form the words to the song— Listen to her!"

"Don't ask me why, but often the ones who can't talk can sing songs they used to know. It's just that way." The nurse turned and swished off.

Whenever she tried to question anyone on the staff, from the chief doctor down to the therapists and nurses, she always came upon a blank wall closing off her march into answers. She began to realize it was not because they were withholding knowledge, but because they didn't possess it. The brain held secrets in its wrinkled gray convolutions, a mysterious organ as stroke was still a mysterious disease.

"Mother, I understand all this is humiliating, but there's no going back. You have to obey these therapists and nurses, no matter how condescending they are. You have to try to walk. You have to try to speak. You have to try to hold the spoon. Things will only improve if you stubbornly try to do things, instead of stubbornly refusing."

NEVER THIS MEAN TO YOU

"Oh, yes, you were." Suzanne snorted. "But, Mother, the only one who can get you out of this damned place is yourself. Don't fight me. Don't fight them. Fight your illness!"

Sunday afternoon, Rachel was there, praying at Beverly's bedside. Beverly must love that, but it sounded pretty, anyhow. At least it was company for Beverly, and soothing to herself. She could be quiet and bask in a moment of peacefulness. Rachel was blooming. She said she had been hiking with Michael. She tanned better than Suzanne, who freckled. Rachel freckled too, but not as extensively. How glad Suzanne had been when the fashion for a mahogany tan had faded in the epidemic of skin cancer and the destruction of the ozone layer. All through adolescence and early adulthood, she had spent a small fortune on tanning oils trying to look the way Elena looked naturally. All she got was blotchy. Her freckles got freckles.

Suzanne watched Michael, trying to collect a sense of him. He could pray just fine, loud and sure of himself with the Hebrew. His Hebrew was more fluent than Rachel's. He wasn't bad-looking, thin, fine-boned, a little awkward in his movements as if his body had grown too fast for him to be used to yet. Beverly was eyeing him too. At one point she caught her mother winking with her good left eye at him. He seemed startled and then forced a smile at Beverly. He was a good boy, to come here from Philadelphia every Sunday with Rachel. She noticed that they seemed to communicate by telepathy like a flock of birds, wheeling at once, turning in the same direction, a unit. She began to suspect this was serious. That kind of communication meant they were sleeping together, perhaps even living together. She never got anything but the answering machine or the roommates at Rachel's apartment. She was disturbed that Rachel had not confided in her, as she always had.

In the hall outside Beverly's room, Suzanne proceeded to try to find out. "I assume you're coming home for Pesach, sweetheart. You can sleep in my room. Would you like Michael to come with you?"

"We thought we'd do first-night seder with you and then second-night with his parents."

"Ah. The in-laws," Suzanne said, watching Rachel's face carefully.

Rachel blushed. She didn't speak. Whoops! As if by remote control, Michael appeared immediately. "I think Rachel and I better get going, Mrs. Blume." That Mrs. Blume was her, not Beverly. "We have a meeting of our Torah study group tonight. We're starting Exodus."

Suzanne was about to make her own exodus to La Guardia, when one of the hospital social workers buttonholed her. "It's time to think of what sort of preparations you need to make for your mother."

"Preparations?" It sounded like a euphemism for burial.

"You have to understand, even if she improves at a significantly faster rate than she has been able to do so far, she will never be able to live alone. Have you considered a nursing home?"

"No! But she has an apartment. . . ."

"She can't return to it. Mrs. Blume, so far your mother cannot feed or dress or toilet herself. She needs a safe environment, she needs continuing therapy long after she leaves us, and she needs care."

Suzanne sat on the shuttle, wanting so passionately to be home already she had the feeling she could rise and rocket home at a greater velocity on her own, without the help of the plane. What was she going to do? She could not put Beverly in a nursing home. Would she have to take her back to Brookline? Even when Beverly was healthy, her mother and she had not willingly cohabited since she was seventeen. How could they possibly manage to live together now?

Suzanne had left home to go to college and returned only for an occasional holiday. Every summer, she had gone to summer school. She had zipped through in three years and then gone to law school. Never had she wanted to live with Beverly after she had gotten away from her. The happier parts of her childhood had been when Beverly was off organizing and she was living with her Aunt Karla. Aunt Karla loved having her there. Aunt Karla thought she was wonderful. Aunt Karla cooked succulent meals, cholents, pot roasts, chickens roasted with vegetables, goulashes—for her husband had been a Hungarian Jew who had died slowly at forty-two after being hit by a fuel truck while unloading boxes on Flatbush Avenue. He had lain in a coma for three months, exhausting Karla's savings. Her soups filled the house with steam that could make Suzanne drunk. Suzanne felt cherished with her aunt, as if her presence were a gift. She was the daughter Karla dreamed of. When she had gone off to law school, Karla had set about finding a little girl to adopt.

Her mother was apt to open a can of chili or chicken soup and call that supper. Her mother did not think Suzanne was wonderful. Her mother was always telling her how to act with boys, how to dress, how to carry herself. Then Suzanne would purposely slump and pick up a book and pretend to drown out her mother's voice with the words on the page until in fact she became so involved that she could not hear Beverly telling her what was wrong with her and how to make it right. Beverly was always trying to fix her, to improve her, to organize her. The way Beverly did things was right, and the way that Suzanne wanted them was wrong—morally, aesthetically, politically wrong!

Her mother scoffed at lawyers and said the first thing to do after a revolution was to shoot them all. Her mother considered she had long ago sold out. Her mother thought teaching jurisprudence was a con, something highfalutin and silly. Her mother thought feminist theory was bad politics. Beverly had tried to make her feel guilty first for marrying Sam and then for divorcing him. How could she bring her mother back to Brookline, to a neighborhood Beverly hated to visit because she called it bourgeois?

There was a message from Jake: he would be in town Tuesday. Could she see him? She taught until three. Her sexual harassment case had gone to the jury, who had only taken two days to give her—or rather her client Sherry—a victory. She was still awaiting a decision on the appeal of the murder conviction of Phoebe, who had tried to protect her daughter. She had preparations to make for Pesach, for her classes. She could steal the time from around four-thirty to bedtime, a block of time she communicated about at once.

She was not nervous this time. She longed to fall into him and be replenished. She was exhausted, she was overcommitted, and he was her vacation. She would never say that to him—she doubted there was a man living who would like to feel he was essentially a kind of recreation program for a woman—but she just wanted to snuff herself out in him for a few hours. She had consulted her gynecologist and put herself on the pill. She was entering menopause, but it seemed a gradual entry, and she could, her gynecologist warned her, still get a nasty surprise and find herself pregnant. She endured occasional hot flashes, but as far as she could tell, she had been too damned busy to actually experience her own menopause. It was creeping past her. When she had a hot flash, she was still astonished and often did not realize till a couple of months had passed that a period had been missed. Her body seemed off on its own adventure, without her mind accompanying it. She felt as if she were being cheated of something other women had begun to study: a colleague in women's studies was writing a book about the change. With her weekends gone, she was behind in everything she did. Her article languished in her computer. Fortunately, she had overprepared her lectures on constitutional law during the last summer, so she managed to stay afloat.

She had not enjoyed a full night's sleep in weeks. Her fatigue reminded her of just after Elena was born. After Rachel's birth, it had been less totally draining, because she had known what to expect, because she had Marta and some help from Sam. With Elena, she had had only herself and a couple of weeks of Aunt Karla's presence, a miracle in the middle of chaos. But Karla had to go back to teaching school and she was waiting for her own little girl to become available. That was Suwanda, tall, lean, now an acupuncturist in San Diego. Karla had adopted Rosella two years later, as a newborn. For a woman who had never given birth, Karla knew a lot about raising kids.

"Beverly glares at me," Karla said on the phone. "I feel as if she hates me now! Rosella came in with me and she hardly looked at us."

"She doesn't hate you, dear. She hates the situation she's in. She hates her body and her brain that betrayed her. She hates the hospital and the staff who treat her as if she's feebleminded."

"She's always resented me. Judged me. You know that."

"Beverly hasn't been satisfied with either of us. . . . That's how she is. But right now, she needs our help. Try to encourage her to work with her therapists."

"The last time I was there, she wouldn't even write answers to us."

She jumped into bed with Jake within ten minutes of meeting him in the lobby, falling into him as if diving into oblivion. They made love much longer than the time before and far more powerfully. She wanted passionately not to think, not to be conscious: a powerful aphrodisiac. She knew she was surprising him, but he seemed rather pleased than overwhelmed. He was a man who liked sex with her, she was realizing with great satisfaction. It was a balm to her confusions. At least here in this rented hotel bed, she was at ease. Who would have guessed it? She did not really have the time to spare to do this, but she did not care. It was the most pleasurable event in her life for weeks.

Lying under him, over him, beside him in a half-destroyed bed, she realized she had never experienced sex the way she did with Jake. Perhaps it was him, perhaps it was simply her long abstinence, perhaps it was the time in her life. Sex with Victor had been potent but far more passive. He was something that was happening to her. He was the event. She was the object. With Sam, it had been mutual but low on their list of priorities after the first couple of months. They did it when they both could arrange the time and energy, and it became less and less frequent until perhaps once a month they got together. They were both so ambitious then and so overcommitted and so involved in whatever cases they were fighting in court that they barely observed each other. All her energy at home went into the baby and Elena, the children who always needed more than she could give, never mind Sam. Neither of them seemed to have the will to force intimacy and sustain it. It just hadn't seemed important enough to work on, until it was gone.

She did not exactly consider Jake important to her, and she was surely just as overcommitted in time and energy now as she had been then with Sam—but she experienced him as her last chance at sex, perhaps in her life. They had created an artificial intimacy on-line that was blooming into a physical intimacy both jolting and sensual. She loved his mouth. She loved the way he entered her slowly, withdrawing and then thrusting in again. She loved the way his head snapped back when she was riding him and he was gone into sensations and she knew he would never, never suddenly open his eyes to ask if she had remembered to turn on the answering machine. Perhaps it was marriage that had deadened Sam and her. Perhaps it was being young and greedy for winning. Perhaps it was having a baby too soon after they married. But this late blooming was rich. Jake's large hot hands on her breasts almost brought her to orgasm again. Her breasts had never felt so sensitive and as able to give her pleasure.

Over supper she stared into his face, trying to understand the power of their coupling. She asked him questions about his life. His daughter had suddenly written to him, sending a photo of herself with a baby boy. His board had agreed that he could try to put together a Boston office if he had enough backing. He would be in charge of it, but he would need a local board of advisers and volunteers and money. Especially money.

"I've got this pesky case pending in California. From a protest about logging old growth redwoods. The local police came down on us hard. That was five months ago. I keep expecting it to be dismissed—after all, the violent ones were the police, not us. But it just drags on and on from motion to motion."

"Who's your lawyer?" She questioned him carefully about the case, but it sounded fairly trivial. At the most he could expect a suspended sentence and a fine, even if his lawyer lost. Nothing to worry about, she guessed.

His dark, intense eyes, close to almond-shaped, were beautiful in his sharp face. His face had something foxy about it: quizzical, feral, alert. He was one of those men who liked to put their backs against a wall and look out at the room. He gazed at her more intently than anyone had in more years than she could imagine. It was hard for her to take an interest in the Italian food, good as it was, for all she wanted to do was get back in bed with him and wipe out her life for another two hours. Yet the conversation was good. It was rare; it was years and years since she had sat talking intimately with a man, talking openly, honestly. She had male colleagues, she had male clients from time to time, she had male students and Jaime, her assistant. This was different. It was what had attracted her to him on-line: the quality of the discourse. The sense of ease.

12

Beverly

Beverly hated the physical therapist pulling on her arm and her leg. It was humiliating to be handled like a sack of trash bundled for the dump. They made her stand up. They were talking at her, the nurse with the frizzy hair and the therapist, a woman half her age with damp pudgy hands and an inane grin. Oh, you think it's funny I hang on to the bed afraid of falling.

"You have to learn to fall, Mrs. Blume. You are going to fall, and you have to learn how to do it correctly so you don't injure yourself."

Grin. Right, it's funny for you, you bitch, to see me crashing to the floor, but it's damned well not amusing to me.

"Take another step. That's right. Now we have a walker for you."

Beverly let herself drop abruptly on the bed's edge. She was never going to use one of those disgusting contraptions. Decrepit old people used them, shuffling along. The nurse and therapist were talking at the same time. When two people talked to her, she couldn't focus on either. They worked with stroke patients, you'd think they'd have learned that she could only hear one of them.

"If you ever want to go to the potty on your own, you're going to have to get up on your two feet and put one foot in front of the other."

Back and forth they made her march like Frankenstein's monster, to the door and back to the bed, to the door and back to the bed. She had to urinate, but did they care? She tried to tell them, but she could only make a moan. She tried to reach for her pad, but they made her keep walking to the door and back, to the door and back. Finally she couldn't hold it, and the warm seep of urine ran down her leg as she wept with her good eye.

The occupational therapist was trying to teach her to dress herself. Beverly kept trying to pull her panties on. She got her legs in the right holes this time, but the label was in front. It was so hard to coordinate everything. Her bra she could not do one-handed at all. She could not go through life with her tits swinging in the breeze. Not that she was as big as Suzanne, who knows where she got that from. Actually Karla had the same oversize breasts. The occupational therapist Nona, a woman whose hair was as short as a man's and whose grip was firm on her, who would never let her drop or think it was amusing if she fell on her face, showed her a bra with Velcro in front. It was the right size. Nona saw her looking at the size. "Same size as the bra you came in with," she said with a slight smile.

Beverly nodded fervently, her head as it always did now, canting to the side. On the third try, she got the bra on. Better.

"We'll skip the slip today, okay? Now I have here a dress you can close with Velcro. It's kind of like a bathrobe, but it's striped, anyhow. Kind of cheerful. I have to show all this to your daughter, if I'm around when she comes in. Do you think she could come in on a weekday?"

Beverly shook her head no.

"Oh, well. I'll leave her a message."

On Thursday she went to the bathroom by herself, got her pants down, even flushed, got her panties back up. She turned on the faucet one-handed and washed her good hand and patted at her useless hand. Then she hobbled back to the bed, step, slide, step, slide, like some stupid ballroom dance she was doing with the metal walker. By the time she got back to the bed, she was so exhausted she slept until the nurse woke her.

Eating was problematic. Food got stuck on the other side of her mouth. She imagined her body as split between her and what she called IT. The Jerk. The Jerk owned the right half of her body. On her half she chewed her food and swallowed it, but food that wandered over to the Jerk's cheek could get stuck there and choke her unawares.

The doctors were thrilled Friday because she felt it when they pricked her thigh, but she couldn't move it. It seemed the worst of all worlds. Her right thigh could hurt but remained as inert as a bag of wet sand.

They had given her special utensils to eat with. She could drink pretty well, although sometimes liquid dribbled out the right side. But it had taken a week before she could reliably get the spoon into her mouth instead of just somewhere near it. Everything she did turned into a mess. Everything she did was hard. Fatigue would drop on her suddenly and crush her to the bed. She thought of exhaustion as a boulder that suddenly fell on her and pushed her flat. In any five-minute interval, she could use up her energy completely and deflate.

She could read for a while. The newspaper was hard, the print too small and the contrast poor. Large-print books were perfect. She felt as if she were reading children's books, but they were normal novels and nonfiction books. She could read for up to half an hour before she wore out. When Karla came next, Beverly decided to be good to her sister this time and nod at her and write messages. She told her to bring some large-print books that were worth reading, something political with substance to it. A good biography of somebody who mattered. Karla seemed delighted to be asked to do something and promised she would return in two days with books. She did. Rosella came with her, carrying the big bag. WHERE TWINS? Beverly printed.

Rosella laughed. She was a small woman, no taller than Karla, and she had married a Black man not much bigger. But the twins were already up to their mama's waist. "They won't let us bring the little ones in here. Maybe they think stroke is contagious."

SCARY? Beverly printed. SCARES ME.

Rosella had brought her a drawing Johnny made, of a stick woman in a bed with a big sun shining over her. Karla put it on her bedside table, propped against the lamp. It was the most cheerful thing in the depressing room.

The speech therapist was a bald man around fifty who wore loud plaid shirts that never went with his trousers. He must be color-blind, like a lot of men, and obviously his wife had left him. Today the shirt was a mauve, magenta, and teal madras worn with a pair of olive khakis. She stared into his eyes, half hidden behind his bifocals, and longed, longed for him to do something magical that would give her back her voice. She could remember her own voice, low-pitched, sexy, men had often told her. She longed to hear her own voice again more than she longed for anything else. She would gladly hobble around, she would wear Velcro clothes, she would eat with funny utensils, but give her back the power to speak and she swore she would be happy again. She stared into his face in silent supplication.

"Now I want you to make me a list of all the words you can think of that begin with S."

Laboriously Beverly carved into the page SHIT, SHE, SALMON,

SYLPH, SHOP, STORE, SAVE, SIGN, SIGNAL, SLAM, SORE, STY-MIE. She had only got that far when he stopped her.

"Sssssssss," he said. He put his hands on her face. "Sssssssssss."

She tried. How she tried. What finally came out was "Shhhhhhhhh."

"That's good. That's very good. Now try to breathe out a sound. Just breathe it. Ahhhhh. Ahhhhhhhh."

No sound emerged, but the breath sounded a little like Ahhhhh. A nonvocalized Ahhh.

"Now try to put it together. Shaaaaaah."

She made a nonvocalized sound that nonetheless was recognizably Shaaaa. Then she began to giggle, because *Sha!* in Yiddish meant shut up. A song of her childhood came to her and suddenly she was singing it rustily in Yiddish. *"Sha! Shtil! Mach nich kein gevalt! Der rebbe geyn sein tanzen, tanzen valt. . . ."*

"It's good you can sing. You should sing as much as you can. It's practice for your vocal cords." He had her sing "Some Enchanted Evening" as far as she could get. He had a deep baritone, nothing like Ezio Pinza, but still, it was fun. They sang some more show tunes together. She loved hearing her own voice. She felt almost human when the session ended. She was wheeled back to her bed and slept. When she woke, she said, "Shaaaa!" Almost a croak emerged. She managed a smile that was perhaps more grimace than smile, but which she totally meant. Dear, dear man. She must learn his name next time. He was her hero. Dr. Fish, that's what the nurse called him. To her, he would be Ezio. She wanted to throw away all the other therapists and work with him all day with as much energy as she could force from herself. "Ahhhhhh." She was croaking. "Shaaaah. Ahhhhhhh. Shhhhhh. Shaaaah. Shaaah! Shaaah."

13

Suzanne

Suzanne borrowed Marta's van to transport Beverly to Brookline for Pesach. After the holiday, Beverly was to enter a local rehabilitation center for stroke patients. Beverly was so excited about leaving the hospital, it was hard to make her understand that she could not go home. Suzanne had moved Beverly's things to Brookline a month before with the help of Karla overseeing Rosella and Tyrone. The landlord was glad to have Beverly leave, so he could double the rent.

Suzanne had been paying Beverly's bills. One of the many things her mother could not do was to sign a check. It felt distinctly uncomfortable to be operating behind Beverly's back, making decisions for her mother, who had never lacked decisiveness, but discussing anything with Beverly took forever and she tired quickly of trying to communicate. She could form few words and no coherent sentences. She would not assess her prospects and options realistically. The easiest thing for Suzanne was to view her mother as a helpless client and make decisions for her—although she felt uneasy.

Thus Suzanne was carting Beverly off to Brookline, where Beverly had visited perhaps three times in the twelve years Suzanne had been living in the house with Marta and Jim. When Suzanne wanted to see Beverly, she went to New York. Her mother was portable in certain ways. When duty called, she went, but visiting her daughter in Brookline made her uncomfortable. It seemed to thrust right into her face everything about them that was different. They had more fights on Suzanne's turf than on Beverly's. Beverly was at home only in New York. She had been born there, grown up there, and never put down roots anyplace else. It had always offended or puzzled her, depending on her mood, that her only daughter preferred the Boston area. Probably she considered it a sign of weak character or a lack of style. She had always made clear that she thought Suzanne lacked style.

The minivan was harder to steer than an ordinary car but had room for the wheelchair. Suzanne had done her best with Elena's help to fix up the room off the kitchen for Beverly. Suzanne's gym equipment was now split between her bedroom and her office, and very much in the way. Every time she used the treadmill, she had to hang a quilt over the corner of her chest of drawers, so she would not hit herself on it. She hoped Beverly would be comfortable in that room for the next three days, until Suzanne could check her into the rehab unit.

It was definitely spring on the Wilbur Cross. The willows had leafed out along the streams. An occasional magnolia or cherry was in bloom. The day was sunny with the temperature in the upper fifties and the air softer than it had been in months. It was a drive she would normally have enjoyed, but she was monitoring her mother with one ear and Rachel and her boyfriend with the other. Suzanne felt sore with anxiety. Unlike most years, she was not looking forward to Pesach. The first-night seder was always with her daughters and whoever they brought, with Marta, Jim, and their son, Adam, and a friend or two. Beverly had never before come to her, although when Suzanne was growing up, Beverly had sometimes trekked out to Karla's in Brooklyn, where Suzanne always went. This year her assistant, Jaime, wanted to come and also Celeste, shattered by divorce, and Georgia, just back from Bali.

She acknowledged to herself that she did not look forward to a seder with Beverly, whom she remembered at Karla's in the old days as quarrelsome, alternately bored and combative. Beverly never felt comfortable with the ritual or pleased that her daughter enjoyed what Beverly considered a forlorn relic of the ghetto. Now Beverly would be quiet, necessarily, but it was no improvement. Suzanne sighed, making her way across the Connecticut River at Hartford. They were all who they were, and she must make the best of it. The hospital social worker had pressed upon her eight different pamphlets. If she did everything the woman urged, she would rebuild her entire apartment, reorganize her life, and hire ten different people to help.

It was still light when she pulled into her steep drive. There was her house on its hill, the little backyard sloping sharply downhill, three stories painted light blue with dark blue trim. Home in recent years had meant quiet and comfort. Now she could not read the meaning of her home. Her life felt at the moment without sanctuary—except for those brief moments with Jake: because, she thought, I do not have to take care of him. I'm not responsible for him. Therefore I can be happy.

Suzanne realized in the next twenty-four hours that she had not really absorbed what the social worker had been trying to tell her. For Beverly to exist at all in the apartment, everything must be changed. In the small bathroom off the kitchen there was a shower, but it could only be used if the controls were lowered to where Beverly could reach them. That meant having a plumber in. They had nothing resembling a bath chair until Elena found a stool in the basement. It was not designed to get wet, but it would have to do. Beverly had to be helped onto the stool and off the stool again. The bathroom needed a railing for her to hold on to. They moved a single bed against the wall to protect on one side, but she could not sit up in the bed by herself and she was afraid she would fall out. If Beverly moved back here after the rehab center, Suzanne would have to buy or rent a hospital bed. Jim found a bookcase upstairs he could lend to the cause, with big square partitions where Beverly's clothes could be stacked, as she could not open a drawer. They gave her a tambourine to summon them when she needed something, and the tambourine sounded every other minute.

It took such effort for Beverly to haul herself in or out of bed that most things she might need had to be within reach of her good hand. Once they understood that, they had to turn the bed around so that her left hand would be on the outside, able to reach the table they placed there.

She never seated people at the seder but always let them find their own places. She was amused to note that Elena put herself in between Marta and Jim, as if she were their child, leaving Adam to sit beside Rachel—which he probably preferred anyhow. Elena had suddenly adopted Marta and Jim as preferable parents, obviously. Long ago, when they had moved into this house, Elena had resented them, imagining they were spying on her, keeping watch on her for Suzanne. Elena had lived in this house for two years until she went away to college, only returning for vacations. Now Suzanne was pleased to see that Elena was establishing her own relationship with them, finally. Suzanne drew a deep breath and tried to relax her shoulders. She so wanted everyone to be happy, to have a good seder, to be together in kindness and joy and maybe even a little bit of something spiritual and enlightening, just a little. She wanted joy in the house, a guest like Elijah, who had his cup set out for him. There had not been enough joy lately.

She had not let Rachel have her way with the food. There was plenty for vegetarians, but Suzanne still made chicken soup with matzoh balls and roast lamb. The tzimmes was vegetarian: carrots, apples, raisins, onions cooked long and slow together, Karla's recipe from her own mother. An heirloom. So were the soup and the matzoh balls. Suzanne enjoyed the sense of being one in a line of women making a particular recipe for a particular holiday, women appearing one inside the other receding ever smaller like the cows on the tin of evaporated milk from her childhood. Beverly used to buy evaporated milk for some stupid reason. It didn't spoil. It was one of those weird tastes from childhood that brought back not nostalgia or pleasant memories but an archaic sense of discomfort, like woolen leggings and rubber galoshes, the smell of the cloakroom in grade school. The sweetish overcooked taste of evaporated milk.

Her mother had always improvised meals, for Beverly suspected there was something bourgeois or overly fussy or perhaps dangerously fattening involved in thinking seriously about food. It was from Karla that Suzanne had learned to cook, not that she ever had time to do it. It was a pleasure for vacations, for holidays, for the rare times she had the energy and the leisure to entertain. Basically, the only time she ever cooked a big meal was at Pesach, Rosh Hashanah, Thanksgiving, or somebody's birthday. Yet Suzanne was proud that she could create a sumptuous spread on the appropriate occasion.

Suzanne relinquished leading the service to Rachel, who had brought a new Haggadah, photocopied in her office. There was a lot of turning of pages back and forth and people asking, Where are we? Too much Hebrew for Suzanne's taste, who considered it like pepper, nice as a condiment, but avoid heavy use. Rachel was running quite long. Suzanne began to fidget about her meal in the kitchen sitting in the turned off oven. Rachel was good, though, with a charm in delivery that Suzanne had never before seen in her daughter, already a performer, as rabbis had to be. Suzanne suddenly remembered Rachel in a play in middle school, wanting to be the heroine but being given the part of the heroine's mother instead. She had been valedictorian of her class, but she had not been asked to the senior prom. She had been president of the Social Issues Club and the French Club, but Saturday nights she went out with her girlfriends or stayed home. She had always been her mother's daughter. Elena had been and still was tighter with Sam than his own daughter. Sam loved Rachel, but Elena knew how to play him. Rachel was too straightforward to charm her father as much as Elena could.

If Sam had married a Jewish woman, it would have been awkward for Rachel this Pesach, because she would have had to decide whether to spend the second-night seder at her father's or Michael's family. Sam's tall slender blond wife did not make a seder, so Rachel was spared the choice. Sam's wife played tennis and golf, gave elaborate dinners and parties for his clients, kept the large house in Weston immaculate with help from a string of au pairs and maids, and raised his second batch of children with every kind of lesson that money could buy, from ballet and gymnastics to soccer and violin. They were precocious edgy children with streaks of violence and anxiety that she could sense like the seep of gas whenever she found herself forced to spend time with Sam's family. That did not happen as much since Rachel had learned to drive. Sam had given her a series of old cars, each good for two or three years before it disintegrated.

When at last she could serve the meal, she watched Rachel with Michael. "Here. Try the tzimmes." She fed him as if he could not take for himself. There was something passive in him, as if he simply waited to be served, to be fussed over, knowing that it would come to him. For Rachel he was the prize of her life, Suzanne began to observe. He was pleasant enough looking, teeth a little too big for his mouth but all right. Beverly kept smiling at him as nearly as she could, with her face only partly under control. Her favorites at the table were Elena, Michael, and Jim. Beverly had seldom met Adam and paid little attention to him. Poor Adam was used to Rachel's full attention. She had always played the role of doting older sister, since she had been ten and Adam, eight. Today her attention was fixed on Michael. Adam had always been prone to whine, and he was overflowing with complaints tonight. The wine was harsh, the tzimmes not sweet enough, the service too long, his favorite song had been left out: but what he really minded was Rachel turned not to him but to Michael.

Unlike Rachel, Michael was not taking a large part in the seder. He was more an observer, looking a little amused, as if perhaps this was not what he considered a real seder, not traditional enough. "Who leads the seder in your house?" she asked him.

He seemed surprised at the question. "My father, of course."

Of course? Why not his mother? She suspected that he was judging them in some quiet way. Was he finding not merely the seder but the family too outré? This was a house of women, and she doubted if the boy was used to that. He probably believed the way he was used to was the only right way.

Elena had always liked Celeste, enjoying her gamy humor, but her divorce had left her shattered, and Elena instinctively shrank from her ravages. Celeste was quiet and morose. When she read a passage, her voice was an octave higher than usual, a child's tremulous voice. Once or twice Suzanne was afraid Celeste would begin to cry, and immediately set her some task. Normally she thought during the seder about her own personal liberation and political issues in which she was involved, but she found herself too wedged between her roles as mother and as daughter tonight to give much thought to anything spiritual. She did not see much liberation coming her way this year.

Jaime followed along with the exotic reading and the exotic food, seated on her left as she had Beverly on her right. Perhaps she was attempting to protect both of them from casual buffeting. Georgia, who was an interior decorator with exquisite taste, had brought her a beautiful scarf from Bali, sea colors, that Elena was wearing. She had immediately claimed it, and Suzanne could not refuse her for she looked stunning in it, worn casually around her shoulders over a sea-green camisole and tight black pants. Jaime eyed her curiously, a parrot perched at a table of sparrows. She paid little attention to him, focused on Beverly and Jim. After all, although Jaime was as beautiful and as splendid as herself, he was two years younger than Elena—and at their ages, that could seem a generation. However, Jaime was observing her.

Georgia was beginning to age, she realized with a pang, her black glossy hair streaked with white. The sun had turned her fair skin leathery. Suzanne had never noticed all those wrinkles around her eyes. She was as thin as ever but had begun to look more gaunt than chic. They were all getting older. People kept telling her tonight how good she looked. She was accustomed to her looks being taken for granted, like the walls and the ceiling, nothing to comment on. She felt like telling Georgia and Marta and Celeste that it was only that she was getting laid for the first time in more than a decade. This glow was her body's delight. It would be short-lived, only a little generator of joy parked out there away from the rest of her roiled-up life.

She became aware Beverly to her right was trying to speak, her face distorting with effort, her mouth drooling. Suzanne felt torn among those needing her attention: her daughters, both of whom usually soaked up her available energy, her assistant, a stranger here, Celeste who was sunk into a dangerous depression, and her mother. She was used to having Beverly command her attention by forceful statements. She was used to fending off her mother's attacks. She was used to pretending not to understand allusions to her bourgeois pretensions and her safe dull money-grubbing lifestyle. She was not accustomed to having to wipe her mother's face and lean close to try to figure out what Beverly was sputtering. She felt guilty because she was put off by Beverly's inability to control her body, her voice, her face. The same thing will happen to you when you're her age, she told herself, and you'll want people to be kind and understanding and accepting, won't you? So get it together, Suze, get it together and be a mensch. This is an opportunity too, to improve that first relationship of all. "You want something, Mother? More lamb? Tzimmes?"

Beverly was pointing. There were various bottles on the table, grape juice for the nondrinkers, Manischewitz for the traditional, like herself, and kosher Israeli dry wine for those who could not stomach alcoholic cough syrup. For Suzanne, the taste of sweet kosher wine was the taste of Karla's Shabbats, of holidays and all the times she had escaped her own mother and taken refuge with her aunt. She realized Beverly was wildly pointing at the dry red wine. She was not sure whether the social worker had said Beverly could have wine or not, but she was damned if she was going to forbid it if Beverly wanted it. Beverly very much did. Beverly sipped carefully and managed not to spill a drop. Then she waved her glass for more.

"Grandma, do you really want more?" Rachel asked, leaning across the table.

Beverly nodded wildly.

"The difference, according to Rabbi Moshe Poleyoff, between drinking wine for the sake of the mitzvah on the night of Pesach and drinking that leads to excess is that the second comes from being empty inside and making wine fill that emptiness. But if we are filled with joy and express that through wine, then the wine becomes the *simchah shel mitzvah*, the joy of the mitzvah. . . ."

Beverly made a derisive noise and carefully drank down the glass. She managed a lopsided grin at Rachel and then at Suzanne. Dessert was never a big deal on Pesach—macaroons, fruit, and a matzoh-based custard cake. The huge meal left little room for sweets. After the food they raced through the tail end of the Haggadah. There was always singing then, which Suzanne had loved since childhood. "Grandma, you're singing," Rachel said, and Elena too turned to stare. In fact, Beverly was singing. "*Eli-ahu ha-navi, eli-ahu, eli-ahu. . . .*"

"Grandma," Elena said, peering around Jim. "Have some more wine! It's a miracle."

Beverly giggled and did have more wine. By the end of the dinner, she was lolling in her chair, breathing in gusts through her mouth, now and then snoring. Suzanne was happy for her. It was probably the first pleasure Beverly had enjoyed since her stroke. For Beverly at least, this evening was some kind of momentary liberation.

14   Twelve Years Earlier

Elena

Elena hated school. She hated all the girls who gossiped about her and called her a slut. She hated the boys who grabbed at her in the halls and begged her to suck their cocks. She hated the teachers who classified her as less than human. She hated the counselor who told her in a sickly sweet voice of pretend concern that she was not performing up to her potential—performing like a trained seal. She sat there, seeing herself leaping up, reaching across the desk, and strangling the woman. Feel my potential, bitch. Basically, Boston Latin was not a hand-holding type of school. If her grades sank too far or too quickly, she would be booted.

Nobody would be begging her to stay. Perform or perish. She kept playing Twisted Sister. She really was a sick motherfucker, according to her
peers, and she sure was the odd one out in her family. She was no longer
passing all those tests they threw at her. She played that record over
and over again in her room, on her headphones.

She hated her little sister, Rachel, who was Mama's girl and always
sucking up to Mother. Rachel was good, Rachel was perfect, Rachel was
a complete nerd. She brought home her report cards like Moses coming
down from Sinai. What Elena did as well as she could with great effort
and sweat, Rachel just zipped through. She did all her homework in
record time and did extra. She always had science projects going in the
room they shared. She never asked for cool clothes or anything fun, but
for books nobody else had ever heard of, and lately she wanted a computer. Who ever heard of a ten-year-old girl with a computer? Only
nerdy boys had them. Rachel thought she was a little genius, and so did
her teachers, and so did Sam, and so did their mother.

Most of all she hated her mother, who kept going on about college,
college. Elena was never going to college. As soon as she was old enough
to get a license, she wanted a car. Like Judas Priest sang, "Headin Out
to the Highway." She had a learner's permit already. Chad got his license
the week he turned sixteen. He was after his father to buy him a car.
When Elena had a car, she was going to get in it with Evan and Chad
and take off. They would go down to Mexico. They would drive up to
Alaska. They would go anyplace but here. Key West. The Mojave desert.
She did not care where. Chad would care and Evan would care but she
just wanted to take off and never look back. She would be with both of
them and there would be nobody to pester them and hector them, and
what they were to each other and what they did together. Only with
them did she feel alive. When she was alone in her room, she wondered
if she even existed. She felt empty, empty. She didn't know who she
was and she wished she was dead. Life stretched before her like a hall
at her high school when she was cutting classes and every room had a
boring class in session and going down the hall, she could hear the stupid
smug bored voices of the teachers in each one. It was a puce-colored
hallway reeking of years of sweat and grease and chalk dust. That was
the rest of her life. A dull dim hallway going between one place she

didn't want to be to another place she dreaded going. It was all shit. It was all shit forever.

Every other day, there was her mother going at her, how she dressed, how she was acting, what was she learning, what did she want to be? Deaf, Mother, for starters. Going on about how she could be anything she wanted to be. Okay, I want to be a rock star, she yelled, playing air guitar. I mean something real, Suzanne went. Nothing about her satisfied Suzanne. Well, she didn't like Suzanne either. What do you want to be? An orphan.

Sometimes when she was high, it felt okay. Sometimes when she was making out or fucking, she felt real, she felt there. When Chad or Evan looked at her, she felt as if she really existed and she was something each of them wanted. Sometimes lost in the pounding roar of the music, carried on its tornado of sound and whirled through the night, she felt alive. She felt for a moment as if it mattered, and then she wanted to die right then while it was fierce and good. Once they had gone off on a day trip with Evan's parents to Mount Monadnock, and the three of them had managed to get away. It was fall and the ground was red as blood with maple leaves and golden under them. They got high sitting on rocks way off the trail where the cliff tumbled down before them. The colors seemed to sing in her eyes. They had taken off their clothes and they were all lying on a rock that the sun had heated and it felt as if they were melting together. She could not tell where she ended and they began. She felt as if her heart was bursting in her, swelling through her whole body and pulsating like the colors of the red, red leaves.

Her mother was always on her back about grades, as if they meant a fucking thing. It was so boring, so mundane. Her mother never had any fun, she just worked all the time and fussed. Always running out with her briefcase under the arm and rushing, rushing, wearing stupid gray suits and running on high heels down to the car or even the T. It was a joke. Her mother's idea of a great evening was to make supper, which Elena was entirely indifferent to, lie in a hot bath for half an hour and read a book with her feet up, wearing her old bathrobe. Her mother had been born boring. Some people were, like Rachel. Her mother was the most impatient woman alive. Suzanne was always asking if she hadn't done something yet. Elena would be doing the dishes, like she was fucking supposed to, when everybody else in the world had a dishwasher, and her mother would come zooming in saying, Aren't you done yet? Did you wash your sweater? Did you make your bed? Do your homework? When are you planning to get it done? Didn't you do that yet? Did you forget to take out the garbage again? How could you lose your shoes? I don't understand. I don't understand. She sure didn't, that was for absolute real.

Elena felt at war with everyone. Her mother was trying to keep her in. She simply agreed and then did what she pleased. Rachel told on her twice. The second time, she took a knife from the kitchen and laid it against Rachel's throat, holding her down on her bed. "If you rat on me again, I'm going to slit your throat. Don't think I'm bluffing. Don't ever think I'm bluffing. It'd be a pleasure. I wouldn't mind knowing what it feels like to cut my little pesky sister's throat."

That scared Rachel. She stopped carrying tales to Mother. Elena looked at herself in the mirror, posing squint-eyed and nasty. She could look pretty bad. She liked the way she looked. She was tall now, and she liked being taller than a number of the boys. She was lean and mean and tough. The three of them were their own family. They were together whenever they could be. It was what they all wanted. It was what she wanted more than life itself. When she was with Evan and Chad, she felt surrounded, protected, enclosed, loved. They got wasted a lot, but it didn't matter because they didn't care about anybody else, anybody outside their tight circle. They were everything to one another. If one of them even thought about anybody else for five minutes, the other two set them straight. They were a unit. As soon as they were old enough, as soon as they had wheels of their own, as soon as they had enough money to run away, they were going to live together. They would sleep as long as they wanted to and stay up until they wanted to go to bed. They would eat when they felt like it, pizza or nothing or greasy hamburgers instead of the tofu and broiled chicken and smelly fish her mother tried to get down her. They would play their music as loud as they felt like and they would fuck whenever they chose to and never worry again about getting caught. They would be happy. They would be in pig heaven.

In their first day's class (they tried to take all their classes together, although they couldn't manage it by half), Chad came in late. He passed her a note as soon as he could. "Old man found my stash. Shit! He says he's going to send me to military school."

At lunch he explained. "He found out somehow I see Mom when I'm not supposed to. I don't know how he found out. I don't think it's past him to hire some seedy private eye. Who knows? Anyhow, after he found that out, he went through my room. He ransacked it. He found my stash of dope and downers."

"So you tell him you're holding it for a friend," Evan said.

"Ha. You think he's that stupid? He called his lawyer and he's trying to get my mom in trouble for seeing me."

"What kind of trouble can your mom get in?" Elena asked. She wasn't eating. She hated to eat at the school. She wasn't about to walk in with a tacky brown-bag lunch and she wasn't about to eat that shit either. Food was overrated. She'd rather just have a cigarette and a Coke.

"He can get his lawyer after her, like he did before. He can get the judge to rule I can't see her even as much as I do." Chad slammed his fist on the table. "I hate him. I never wanted to get her in trouble. I just wanted to see her." Waves of intense emotion beat off him.

It was exciting to feel all that raw emotion discharging. It was like an electrical storm at the table. Elena had always loved thunder and lightning. Rachel would stop up her ears, but Elena would run to the window, almost hoping the lightning would strike near, would electrify her. It was so beautiful. Chad felt like that. She wanted to feel that emotion consuming her. She put her hand over his on the table, but he didn't notice. He pounded the table again. He looked as if his face would break open and molten tears pour out, but of course he could not cry here. He could only beat on the table.

A monitor came over. "Don't pound on the table, weirdo."

Elena said, "Let him be. He's got problems today."

"He's my problem right now. Lay off the table or I'll send you to the principal."

"Get lost, dick-face," Evan said. "Or you'll have a problem."

But Chad stopped. They got through the rest of the day. After school, they went to Elena's. Chad didn't want to go home. Rachel was at swimming class. Another mother took her, and then their mother picked her up at six. They shut themselves in Elena's bedroom. She opened the windows before they lit up. Saved airing it out later. Chad wasn't about to be chilled by dope or anything else.

"She explained it all to me before she left, how he was just too cruel to live with. How he was always putting her down, just the way he does with me. He likes to stick pins in you just to see you flinch."

Elena frowned, focusing with difficulty. "Why didn't she take you with her?"

"She didn't have any money. She didn't even have a place to stay. Then she wanted me to come, but he got the court to give him custody. He had like four lawyers and she had this cheap jerk who hardly bothered." He scrubbed at his eyes, dry and bloodshot. "She should've taken me with her anyhow. She should have!"

That woke Evan up. "You don't know that your father and his lawyers would have let her take you," he said gently. Evan hated it when people blamed others too much.

"He's killing me. He won't let me see my mother. He doesn't give a fuck about me. I'm just a piece of property. I'm just a club to beat her over the head. I'm nothing to him. He doesn't care how much I hurt. He doesn't care what I feel. All he wants to do is win."

"Maybe we could run away," Elena said tentatively. Both guys stared at her. "We could go away together."

"Where would we go?" Evan asked.

Chad stood. "What does that matter, so long as it's away from here? I hate him. I hate my life. He's going to send me to military school."

"He's just threatening you," Evan said, trying to cool everybody down.

"No. He had his secretary send for all these applications and brochures. He's threatened before, but this time he's been on the phone to some place in Virginia. He's going to send me to some damned military prison school. I'd rather die."

"How could we get a car?" Elena poked him, to get his attention back.

"I can take one of my father's cars. He has three. I know where he keeps the keys."

"Just don't take the Porsche," Evan said. "That's too conspicuous and too small for three of us." He was in. He could not resist the idea.

Suddenly Chad was up again, ready for anything. "California. I love that place. Northern California—north of San Francisco. I have friends there who have a house where it's like you're walking in a pasture with their two horses and suddenly the world drops away and you see you're on top of this cliff. Bam, down below there's these breakers crashing in on the rocks. You just want to step off. Step off into that blue air."

"I want to go for real," Elena said, putting her hands on both their shoulders. "Not just bullshit around, like talking about robbing a Brinks truck. I want to do this."

"For real," Chad said.

"We're always real," Evan said. "That's what we are together. Brute reality. Let's go to bed."

The next day, Chad took his father's BMW, to show them how easy it was. They went off to Rhode Island and each got tattooed—it was illegal in Massachusetts. Chad got a winged skull, Evan an eagle, and she chose a red rose with a thorn dripping blood. The guys put theirs on their arms, but she chose to have hers on her hip. They were not big tattoos—Chad was charging them on his credit card—but they were perfect. She wouldn't say a thing to Suzanne, but at some point, her mother would see it—probably the first time she wore a bathing suit. Suzanne would go ballistic. Elena loved her tattoo. That night she kept looking at it with a flashlight under the covers, the way she used to read comic books when she was a kid.

Suzanne had had it easy. She had gone to high school when things were upside down and the kids felt powerful. Kids seemed like this great force, all of a piece, what they called youth culture and hippies and yippies. They were so sure they were right that they scared the shit out of teachers, principals, parents, bosses. They just took over the streets and the parks. Suzanne had a lot of practice feeling right and justified by the time she was going off to college.

But Elena knew she was just a burnout. There was nowhere to go and no one to turn to except her little family of Evan and Chad. The good kids didn't smoke. They stayed on the other side of the smoking line outside school. Passing beyond that line as Elena did every day was to brand yourself a slut. She knew what made her feel good, but everybody around her with any power over her told her that sex and heavy metal and whatever they could get their hands on to get them high, all were bad and dirty—and so was she.

15

Beverly

Beverly dreaded going into the rehab center because it sounded like a nursing home, someplace to park her. Someplace to stash her where she wouldn't be in Suzanne's way. However, by the time Suzanne drove her there, she was so exhausted she only wanted to be in a quiet room away from all of them. It was just too hard, too much. Everyone talked at once and they didn't understand she could not follow multiple threads. It was unbearably noisy. Music pounding. Everyone talking at her and each other, their voices a mad loud jumble in her ears. It was all so complicated, things in the way, furniture sticking out. The toilet wasn't within her reach. She could not hobble toward it with the walker she hated, for it caught on every piece of furniture, and there was too much furniture, stuff everyplace she tried to pass. Things kept falling down as she went by. They shouted at her, as if she were deaf. They thought if they yelled at her, she would understand them, when she only wanted them to speak slowly and pause while she caught up with them.

She could talk some now, she knew she could, but no one there gave her a chance to mouth the syllables she could manage. She could do all the vowels. That cute man with the mismatched clothes, Dr. Fish, back in New York had taught her she could make those sounds perfectly well. Shah, shay, she, sheh, shy, shih, show, shoi, shau, shew, shuh. Wonderful sounds. And "m." She could say perfectly good things like "show me," if they would only wait long enough and give her a chance. But Suzanne had always been impatient. She remembered she herself had been impatient, back when she had been a full and real person. Yes, she too had always been in a hurry, but now everything took time. Just getting dressed required at least half an hour, and another fifteen minutes getting to the toilet, getting up and back. Every little excursion and every little activity, like eating ice cream, wore her out till she needed to rest. But in Suzanne's house, there was little rest. All those people milling around shouting at one another, doors slamming, water running, the phone burring, the fax beeping, people thundering up and down to the flat upstairs. All those faces she did not know or could not remember.

She would miss Mao. He had been overjoyed to see her. He was the one who loved her as she was. He got into bed with her and purred and purred. He kneaded his paws against her arm, and she felt as if she could almost feel him vibrating, as if the arm had a little sensation. The other cats, the orange ones, came to examine her, and they too were friendly, but Mao ran them off, hissing with his black fur on end. She was his. She wished she could take him with her to the rehab center. He still loved her, when nobody else could. Even her favorite, Elena, kept away from her. Spoke to her from a distance and fled. Everyone wanted to turn away from the ruin she had become.

Therefore, although she had not wanted to come and had tried to object to being parked here, as she lay in the hospital bed in the pale green room, she was relieved. It was manageable here. Ten steps to the bathroom and rails in place. A stool in the tub and railings. Railings on the walls. Wide doors her walker could pass smoothly through. Ramps. The remote for her TV was within reach. A tray swung over the bed on a balance spring so that she could easily swing it down or send it away. She could print notes on it, could prop up a large-print book. She was expected to make her way to meals, although she would much rather have had them in her quiet safe room.

Meals were depressing. Most of the patients or inmates, those stored here, did not try to communicate with one another. The right-brain-damaged ones could be talkative, but that didn't mean they made sense. The white-haired lady across from her, fragile and rosy as a porcelain shepherdess, sat there swearing, "Goddamned motherfucker son of a bitch bastard." Some switch in her brain had frozen into curse mode. A middle-aged man with a twisted face was singing to himself as he stabbed at his food. Their food had a tendency to get away. Eating took every bit of concentration she could muster, a fierce battle not to get food into her lap or her hair or on her sweater, but carefully, avoiding choking, she spooned a little at a time into her mouth. Meals were very slow because they were difficult. None of them ate easily.

The rhythms of the day were different here than they had been in the New York hospital but just as repetitive and marked. Bathe and get dressed, rest. Eat breakfast, rest, go to physical therapy, rest, go to speech therapy, rest, lunch, rest, go to occupational therapy, rest, be parked by the TV, rest, supper, be parked by the TV, go to bed, and start again. Yet she did not mind the routine, because the chaos at Suzanne's had tired her to desperation.

All around her were people with various degrees of stroke, various stages of recovery. When she thought "recovery" she put mental quotes around it. She heard from her various therapists about people who had regained use of their legs, their arms, their hands, their speech apparatus, their ability to live a normal life, but all around her, she saw the broken and the blasted. Like herself. If they did not often reach out to one another, it was partly because it was so much work to make contact with another person who was not a therapist assigned to you, and partly because looking at another person with a similar problem was depressing. She began to notice, to realize, that often a stroke was only a first stroke, and that others minor or major might readily follow.

She no longer fought her therapists but tried, stolidly, in a daily routine of attempts and frequent failure. The one therapist she approached with passion was her speech therapist. This one was a woman, Nancy Wright. I WANT TO WRITE, NANCY WRIGHT, she printed painstakingly on a piece of paper. Suzanne brought her steno pads and marking pens. "First we'll work on your speech, Mrs. Blume."

A speech pathologist had examined her for a good part of an afternoon until she wept with frustration and fatigue. The verdict was that there was no injury to her vocal cords or her pharynx. It was all in the brain, that gray globular organ she increasingly resented. She imagined a hole in it where the speech machine had once effortlessly worked, spitting out words, sewing together sentences. She had been such a talker. Her mother had called her The Mouth when she was angry with Beverly.

"A *bayzeh tsung iz erger fun a schlechter hant.*" A wicked tongue does more harm than a wicked hand. That was her mother talking. Suddenly she was at the table in their Lower East Side apartment on Twelfth Street next to the Jewish old folks' home. They lived on the third floor back. The table was actually two tables stuck together when the whole family was home for a meal. She had three older brothers and of course her sister, Karla. Al went down in the Pacific on a destroyer. Davey died of pneumonia in the hospital after he was mugged outside his record store. Gene perished of a heart attack just five years ago, playing golf outside Las Vegas. They had never had much to do with one another, except Gene, who had been her favorite. They had little in common. Different paths. But she could see them around the two tables stuck together along with her Aunt Hannah, who was some obscure cousin brought over to save her life, and also their Zeydeh, who seemed to her even then ancient and weird, who spoke almost no English. They were all crammed around those two shoved-together tables singing the blessings and then digging into the good and plentiful food of Shabbat. She could smell the soup her mother made with eggs from inside the chicken, the eggs without shells.

Then she was even younger and helping Mama pluck the chicken from the kosher butcher's. They were plucking the feathers, and what did they do with them? They saved them till Mama and Aunt Hannah made feather dusters they sold at the Sunday market. Nothing went to waste in that house, not a scrap of vegetable peeling, not a bone, not a bit of fat. Everything was used. Not like the piles of trash that went out of Suzanne's every day, mountains of garbage, things tossed out. No, they used every tiny scrap.

Then they did not throw away people, not her weird Grandpa who had a head injury from a pogrom in Lithuania and could only do rote tasks. Not Aunt Hannah who woke everyone in the house with her screaming at least one night a week, nightmares from the Nazis. Sometimes a hungry neighbor or a cousin passing through or someone in some kind of trouble joined the meal. She could smell that soup. She had not remembered it in years. It was a soup that belonged to the days a chicken had feathers and feet instead of parts wrapped in plastic film. Kids like Rachel were turning into vegetarians because it came as a shock to them that all those objects that came so neatly from the supermarket were not Disney creatures marching with a dance step into their pots, but real animals who had died to feed them. She had never been kept in the dark about that, you ate to live, so she accepted it. People overprotected kids nowadays, so they grew up inept and unable to deal with adversity. That was a subject she felt strongly about, and she opened her mouth to speak to the old guy snoozing beside her as the TV played some stupid sitcom about twenty-year-olds with no politics and no sense trying to decide who to fall into bed with. Then she realized she could no more make the speech about child raising than he could understand it.

The scent of that soup tickled her nostrils. She could smell it more clearly than she had smelled anything since her stroke. It was a rich smell, luscious. Perhaps she had never eaten anything so good since. She could taste it. Her mouth was filling with saliva. She could feel the hard wooden seat with its center ridge pressing into her buttocks and she could feel the rough cotton of the white Shabbat cloth under her elbows. Yes, Zeydeh was bent over his bowl of soup, nose almost in it, and Davey was imitating him and poking her in the ribs. She could smell the fragrance of the challah fresh from the oven. Broken open, its yellow softness revealed itself under the glaze of the surface. It was almost more cake than bread. It melted in her mouth. Why hadn't she bought herself challah in recent years? A bakery in the next block to her apartment made perfectly good challah. Mama roasted two chickens so everybody could have two pieces. She always got a wing and a back. The boys got the legs. Mama, Papa, and Zeydeh split the breasts, and Papa got the other leg. Aunt Hannah, Karla, and she divided up the rest. She remembered how when she had left home and was making money as an organizer for the ILGWU, she ordered half a chicken in a restaurant and she ate the whole thing, every bit of it. She could taste that too. It wasn't like Mama's, which was a kind of chicken pot roast with celery and carrots and onions and garlic. Karla knew how to make it. No, this restaurant chicken was roasted like the goyim made but very good. She ate it all down to the last bit of skin and sucked on the bones, picking up the bones in her hands, not like a lady. She could taste her mother's chicken in her mouth and at the same time she could taste that roast chicken in the restaurant, from her first union paycheck.

Tears trickled from her left eye, her good eye down her cheek, leaving trails of salt. How could she ever have imagined she would be reduced to sitting in a dimly lit room in front of the TV no one was watching with a bunch of old people nobody cared about—including each other— and crying about vanished chickens? I've had my life, damn it, she thought, I've had my life. It was a damned good life, even when I was scared, even when I was in danger, even when I was crying my heart out. Why can't it just be over? I don't regret it, but for this empty epilogue. I had as much living as anybody could ask for, so let me out of here. Let my body go!

16

Suzanne

"Are you sure you're not rushing into marriage because you're nervous about going to Israel by yourself? You've never been out of the country alone. You've always been with me or with your father."

"Really, Mother, I'm looking forward to Israel, I'm tremendously excited about going. I've traveled by myself." Rachel was using the ultra-reasonable tone of voice Suzanne had often heard her use with Elena. "When I was thinking of going to school in California, I went out there alone. I went to Santa Fe with a friend. You're just upset because I want to get married during my year there."

"But how long have you known him? Michael." She made herself say his name. She did not like the way they doted. She did not trust doting. She did not like his vaguely superior air, the sense she had of him judging them.

"I've known him since my first year in rabbinical college. We were in Hebrew Ulam together. We started studying together that first year." Rachel put down the underwear she was sorting—what was to be taken with her, what was to be put away. "Really, Mother, what have you got against him? What more suitable husband am I ever likely to meet?"

"I like him," she said defensively. "I like him fine. I just think marriage is something you should wait till you're done with school before you rush into."

"Who's rushing, Mother? We've been talking about it for months and months."

But not to me, Suzanne thought sourly. When did you stop telling me?

* * *

Suzanne was putting away the woolens Rachel had brought home. It always moved Suzanne to handle her daughter's clothing. She was sorting the things that needed to go to the cleaners from those that could go into old suitcases in the basement at once. A few smelled of the simple light floral perfumes Rachel liked. Others simply smelled of her daughter, a particular scent she could not have named but would have recognized anyplace. She buried her face in a blue woolen turtleneck, and for a moment she felt like crying. Menopause, Marta would say. Marta blamed all moods on menopause, as if the world wasn't knobby with problems and irritants. Rachel's body scent was a clean gingery bready smell. Flesh of her flesh. This morning she had heard Jim and Marta fighting upstairs. Marta had a low flash point, a temper that sometimes caused her to break things she had no desire to break. Jim was slower to anger but far, far slower to forgive; and he never forgot.

She remembered when the girls had been small, how much their little clothes had pleased her, like the clothes made for dolls. Rachel had been a plump baby, good-natured, easily moved to giggles or tears. When she was older, she liked to color. She used to get so excited when she saw the ducks in the Public Gardens, the swans. She loved the swan boats. Elena had never been interested in them. She liked rides better.

Rachel had loved stories about animals, heroic dogs, wise or foolish cats, mistreated horses, mischievous goats. Elena had been more musical. She had responded to music from the time she was a baby. At one time, Suzanne had imagined that Elena would be a musician. Or a dancer. Even in financially difficult days, Suzanne had managed ballet lessons for Elena. She could remember her flickering across the stage like a dark flame. She had always been lovely. She was one of the only women Suzanne had ever known who woke up pretty. Sleep seemed to lie on her lightly and never to rumple her excessively. Yet she slept profoundly. When Elena was an infant and then a toddler, sometimes her stillness in sleep frightened Suzanne. Elena would sink into sleep and lie in it as if on the bottom of a pool. More than once, Suzanne had wakened her out of fear that something was wrong, fear that her baby had died.

She had been a far more anxious mother with Elena than with Rachel. By the time Rachel was born, she had Sam and Marta to help. She had some experience. But when Elena was born, she realized she had never held a baby in her life. She ran out and bought Dr. Spock and every other book she could see that might serve as manuals. The more she read, the more things seemed able to go wrong. Sudden infant death syndrome. Colic. Meningitis. Choking. Smothering. Being dropped on the head. Some nights she had sat and wept, overwhelmed with the responsibility, overwhelmed with fear. Sometimes she felt as if Elena were not a baby but huge, bigger than she. Then she would feel guilty. Motherhood had not been joyous the first time. She had felt inadequate. She was finishing law school, she was on the *Law Review*, she was studying hours every night while holding the crying Elena on one arm. She wondered why she had not gone mad. Perhaps she had. No, she had survived and so had Elena, but when Elena got into trouble, Suzanne had been sure it was her fault, her failure as a mother.

"I think it would be good for you to be on the board," Jake said, dipping bread into sauce from the pot roast. "I know it would be good for the board."

"But I'm overextended as it is. I'm teaching, I'm practicing law, I'm still involved in the clinic, I'm mentoring several students, I'm trying to finish an article on appeals in battered women syndrome cases . . ."

"The board will meet only once or twice a month. You could manage that. An evening now and then."

"But you don't want me just as a warm body at meetings. Do you?" She wished she did not have a tiny suspicion that one of the reasons he was attracted to her was because he wanted to recruit her legal talent for his organization. Gratis, of course, legitimate pro bono work, if she had the time. But she had that little suspicion, and she did not enjoy it.

"You're a crack litigator, Suzanne. We could use any help you could give us. We're always in court. We're always suing some lumber company or power megalith, or they're suing us, or both."

"Just when did you think of asking me? How long have you had that in mind?"

They looked at each other in a heavy silence. Between them lay the half-eaten meal and the question she did not quite ask, but which he understood.

"It's an obvious idea, Suzanne. I'm not at all sure it was my idea originally. I imagine when I mentioned meeting you, one of my directors made the suggestion."

She decided to ignore the messier possibilities for the moment. "I have no idea how much time and effort my mother is going to take. For the moment, she's in a good rehab center. But that's temporary. She's going to need lots of help. I don't understand what's involved, frankly, except that I suspect it's a lot more than I can imagine."

"Well, how about you go on the board and we put off asking you for anything more until you have your mother settled?"

"How about you give me some time to see what having my mother in my home entails?" It was always easier to maintain a relationship in two busy lives when at least part of those working lives intersected. However, she felt too overextended to agree to anything. "Right now I wouldn't baby-sit a friend's goldfish for a weekend. I'm pulled out of shape."

"It would be good for you to get involved. I know you'd find it more interesting than you can guess."

"I just need some time without any more new demands."

"I can wait." He grinned at her.

Why did that make her so uncomfortable?

17   Twelve Years Earlier

Elena

Elena was annoyed the guys were hogging the driving. Ever since Chad had taught her, she loved to drive. Her mother saw no reason for her to start driving at what she called below the age of reason, but Chad had brought her in for her learner's permit. The guys would tire eventually and let her take over. They had borrowed Chad's father's BMW, which was hardly inconspicuous but made good time on the night interstate west. They had left in the morning at the time they were all supposed to be going to school, to give them a full day's head start before any of them were missed. Now it was 1:30 A.M., and they were just crossing from Ohio into Indiana with Judas Priest shouting that song they kept playing over and over, "Rock Hard, Ride Free."

She wakened curled in the backseat to find that Chad was checking them into a motel. They all fell into the bed and more or less slept until it got noisy in the morning. Then they all took turns in the shower and Chad shaved.

"How come you aren't shaving?" she asked Evan.

"I'm going to grow a beard. Great disguise. I look older with five o'clock shadow."

She made a disgusted grimace. "Just don't expect me to kiss you!"

He grabbed her and rubbed his cheek against hers. "Kiss, kiss, kiss."

They were both giggling as they fell on the bed. Chad came in whistling. "Leave you guys alone for five minutes, and you're at it. In permanent heat, that's what you are."

Elena said, "I think we should all do something to change our appearance."

Chad shrugged. "Who's looking for three kids? Runaways are a dime a dozen."

"Your father's going to want his car back."

Chad waved that away with an airy gesture. "We'll have to ditch it at some point and get another."

"Oh, sure. We can trade," Evan said. "Hi, want to trade your old Ford Escort for a nice BMW, no questions asked?"

"For the time being, let's get as far as we can in it."

"I've never been to California," Elena said, curled up again in the backseat with a bag of potato chips that would do for breakfast.

"I have," Chad repeated. "We lived in Sacramento for two years when my parents were still together. Mom and I used to go for picnics on the American River. My mom taught me how to paddle a canoe. We would pretend to be Indians."

"Your mother used to, like, play with you?" Evan asked in surprise.

"Yeah. She had a wild imagination. We always played together. Now I'll never see her again, ever."

"That's silly," Elena said. "She wouldn't tell your dad where you are. She wouldn't rat on you."

Chad didn't answer. Elena tried to imagine her mother playing with her. Actually she remembered Suzanne crawling around the floor with her when she was little. They were bears under the dining-room table. She could hardly believe Suzanne had done that. Growled and eaten berries. Yes, they had eaten blueberries out of their hands under the table, her mother's face stained with purple. In the memory, Suzanne was young and almost radiant. She remembered the same table as a tent and her mother and herself under it—were they Indians? Bedouins? That was fun. They ate under the table from a can of tuna fish. The cat Big Boy had come and eaten some of it too and made Elena giggle. Big Boy was a huge brown tabby from the street who slept with Elena, always, his big grizzled head on her thigh. She wondered if he was missing her. He was an old cat now and set in his ways. Would he start sleeping in Rachel's bed? Would he cry for her, looking around the house and in the closets? She felt almost angry at these long buried memories of childhood. How could Suzanne have been that way and now be the way she was? Now she never understood a thing but kept pushing Elena to be somebody else, an older version of the perfect Rachel. Her mother just did not love her. She was trying to train her like a recalcitrant dog.

After weeks of making idle plans for running away together, Elena herself precipitated their leaving. She received a midsemester grade of D in physics, which she had taken just to avoid chemistry and its bad smells. Physics seemed cleaner. But she hated it. Everything had to be so diddly-shit precise. She had expected it to be exciting, like time and space and warp engines and stars exploding. But it was all boring. It was measuring things nobody needed to measure, displacements, specific gravities. All this crap was because her mother insisted Elena go to college, which was pointless. It was pointless like school and adulthood and every meaningless thing people filled their time with: 6:45 watch the news; 7:30 get married; 8:05 talk to investment broker; 9:00 watch TV. They would all be dead soon, like some terrorist would set off the big one and they would combust or else die hideously with awful sores and their hair falling out. Or some other terrorist would drop a plague virus in the reservoir. There was nothing to look forward to anyhow except growing up and getting a boring job and paying taxes and having babies you could force to act the way you wanted them to, so they too would grow up doing what they found just as boring as you had. As Chad was always saying, it was better to give them the slip. Head out. Get off the bus. If you followed their plan, all you got every day was older.

But she knew her mother was just going to kill her for getting the D. As if it mattered. She could hear it already, the speeches about living up to her potential, the speeches about how important it was for a girl to do as well as she possibly could—like she was some kind of super Girl Scout leading a charge of females up a hill against a guard of macho men. Her best friends were boys. Her mother didn't understand guys. She was always going on about discrimination and quotas and affirmative action and self-esteem. Elena's self-esteem was just fine. She didn't need some stupid grade in a class she hated to prop it up. Her mother didn't care about her anyhow, only about performance. Suzanne just couldn't endure to wait until Elena grew up. She wanted her to act a certain way, to dress a certain way. The first time Suzanne saw her new bathing suit, she was ripshit. "You have to shave your pubic hair to wear that."

So what? Like did her mother think she was going to slip with the razor and perform a clitoridectomy? When Suzanne saw her tattoo—her gorgeous rose with the thorn and the drop of blood—she just went ballistic. She spent a whole evening investigating law governing tattoos on minors in Rhode Island before Elena persuaded her to cool it. Then Elena heard her on the phone to her friend Marta asking about how one got tattoos removed. Elena just couldn't stand the fuss that was going to happen when her mother saw her report card. All that guilt, all that screaming and moaning. So she said to the guys, "If we're ever hitting the road, it better be now. Chad's facing military school and I'm facing the electric chair."

Now here they were, driving across endless expanses of nothing in particular. They could hardly find a place to pee, it was so vacant. It felt like high school in the form of a landscape. Nothing at all for a hundred miles and then a fucking Hardee or a Kentucky Fried Chicken and a gas station. They didn't even have Burger Kings. They were playing Mötley Crüe's Shout at the Devil. Every time they sang "Bastard," she felt they were singing to her. When Chad changed the music to Iron Maiden, they all shouted with the tape on "Runnin Free." They were running free. The other song the guys kept playing was Scorpions, which was not her favorite group, "Bad Boys Running Wild." She was just as wild as them.

They were past Iowa and into Nebraska at a service plaza. They always tried to sit by the window because it was more interesting, and they could keep an eye on the car and stuff. They saw the state troopers stop and one of them walking all around the car. He looked at something and he was reading the license plate.

"Come on," Evan said. "The Greyhound is loading. We can get on and pay for our tickets on board. Just get on. We can say we were hitchhiking and got stranded. The driver won't throw us off in the middle of nowhere."

They boarded the bus with the other passengers. They couldn't sit together, but they got it straightened out and went as far as Denver, where the bus was going. Chad paid for all their tickets. He had cleaned out a money stash at his house. The main things she missed were her clothes and the tape player. She still had her Walkman and most of her tapes that were in her backpack, but a lot of the tapes had been in the BMW, including the Iron Maiden tape with "Wrathchild" on it.

Denver was kind of cool. They could see the mountains the next morning, after they walked around during what remained of the night. Soon it was too smoggy to see, but they knew the mountains were there. They had no luggage, because when they had left the car, they had left everything. She had only the clothes she was standing in, jeans and a T-shirt and her leather jacket and sneakers, plus the few things in her backpack.

"What are we going to do?" They were sitting in a café that had opened for breakfast. They were eating a big breakfast because they hadn't eaten much the day before. They had been scared in Nebraska and they were still nervous. Before they left the café, Elena washed her hair in the basin in the women's room, with the weird liquid soap. She patted it with paper towels. It would dry as they walked around.

"We should cut your hair off and pretend you're a boy," Chad said.

"Nobody's going to think I'm a boy and keep your hands off my hair."

"What are we going to do now? Keep taking buses?"

"That is distinctly not cool," Chad said. "We need wheels."

"Do you know how to hot-wire a car?" Evan asked. "I don't."

Reluctantly after a couple of minutes, Chad admitted, "No. I don't either."

"I don't see charities ringing their bells on street corners to give away used cars," Evan continued. Maybe he felt the other two had dragged him into this mess. Evan had swiped his old man's American Express card, but soon his old man would put a halt on it. Plus if they used it, it would be like a big sign to the cops as to exactly where they were. They had already gone close to the limit on Chad's Visa, and that too would leave a paper trail. They had to buy a few clothes, and all three got matching nose studs. It was like a wedding ring, but cooler. It said they were one another's people, a family. This was all the family she would ever want or need.

"There's worse places to be," Elena said in a conciliatory tone. "It's nothing like Boston or New York or Washington. I like the Spanish I hear in the streets." That was the only class she missed from high school, except English. She wanted to be smooth in Spanish so that if she ever met her father, she could impress him. "Maybe we could like go up into the mountains. They're so fucking awesome. Why not? There's a lot of ghost towns here. We could just find some old deserted cabin and move in."

"We could go to Mexico," Evan said. "I was there once with my parents in Acapulco, but I barely remember it. I think I got sick and threw up."

"Well, then, we don't want to be going there," Chad said sarcastically. "Poor little Evan. Besides, if we don't get wheels, we aren't going anyplace."

"I just said, I don't see why we can't stay here for a while. . . . I think it's cool."

"We said we were going to California. I have friends in California. They can help us."

"Oh sure, they can give us their allowance. Loan us ten bucks. I can hardly wait," Evan said.

"Guys, we're getting cross. I think we all need sleep. We got to find a place to crash," she said. It was real important to her that they all get along, not carp like married people. Mostly they all did get along, because they loved one another, but when things were hard, then the two guys would start sniping.

They walked around for a couple more hours, getting crankier and more and more silent together, until finally they found a cheap hotel that did not give a damn that there were three of them sharing a room. In motels, it was easier, because just one of them checked in. It all came down to Chad's being right: they had to have a car.

Around eight that night they woke up and went out to eat. Elena got them to try a Mexican place. She hardly ever had Mexican food. Her grandma had taken her out for it a couple of times in New York, but Suzanne didn't like hot food. But at least, thanks to Beverly, she could pretend to having eaten it all her life. It was greasy but good and definitely cheap, which helped a lot because none of them had much cash.

They walked around and looked at people and stared into store windows. They bought a couple of T-shirts and some underwear and socks and the Rising Force tape. Chad tried to buy beer, but they wouldn't sell it to him. Evan said, "When my beard grows out, I'll look much older, and they won't ask for ID."

Chad said, "We can always pimp for Elena. That should support us."

"Fuck you, Chad. I don't think that's funny. I won't do that. You go sell your ass."

"Nah," Evan said. "Nobody'd pay for her. We'd have to pay them."

They were both grinning now, bonded over teasing her. She pretended to be upset, but she was glad they stopped being cranky.

Back in the hotel room it was stuffy and dim. Chad stood in the middle of the floor looking at both of them where they sprawled on the bed, Evan's head on her breasts. "I have the solution to our problems right here. Never pays to doubt the Chad."

"Your credit card." Evan threw up his hands. "We can use it maybe twice more and then they'll be down on us."

"No. This." Chad reached into his jacket and pulled out a gun.

She remembered it. It was from his father's bedroom. The Smith & Wesson .357 Magnum, he had called it. It lay there in his hand, large and deadly.

"What's that for?" she asked, not wanting to hear.

"Freedom. If they corner us, I'm not going back." He raised the pistol to his temple and mimicked firing. "Fast death, sure and sweet."

Evan hefted it dubiously. "Exit? Bang bang, an emergency measure? Is that why you brought the damned thing?"

"No, man, it gives us a chance. That's our ticket to California."

Elena hated guns, but she didn't speak. She would sound like a wimp.

* * *

Elena and the boys spent a week in Denver, arguing about what they should do. The money was going. "We could always rob a gas station or a convenience store," Chad said. "People do that all the time."

"That doesn't make it right!" Elena said with a fierce conviction that surprised even her. "You can't go sticking a gun into the face of some guy who's just pumping gas. Just an ordinary working guy. That's not right!" It could have been Suzanne talking, she knew it, but she couldn't help her upbringing. Or Grandma Beverly, who was as cool a grandma as anybody ever had. Elena couldn't condone casual crime committed against ordinary people just for money.

"I never thought there was any use having a gun along," Evan said.

"It's a way out," Chad said. "I won't go back. I'll never go back."

Evan shrugged. "Don't be so dramatic. If we're ever going on to California, it should be before all our money runs out. Maybe we should just take a frigging bus as far as we can go."

Chad grimaced. "I hate buses. They stink."

"Well, do you just want to stay here until our money's all gone?" Evan demanded.

Sometimes she hated Chad. They were out here because of him. Okay, she was scared for Suzanne to find out she was flunking physics, but Suzanne wasn't about to do anything more than guilt-trip her and make up some stupid punishment, like doing the dishes for two weeks straight. But Chad had all these complications, like his mother he wasn't supposed to see and his father who wanted to send him to military school and he suffered all the time at the top of his lungs. He'd bullied them into coming. They had just been daydreaming about it like kids would talk about setting fire to the school or robbing a bank or a beer truck. It was like imagining you were Batman or something. It was like getting high. When it was over, you were still home and everything was the same. But here they were a couple of thousand miles from home and a mile high in a city that felt terribly dry and made her heart pound when she ran up the stairs at the hotel. They were dirty and had no nice clothes. The beds were awful and the mattresses were lumpy and smelled of stale urine. Her face was breaking out, which just never happened to her. It was all the greasy food, her mother was right. Too many french fries did ruin your skin. There was a special shampoo she used at home she didn't even see in the drugstore here. It made her hair shine. Now her hair hung there dull and limp. She didn't even have a hair dryer to blow it out the way she wore it. No wonder when she saw herself in a mirror or a shop window, she just didn't want to look. She worried about Big Boy, that Rachel and Suzanne wouldn't give him his medicine twice a day and would forget to get the special food he needed from the vet.

Evan was getting grumpy, her Evan who was always above the fray. The situation was out of his control. He knew it, she knew it, and neither of them liked it. She liked it better when Evan ran things, when it was his ideas they followed—although it was Evan's stupid desire to fuck Chad that had got them into this mess to begin with. When they all had sex now, she didn't come. She was too angry. She lay there bored and a little sore. Mostly Evan wanted to fuck Chad and Chad wanted to fuck her, and they both wanted it too often to suit her. Chad was always wanting to try new positions with his feet in her face or her straddling a chair that was uncomfortable anyhow. Lately whenever she peed, it burned. The guys were so noisy together they gave her a headache. If she could only be alone sometimes, quiet, peaceful.

She wished they would just lay off her until they got to California. She saw the golden state in her mind, beaches, orange groves, cable cars, movie stars, waves rolling in. If they could only finally get to California, everything would be better. Chad had friends there who'd help them. They would be okay. They would all live in a little shack on the ocean and get brown and happy together. In the meantime, she felt like they insisted on sex all the time because they were bored shitless, the same as her.

"Pack up. We're going," Chad announced suddenly, clapping his hands together. "Let's move on out."

Everything they had, what little it was, fitted into the backpack Elena always wore, only now Evan kept it on his back. They sneaked out, because they owed the desk for the last night. Elena had been sent down to give him a story about how they were waiting for money to come. He'd leered at her but said he'd give them until the next day at noon. It was evening. They took a bus to a mall where they ate burgers and ice cream.

Elena didn't know what Chad had in mind and she was sure Evan didn't either, but both of them were scared to ask. Maybe if she knew, she'd have to try to stop him, and then what would they do? They were running out of options. It had seemed to her before they left that they had so much money. She had taken three hundred dollars out of the savings account set up for college. The check had to be cosigned by Suzanne and her, but Evan was expert at forging Suzanne's signature. He had been doing it on absence excuses for two years.

Food used up money fast. Gas, when they had had the car. It had needed a lot of gas. "If we do get a car," Elena said, "it shouldn't be so gaudy, so conspicuous. And it shouldn't use so much gas."

"I better check the consumer's guide ratings on gasoline consumption before I lift us some wheels. And don't you care about emissions standards? We shouldn't like drive a car that pollutes," Chad said, slapping her butt. She hated when he did that, and he knew it.

They walked around the mall until the traffic thinned out. Finally Chad saw what he was waiting for. A guy pulled up in a dark blue Ford Taurus. His girlfriend was waiting in the passenger's seat while he ran into the liquor store. He left the engine running.

Chad yanked open the door on the passenger's side. "Out." He shoved the gun into her neck.

"Don't hurt me!"

"Don't scream, or I'll shoot. I don't want you, just the car. " He pulled her out. "Evan, drive." Evan flung the backpack behind him and fumbled for the parking brake.

Chad motioned Elena into the backseat, and they lurched off. "Okay. Elena. Where do we go?"

"Turn right at the light." She turned on the overhead and looked at the map Evan had bought. "Okay, just keep going. We're heading for the interstate."

They drove all night. Before they climbed into the mountains, they had to buy gas. "That jerk had less than a quarter of a tank. I used to know this guy who never put more than a quarter tank in his wreck at once, because he always thought it was going to die on him." Chad sounded almost cheerful. The tapes in the car were country western crap, and Elena threw them out the window as they roared upward. The one tape she kept was Kiss, who were okay. It was an old tape but it had "Partners in Crime."

She finally got her turn at the wheel. Evan tried to stay awake to talk to her but he dozed off, his head against the passenger seat window. She drove just five miles over the speed limit, the way Suzanne always did. They didn't want to be stopped by police. She had a brief fantasy that they would be, and then she could go home and take a real bubble bath and change her clothes and sleep in her own clean bed with Big Boy. But she didn't want them to get caught while she was driving. The guys had waited all this time to finally let her drive, so she wasn't about to fuck up.

She drove on through the dark shapes of the mountains, the engine straining sometimes. She had to turn on the heater, it got so cold in the car. She could see patches of snow and then more snow to either side of the car. Then white banks of snow hemmed them in. In the headlights of oncoming trucks, she saw a whole winter of snow around them. Then finally they were coming down and down. The snow disappeared and the sky began to lighten over the mountains behind them. She was tired now but she wouldn't admit it. She gripped the wheel hard. Chad was snoring in back. Evan lay against the windows, his head at an awkward angle as if his neck were broken. What was going to become of them all? Suppose they did get to California? So what? Kiss was singing "Nowhere to Run," which matched her mood.

Still, she had flown through the dark. She had driven all night and her exhaustion was like a drug singing in her veins. There was no going back now. They were across the first high mountains and she would never be the same again. She had come into a new country of the damned. She was not who she had been, but new and dangerous and desperate. They had stolen this car, they had stolen their new life. They were real criminals now, outside the law, outside the prefabricated flat lives she scorned. She loved them both passionately, Evan, who was a part of her, and Chad whom they both adored and who ruled them like the sun, as they turned about his fire and ice. Her desire for him slowly returned as she drove on into the pasty predawn, the air like congealed grease around them. He had been right to yank them out of their boring lives and turn them loose. On to California, where they would live together and there would be no one else they would have to please—only themselves, only each other. They would be free—together.

18 Twelve Years Earlier

Elena

Elena said, "So what's going to happen in California, when we get there?"

They were camping in the desert under a sky that had more stars than she had ever seen. They were partway across Nevada. They had got gas in Elko and got back on 80. In Battle Mountain, they bought Cokes from a machine. The last time they ate was in Utah. They were scared to get out of the car in a town, scared to go into a fast-food place or a restaurant. They were trying to make the money last and trying to avoid being seen, because they were sure they were wanted now. The night was cold. She had her jacket but she was still chilled through, pressed against Evan's bony side. He had been increasingly silent all day. Now he spoke up. "Yeah, Chad, what's in California?" There was an undertone of confrontation in his voice.

"Nothing," Chad said. "But wouldn't you like some real honest nothing?"

"What does that mean?" Elena asked.

"What do you think of your life so far?"

She laughed harshly. "Shit. Pure endless shit."

"What do you think the rest of your life will be?"

"Shit. Pure boring shit."

"So?" Evan huddled farther into his clothes. "What do you propose?"

Chad was quiet for perhaps five minutes. The stars were huge over them, like animals in the indigo sky. Not all of them were white. As she lay back staring at them, she could see blue and yellow and red. It was as if they were in outer space looking around. It did not feel like earth. She felt as if they had left behind everybody else, and there was no one alive, really alive, except the three of them who were one unit, one self. She touched the stud in her nose, a sign of their union, that their bodies belonged to each other as their souls did. It felt as if they were on the moon, or some asteroid private to them.

"I think we should go as far as we can, because it's fun and we're together, and it's the best game I ever played. But if they're going to catch us, or the money runs out and we're at the end of our game, then we should end it." He clapped his hands together, a sharp report like a small explosion.

"You think we should kill ourselves," Evan said.

"Some combination of that," Chad said calmly. "I'm not going back to my old man. I'm not going to let him destroy my mother and put me in military school. I'd rather die. It's that simple."

Evan was silent, tense. She could feel his body drawn into itself, coiled. She did not want to speak until he did. She felt calm about the idea of killing herself. It sounded curiously neat and soothing. She could imagine how sorry Suzanne and Rachel would be for the way they had treated her.

"Of course, if you're scared . . ." Chad said. "It takes nerve."

She could imagine how impressed all her classmates would be. She would go from slut to heroine. She would be a story no one would forget. That's how it was, if you really did it.

"I've thought about it," Evan said. "Ever since I can remember, I've thought about it. But then I used to think all the time about flying."

"You couldn't fly," Chad said softly. "But you can walk out that door."

"There's always that," Evan said.

She tried to imagine it. Like a huge orgasm. A crashing into sleep. She thought of what Suzanne would say, and how her sister would cry and cry. Everyone would think how mean they had been to her, and they would feel guilty. Suzanne would think how she had yelled at Elena about the dishes and her room and smoking and grades and clothes and her tattoo. Suzanne would really be sorry, but it would be way, way too late. After the assembly in school, counselors would come in to tell the kids it was all right, but nobody would think so, not the adults, not the kids. A month later, some other kids would kill themselves in homage. A copycat suicide. But theirs would be unique. "We can't let them catch us and put us in jail," she said aloud.

Evan said, "We're underage."

"I'm not," Chad said. "I'm sixteen. I'd go to jail. But I won't."

At dawn, he showed them all how to load and fire the gun. It hurt Elena's ears. It really hurt. But she learned to hold the gun.

"It isn't like you have to be a good shot," Chad said. "It isn't like you're trying to hit a target forty feet away." He held the gun to his temple, and Elena thought for a moment he was going to do it right then.

"I'm hungry," Evan said. They had hardly slept all night. "Do we have anything left to eat?"

"We'll stop in the next town. We need gas anyhow," Elena said and began walking toward the car. She did not want to die, not particularly. Not right then, anyhow. Later. Now the wind was fresh and cold as a fish's belly and the east behind them was a lemon stripe at the horizon. It was strange how in the desert, she thought of the sea. The mountains she was staring at looked near, but they had driven until well after dark across the desert surrounded by ridges of mountains they climbed and then descended and back onto the desert again. She felt like an ant crawling over a bedspread. But she did not care. She walked in the middle, with her arms around each of them.

"If they catch us," Evan said, "they'll separate us."

"Of course," Chad said. "But we belong together."

"We're a set," Elena said happily. "A family. A unit."

"Don't call us by nasty names like family," Chad said, slapping her butt. "We're loving to one another. My father never loved anyone but himself and expensive whores and expensive cars. Never. We're not a family, we're a little tribe. A tribe of three."

"I don't think I ever loved anyone but a spaniel I had named Audrey, my grandmother, who died when I was twelve, and you guys," Evan said. "My grandmother was so warm I always wanted to be with her, but my parents could barely stand her. She had an accent. They called her ignorant, when she spoke five languages."

"Whatever we are," Chad said, "we stay together. If we need to, we die together."

They had driven for maybe half an hour. A police car had passed them going the other way right after they pulled out onto the highway, but it didn't seem to pay them any mind. It wasn't really light yet, just gray dawn with the sun not yet up over the last mountain range behind them and the sky still dark ahead, westward where they were going. Elena was curled up in the backseat, using the blanket that they had found in the trunk. Chad was driving and Evan was sitting beside him. Then they saw a police car coming behind them with its lights rotating. They couldn't hear the siren. No cars were in sight before them, just a couple of trucks on the other side of the highway. Chad stepped on it, but the police car was gaining on them, still far behind but getting bigger as she knelt on the seat facing backward. "I wish we had the fucking BMW," he muttered.

Suddenly Chad swerved off the highway. The car spun around, rocked as if it would go over but then finally came to a halt facing back toward the police car still getting bigger. Chad pulled the gun out of his jacket. "This is it," he said. "I'll go first. Then, Evan, take the gun, do Elena and then yourself."

Evan made a noise that sounded like a yeah, but he was probably as scared as she was. She felt a weird elation and total panic at once. This was it, like Chad said. The end. The finish. The final scene in the movie. She imagined music and she wished they had the tape deck on.

Chad was facing away from her toward the police car. She saw him lift the gun and put it to his temple. There was a noise so loud she bit her tongue. Her head rang and her eyes dripped tears. Then she felt something wet and slimy on herself. She looked down. It was his blood, and some gray matter like snot. "His brains," she screamed. "His brains are all over me!"

Chad slumped forward over the wheel with part of his head gone and blood and brains all over her and the seat and the window. It was horrible, not at all the way she had imagined. He had turned into garbage. She pawed at herself, but she could not bear to touch the stuff. She realized that Evan was screaming. He had blood all over him. Chad had fallen on him and he was frantically pushing him away.

She opened the door and stumbled out, vomiting. It was a dry vomit because they hadn't eaten for twelve hours. But she kept heaving, bent over and then rising to her feet and staggering onward. She was coughing and crying and trying to vomit but on her feet because she had to get away from that thing in the car, she had to escape it.

The police car had slowed down and was pulling off about thirty feet away from them. Two state patrolmen got out, one from each side, and started toward them. She stared at them as she lurched forward and it seemed to her as if she were traveling toward them and gazing at them for minute after minute. One was taller and wore sideburns like Elvis. The other was stockier and had light curly hair that reminded her of Rachel. It felt as if she was moving ever so slowly toward them and they were staring at her as if she was something fierce and wild, like a bear. Then they both looked past her. Evan got out of the front passenger's seat. He had taken the gun but it hung loosely in his hand.

"What are you doing with that?" she screamed at him. "Are you really going to shoot me?"

Evan didn't say anything. His mouth was hanging open and he looked as if he might throw up too. Chad had fallen half out of the open door, blood all over him. The cops were coming toward them. "Drop the gun," one of them shouted. "Put the gun down. Put your weapon down on the ground now! Then raise your hands. Put your weapon on the ground." They had their guns trained on Evan. One cop had dropped to a knee and held his gun in front of him in both hands. The other was still coming forward, also holding his gun out with both hands. Evan just kept staggering toward them. Then he made some kind of gesture. She was sure he was raising his hands to surrender, but he still had the gun and the cop in front shot, then the other trooper. The gun in Evan's hand went off as he was hit, but the shot just went into the earth. Shot after shot. She could not tell who was shooting, but she saw Evan jerk and spin. Then he went down. She ran to him. The cop was on her and grabbed her and pushed her against the car. She was screaming. She did not even feel herself slam into the metal.

She heard the cop who had shot Evan say, "He's dead." At first she thought he meant Chad. But she kept screaming. She couldn't stop. She didn't think she would ever stop. They had shot Evan, who hadn't wanted to die, who hadn't had any intention of shooting her or them or anybody, anybody at all. Who was just so freaked-out at what Chad had done, for real, that he wasn't even aware he was holding the gun. They had shot him dead. She waited for them to shoot her too. Why should she care?

19

Suzanne

Suzanne was sitting at Marta's kitchen table, her head in her hands. "I don't see what else I can do."

"You haven't considered a nursing home?" Marta was still dressed for court. She hadn't yet changed, except for kicking off her pumps and removing her suit jacket.

"Marta! You know Beverly. She isn't senile. She'd go mad in a nursing home. I can't do that to her."

"But neither can you stay home and take care of her." Marta was sensuously caressing her own toes, freed from her court pumps.

"We'll have to see how much taking care of she needs. I can hire someone. Marta, what else can I do? She can't live alone. I let her apartment go months ago. I have to move her in. I have no other choice I can see, no other viable and reasonable choice."

"Beverly and you under the same roof. You'll move up here."

"Maybe we can reach a rapprochement. She needs me. I always wanted her to give me her approval. I'm aware of how childish that is, but it's been there forever. For her to say, Yes, you are a good lawyer, you did know what you were doing. You are truly a political person whose standards I can respect. And so on and on and on."

"And you seriously think moving her into your flat is going to accomplish all that? There'll be the wrong room, wrong furniture, wrong city, wrong food, and so on and on and on."

"Realistically I know that. But my fantasies come into play. And I want to do right by her. She deserves being taken care of. She has been a good person, she has given her life to good causes. Now I should throw her in the garbage because she's damaged?" Suzanne thought of a new line of argument. "How about your own mother? If she hadn't died of breast cancer . . . suppose she'd had a stroke?"

"But, Suzanne, I was close to her. I never stopped being close. I could have lived with her. It isn't the same thing. She was my bud."

The carpenters came to put up railings and ramps. Her house was in utter chaos for days. Elena flirted with the younger carpenter. Suzanne would come home from work to find him still there, sitting at the kitchen table looking into Elena's eyes while she practiced her Spanish on him.

"Are you interested in him?" Suzanne asked cautiously.

"If what you mean is, am I screwing him, no. He's awfully young and naive, frankly."

Then the plumber, the electrician. Then the carpenters came back. Then Elena and Suzanne repainted. "You think she's going to give a damn if the paint is white or yellow?" Elena asked, her hair tucked under a red scarf.

Suzanne shrugged. "I don't want her to feel that anything is shoddy or that we don't care to make it right."

"I will never let myself fall apart! It's because she smoked all those years." Elena shook her head. "Even I stopped smoking finally."

"Well, she did cut down on her smoking. Beverly's always been healthy. She had more energy than six other women put together."

"It used to be so much fun to run around New York with her. She always knew bargain shops and cool places to have espresso or Chinese-Cuban food."

"She never spent much money on herself, but she always looked good. She had dozens of friends." Suzanne found herself on the verge of breaking into tears. They were talking about Beverly as if she had died. She sniffed hard and rubbed her eyes. "Anyhow, I think this pale, pale green will suit her. She's always said her favorite color was green. To match her eyes."

For three weeks, workmen had been in the house almost every day. She tripped over her treadmill when she ran to check a fax. In the middle of the night, when she woke up to pee, she ran into the exercise bike. Everything felt overcrowded. Constricted. She must endure it and not complain, not be martyred. Never let Beverly feel she was putting anyone out. The room next to the kitchen—which had housed a student who had lived with them for the year after Elena's disaster, which had once been her office, which had recently been her gym—was now fixed up into a sickroom. It had a hospital bed, railings. Everything was designed to be reachable from the bed or easily gotten to. The bathroom off the kitchen had been modified with a chair in the shower, a new higher toilet, faucets that turned on or off at a touch. The kitchen had been changed to make it more accessible. The front porch had a ramp, since Beverly could not climb stairs with her walker or her wheelchair. The ramps too had railings.

Suzanne's house, her refuge, her aesthetic retreat, her comfort hole, was all changed around to meet the needs of her mother, with whom she had not lived since she had gone away to college. She could still remember those fights. They had been fighting since she was eleven, but the fierce arguments reached a crescendo her senior year of high school. "What's wrong with City College?"

"I have a scholarship to Brown." She could scarcely say that she had applied to thirty colleges to get away from home. Brown was the most prestigious place to take her and offer tuition as well. Suzanne had earned a four point average, was class valedictorian and coeditor of the high school paper, and was terrific at taking tests. Her SATs had been gorgeous. She was convinced to this day she had done all that not so much in order to succeed as to escape. Now they were about to become roommates.

Mud slides and more mud slides. I was supposed to go to a conference in Big Sur, but Route 1 is closed again. The meeting got moved to a hotel in San Jose.

My friends are buying me out of my half of the house. The wife's pregnant again and they think they can fill it just fine. It isn't divided into apartments, like your house. We just all shared the kitchen and the family rooms. I'm glad we don't have to put it on the market. It should make clearing out of here easier.

Have you thought about joining the board? There's a lot of enthusiasm here for the idea.

I haven't had two minutes to think about your board. My apartment is full of carpenters, plumbers, plasterers, electricians, all because my mother is coming to live with me in approximately two weeks. I am considering taking on one of the trickiest appeals I've ever faced. I wonder when you first had the idea of my joining the board?

I will not let it bother me, she thought, if he is trying to recruit me in bed. She promised herself she would not take it seriously. If he did not want her skills, she would never have come alive again sexually, would never even have guessed it was possible for her. After all, everybody had motives, everybody had his or her own agenda. Still, it felt a little tarnished. It made her wonder if she could possibly continue to carve out time for him if he did move east. Whenever he brought up her joining the board, she took an emotional step backward.

When I came back from Boston and mentioned I'd met you, immediately my boss got excited. He suggested I ask you at once. I still think it's a great match of talents and need.

She was not convinced, but she was mollified.

Basically, Beverly had to be taken from the rehab center because Medicare and the insurance covering rehabilitation had run out, and with Rachel still in college and Elena at home, Suzanne could not pay for a continued stay. Plus every time she visited, Beverly whispered in that strange cracked voice, painfully forming the words or something like the words, "When go home?"

She was not sure that Beverly understood that home, meaning the old apartment, was gone forever, but surely a room of her own in Brookline would be a lot better than this dreary room with a partially deranged roommate who kept babbling about events in her distant past and sometimes calling her dog for an hour at a time. Suzanne had saved her mother's things—some pieces of furniture, lamps, bric-a-brac, books, clothing—and they were waiting for her in Brookline. Perhaps those familiar objects would help make Beverly feel at home.

The day arrived when the move could no longer be put off. It was a Saturday in late May, a cool overcast day when colors, instead of fading in the mist, seemed to glow as if lit from within. The pink dogwoods on the lawn of the rehab center looked as if they might explode. Suzanne was wheeling Beverly to the curb. She had borrowed Marta's van to transport the wheelchair and the walker and the other paraphernalia. "Look, Mother," she said, pointing at the pink dogwoods.

"Suburbs," Beverly said and shrugged her good shoulder.

Suzanne did not speak again as she got Beverly to the van, helped her from the chair to the seat, protecting her head as she had been taught and collapsed the wheelchair before adding it to the heap in the back. Then she paused, feeling an insane desire to flee, to run off into the misty morning and vanish, perhaps turn up in California on Jake's doorstep. It's your fucking duty, she thought. Beverly is your mother.

A little voice said, some mother she was. But sometimes she was a good mother and loving and always Suzanne was proud of her. When she came to school, it was an occasion. Here comes the charming Mrs. Blume. Her mother was always special, dressed up a little Bohemian but always attractive, her hair glowing, just enough makeup and never too much. The male teachers lit up. The principal would see her at once. She had that rich throaty voice that made everyone want to stop and listen—unless Beverly had a political bone to pick, like her objection to school prayer long before it was a cause everybody had heard of. Her mother might not be a practicing Jew, like Aunt Karla, but she was well aware of how the dominant culture tried to assimilate her daughter forcibly with Easter songs in school assembly. Then her mother's visits raised hell, but a kind of hell that Suzanne was not embarrassed by. She had always agreed with her mother then, politically. It was not until Suzanne became a feminist that their fighting spread to the political arena. "I have no common cause with suburban housewives," Beverly proclaimed. "Ladies in pearls are not my constituency."

"I have no common cause with macho politicos who use women like toilet paper," Suzanne had yelled back, just as strident, just as angry.

Suzanne's becoming politically active had not brought them closer but given them one more thing to argue about. But after age seventeen, she had always been able to walk out the door, to escape. Gritting her teeth, she went around to the driver's side of Marta's van and climbed in. This time there was no escape.

20

Beverly

Beverly had been invisible for months. She spoke and no one heard her, for none had the patience to listen while she carefully, deliberately sculpted the words out of pain and air. She made gestures and faces no one noticed. She had no opinions or ideas, since no person listened to them, argued with them, was swayed by them. She was without purpose or effect.

She hated the physical therapy but she went through the motions. The speech therapy she gave herself to wholeheartedly. The occupational therapy she worked at. It was humiliating to be learning like a retarded toddler to dress and undress herself, take herself to the toilet, clean herself, feed herself, get in and out of her walker and her wheelchair. She could use the walker on even ground, but she tired quickly. The wheelchair appeared in some ways more dignified and certainly more comfortable, but it was too wide to pass through many doorways.

Her anger was feeble and throttled. She was often angry, but it was hard to express except by throwing things on the floor, again like a toddler in a high chair. She remembered King Lear, so angry, so foolish, so weak. She thought of herself as Queen Lear. She had lost everything and would gladly die on the moor.

Her speech therapist was a fat woman to whom she had taken an instant dislike the first day, but at the end of a week, she had to admit that Nancy was better than that Dr. Fish she had thought so wonderful in New York. Nancy pushed her hard. She began to get out not only almost every sound she needed to truly speak, but to form complete sentences, even if it took her five minutes. She came to respect Nancy, even to feel warmly toward her. She wished she could go on seeing her even after she left the facility, but it was too far away from Suzanne's house. She'd be seeing a speech therapist whose office was a few blocks away.

Now Suzanne had finally come to get her out of this pastel prison. But Suzanne had lied to her, had never told her she had let go of Beverly's home, the apartment where she had lived for the last thirty-one years, in the neighborhood where she knew everybody and everybody knew her. Here she was nobody, just an old lady in a wheelchair who drooled sometimes and couldn't talk right. There she had been a character with politics, with a history, with a circle of friends—friends she would never see again. People she cared about. When Suzanne had blithely let go of that apartment, she had killed Beverly's identity, her selfhood, her past. She was furious whenever she thought of that act of cheapness. Suzanne had no right to do that to her.

Now she was going to have Suzanne's choices thrust down her gullet. Even the house was wrong, a big wooden object with trees and dark ominous rhododendrons and yews all around it, a huge waste of space. It was depressing, a turn-of-the-century monster upper-middle-class people had lived in with servants when her mother had come to this country. It was as if Suzanne had some nutty nostalgia for what Beverly's mother had never enjoyed: the good life circa 1910 on a street occupied by professionals, yuppies, their precocious children, their computers, their pedigreed dogs and cats. Even their hamsters had pedigrees back twenty generations, all the way to 1994. They drove BMWs, Volvos, Jeep Cherokees, the higher range of Toyotas with an occasional Land Rover and Lexus. Someone else, usually Black or Latina, cleaned their houses. Sometimes another service person, usually white, walked their dogs for them. Beverly did not belong here. Even if she could speak fluently and forcefully, she would have nothing to say to people who lived like this. They had built a ramp so she could wheel herself into the maw of the dark enveloping house. The thought of actually living here was so depressing her eyes burned.

"You should be grateful," the social worker said, "that you have such a good daughter. She's taking you in. She's remodeling her house so you can get around." They kept telling her she should be grateful, as if to be forced into a corner of someone else's life when she had always had her own, was something to grovel and mumble thanks about.

"Why . . . move out . . . good apartment . . . South End," Beverly spoke slowly. It took her three false starts to get out the question.

"Mother, I haven't lived there in twelve years! You know why I left."

"Why?"

"I had to get Elena out of that neighborhood."

"Should've . . . sent her . . . live with me."

Suzanne said nothing, her mouth thinning as it did when she was angry.

"Marta . . . kept her . . . from jail," Beverly said.

"She did, yes," Suzanne agreed. "I'm glad you remember."

"I remember . . . all," Beverly said. "You think I lost . . . brain?" She wanted to say another word, but she could not recall it. She was always having to substitute one word for another. She knew Suzanne was trying to listen, trying to be patient, but sometimes while she was putting a sentence together like building a wall one brick at a time and then attempting to force those words out through her reluctant apparatus, Suzanne went off to another task, answered the phone, began another conversation.

She was put in a little room off the kitchen. She supposed it had been the maid's room when this house was built. She imagined an immigrant Irish maid huddling there in tears after a sixteen-hour day of work. It had its own bathroom, whose door had been widened. There were railings everyplace. At least it would be far easier than when she had stayed here at Passover. She slept in a hospital bed, which she would never share with any man as long as she lived. She would never have another lover. No one would ever stroke her breasts again or touch her there or talk silliness to her late at night or in the morning. She would never be held in strong or wiry arms, never press her breasts against a broad hairy chest or feel an erection hard against her belly or thigh.

But her cat was waiting for her. Mao was thinner. His coat felt coarse. They weren't feeding him right. Probably those two huge orange tabbies took his food away. She would fix that. He was ecstatic to see her, kneading her side, vibrating as if he were all purr-engine. She moved him to her good side where she could hug him. A little feeling had come back on her numb side, but she still could not move that hand. The leg she could move crudely, roughly, dragging it more than walking normally, but at least it supported her.

She was exhausted from the move and she napped, Mao pressed to her side. Whenever she woke, he was there purring. He was the only friend she had left now, the only remnant of her own real life that had been stolen from her. Grateful, they wanted her to be grateful, for what? Grateful that Suzanne hadn't thrown her out on the street? She had known bag ladies in her old neighborhood, and she was not convinced their life was any worse than hers right now. At least if she were a bag lady, she'd be in her own neighborhood. Her friends would help her out. They always had.

Karla, her silly sister, had always said she believed in an afterlife. What a word, after life. Well, that was what she was enduring: this was her *after* life.

21

Suzanne

Alexa appeared at Suzanne's office. "Suze, we better have lunch together—somewhere with a bit of privacy."

"Sorry, I can't today. I just moved my mother in, and I have to interview some possible caretakers from an agency. How about we talk for a couple of minutes here?"

Alexa shut the door, looking around in the hall first. Suzanne assumed this was about Alexa's battle to get tenure in the political science department, but Alexa looked at her accusingly. "Is it true you're taking the Rodriguez appeal? Tell me it isn't true."

"News travels fast. I only decided last week to consider it. I've only begun to review the transcripts." Suzanne sat down, trying to glance surreptitiously at her watch.

Alexa was a stocky blond woman who wore voluminous clothing, as if she were fifty pounds heavier than her real weight. She had a pretty face, round and motherly, and had recently married a chiropractor. "Suze, you can't do it. It's dirt. Dragging those children and their families through that trauma again. Let some cold-blooded shyster have it."

"Alexa, I don't think she's guilty."

"How can you believe her instead of twenty children?"

"I'll be able to answer that question better, after I've read through the records. I haven't committed myself yet. I need to know if there are genuine grounds for appeal."

"That woman abused little children left in her care. If you get her off on some technicality, how could you live with yourself?"

"I can't really discuss the case until I know the facts and the context. I'm not convinced she abused anyone. Have you read the transcripts?"

"I've read the papers. I think she should be hanged. The sexual abuse of children is one of the worst crimes an adult can commit, girlfriend, and you know that in your conscience."

"But sending a woman to prison for thirty years for a crime she didn't commit is also a terrible abuse, Alexa. Suppose somebody heard you calling a student Girlfriend and decided you were having an affair with her?" Suzanne stood. "I really have to keep that appointment at the agency. I can't leave my mother home alone. Elena's with her today, but most days she works as a receptionist."

Striding down the hall with Alexa bobbing beside her, she was annoyed. Everybody assumed Maxine Rodriguez was guilty. Perhaps she had even assumed that herself before she had met the woman out at Framingham last week. Maxine came across as a dedicated woman whose life had been destroyed. She was gaunt and distraught, desperate, but Suzanne felt that pull, something that often made her take a chance on a client whose case felt reasonably hopeless. Suzanne had not decided to take on the case. The court of appeals had refused to review the previous appeal. She would need new grounds. However, in the advances of appellate court opinions she had been scanning just the week before, she had read an opinion overturning a similar case on the grounds that the children's testimony had been rehearsed, prepared, essentially scripted for them. Alexa's using guilt on her for considering the case made her even more determined to examine the record with care. Alexa was her friend, but she was also prejudging. Children were the sentimental heroes of this story, but Maxine also had rights and feelings and a life cut off at the roots.

Suzanne stood in the doorway of Rachel's old room, where Elena was staying. Elena was being difficult about sharing the room with Rachel, who was home between returning from school and going off to Israel. Elena kept demanding Suzanne move out of her office and let Rachel stay there. "Look. I'm a lawyer. This is my law office. It is not anyone's bedroom. You've been staying in Rachel's room, and now Grandma is in the room downstairs. The two of you will just have to share a bedroom until Rachel leaves. It's only ten days, Elena. Try to be reasonable about this."

"I do not share a bedroom. I do not share a bed with a woman, even if she is my sister. I am not a child, and I need privacy."

"Well, there isn't any to be had."

"Why don't you sleep in here with her?"

"Elena, I'm glad to have you here, but you moved back simply to have a place to live. I also have Beverly now. I am not moving out of my office and I am not moving out of my room. I just rearranged and rebuilt half the house. I'm not about to rearrange the other half."

"Fine! I'll find someplace nice and private to stay. You'll see!"

"Elena, if you want to stay with a friend for the next ten days, that's fine with me. But we all have to make allowances for each other."

"You make me feel like I don't matter!"

"Elena, of course you matter very much to me. But you know that I have classes to teach, people depending on me to get them out of prison or to win appeals, your grandmother helpless downstairs. I have to live my life. I can't just sacrifice it to you."

Rachel was far more accepting of the situation. They were packing up some of her things for storage and others to go with her to Israel, or to follow her.

"I'm so sorry it doesn't even look like your room any longer," Suzanne said. "Nothing seems to be working out to anybody's satisfaction."

"It doesn't matter. I'll never live in this room again."

"Rachel, why do you say that?"

"We're getting married, you know that. You don't expect Michael to move in here."

"In Israel."

"We want to be married in Jerusalem. What could be more special? You'll fly over with Grandma. Elena if she wants to come. Daddy for sure and maybe his family."

On one hand, Suzanne was glad that Rachel was not marrying right away. They had time to reconsider. More selfishly, if she had to manage a wedding right now, she would explode. She could not imagine where the time and energy would come from. On the other hand she wished Rachel were not going anyplace, particularly into danger. The logistics of a wedding that far away (all those expensive plane fares and hotels) made her taste anxiety in her throat like acid.

"Wouldn't you rather put off worrying about marriage until after you get done with your year in Israel and get married when you come back home? You have a lot to learn this year and a whole new culture to get used to, without having to learn how to be married to each other."

"We know we want to marry, Mother." Rachel gave her a sweet smile. "We won't change our minds. We've been talking about marriage for months."

Suzanne found herself quietly weeping as she packed Rachel's clothing for a year's storage. They had never been separated by such distances, thousands of miles. When Rachel had gone to Europe, it had been with Suzanne, who loved traveling with her younger daughter. Rachel was a patient traveler. Unlike Suzanne herself, she did not mind when a plane or train was late or when they had to wait to get into a hotel room. She liked almost everything except men bothering her in the street. She liked strange foods (she had not been eating kosher yet); she liked museums; she liked city streets and markets and churches and shuls; she liked mountains and seas and rivers and forests. Rachel didn't complain about the blistering heat in Arles or the early snow in Bergen. She didn't mind the traffic jam on M-1 outside Heathrow so that they almost missed their plane trying to return a rental car to someplace with ambiguous signs. She liked traveling by plane, she liked traveling by train, she liked taking the underground or the metro or whatever. She was a perfect equable traveling companion. They would never travel together again, she thought, wiping her streaming eyes.

They were both in an elegiac mood. Do you remember, was the theme of their chatter. Suzanne was glad she had some time to spend with Rachel in between the end of school and the beginning of summer quarter. She had not planned to teach this summer, but after Beverly had her stroke, she volunteered, convinced she would need the money. She had not guessed the half of it. She would need to put a lot of work into Maxine's case, which she had almost decided to take. It was a political hot potato, and although Suzanne's appeal would be strictly on procedural grounds, she did not doubt that the ambitions of the state attorney general and the lieutenant governor were as relevant to the case as any of the children's well-rehearsed testimony.

"Do you remember how you used to cry when moths got into the apartment on Rutland Street and died there?"

"Oh, Mother, I'm sure I didn't go around weeping about moths. But I do remember when Big Boy got sick and died, how terrible that was."

Then a little later, "Mother. Do you remember how we rented a little house with Daddy up in Maine? It was out on a rocky peninsula. Once with a friend I tried to find it, but I discovered that Maine has maybe two hundred rocky peninsulas, and I couldn't remember where it was."

"It was on a peninsula near Bath. Called something like Five Towns. You were almost six. . . ."

"You and Daddy seemed so together. When I remember it, everybody is always laughing. Everybody is glowing and happy."

"It was just a week. You can be happy with anyone for a week, I guess. I just wish I could make Beverly happier."

"I think she needs more and brighter lights in there. It's hard enough for her to read without sitting in twilight."

"More light." Suzanne was pitifully eager for any ideas that might help. Rachel had concrete suggestions about improving Beverly's situation: get her a computer with an extra large screen. One with big keys. Then she can communicate more easily when she's tired and she can find stimulation on-line.

To Suzanne's surprise, Beverly did not reject the idea. "Can learn!" She hit her chest with her left hand. "Learn!"

Then suddenly the preparations were all made, the time was used up and Rachel left for New York, where she was meeting Michael to fly to Israel together. It had been hanging over Suzanne for months, for weeks, for days. All at once the day, the hour arrived and she saw off her daughter. Rachel looked so small and vulnerable heading for the plane. She appeared very serious, with a briefcase in one hand, pulling a carry-on with the other. Rachel had worn that same expression since she was a toddler making mud pies and sand castles in the park. Suzanne could see Rachel with her sturdy little legs stuck before her in a V looking at a doll in her lap with that full measuring stare. Rachel had been born good-natured and serious, in equal measures. That night, Suzanne wept

again, intermittently. Beverly held her hand in her good hand. "Will
. . . do . . . fine."

"She may. I don't know if I will. I'm closer to Rachel than to Elena.
Rachel always preferred to be with me rather than her father. We never
had the same kinds of bitter gouging fights I'd still have with Elena if I
let it happen."

"You love, both . . . diff . . . rent ways."

They had a rare moment of communication, even if the content was
simple reassurance. Rachel was too young to marry. Why couldn't she
wait? Why did she want to join her life to that rather innocuous stiff
young man?

Suzanne often found her own house uncomfortable lately. Elena's music,
Beverly's needs. She hired a woman to come in for Beverly eight hours
a day Monday through Friday, to take her out for a walk when weather
permitted, make her lunch, whatever. One of Beverly's main problems
was boredom. She was not about to park herself in front of the TV and
watch soap operas all day. She would watch the news and CNN for a
while, even a cooking show occasionally. Suzanne found that ridiculous,
as Beverly had never cooked anything more complicated than a hot dog.
Her usual style was to open a can of soup. Spaghetti was pasta boiled
too long with a can of tomato sauce or tomato soup dumped over it.
Maybe cooking shows were like sitcoms to Beverly, a series of jokes.

Suzanne was helping Jake find an apartment. The move was happening. He would be here most of the time for the next few years. He was
fully capable of finding his own housing, but it distracted her from her
continuing funk over Rachel. It was mildly amusing to look at places to
live, and probably she would be spending some evenings and weekend
afternoons there, so she might as well help in the search. Both of them
put in such long hours, and had so many meetings to attend, that working on the apartment problem was a convenient excuse to spend time
together out of bed.

"All right, I'll be on the board. But it may be pretty nominal, Jake. I
haven't got days or even hours to give."

"You might find it more interesting than you suppose."

It was Jake she found interesting, and if the price of peace between
them was to go on his board, she did not like it, but she acquiesced.

The sex was strong. She enjoyed surprising herself and sometimes surprising him. It was Tuesday and she had an appointment at three, but she was free until then. They had looked at two places, one ridiculously overpriced and the other, possible but small, cramped. "But I don't need much space," he said. "I travel light and I live lightly. Some books, a bed, a computer on a good desk, music and a little kitchen and I'm set. I'd rather live in a smaller place I can afford." He was tight in surprising ways, she noticed. He hated to waste money. Maybe that came from running a political organization on erratic contributions. He had the recycling habit. When he wasn't using the computer and actually had to write on paper with a pen, he used the backs of circulars and form letters. When something broke, her impulse was to discard it and his was to tinker with it. The too small apartment was in Brookline ten blocks from her house. "You want to stop by my house? I think we can grab a little privacy."

It was eleven-forty-five when they arrived. "I think it would be nice to take Beverly out for lunch today," Suzanne said to the West Indian aide, Sylvia. Sylvia was just a few inches taller than Beverly but had eighty pounds on her. She was a broadly built woman with light brown skin and hair cut really short. She was skilled at getting Beverly to do what was needed. Suzanne handed Sylvia two twenties and Sylvia set about to bundle Beverly out to the Greek place, the diner, or the Jewish deli, as Beverly chose. It would take them at least an hour and a half, including the time to toddle down the block.

They had just got into bed in the otherwise empty house when Suzanne heard voices and footsteps. After they made love, when they got up to shower, she looked out and saw Jim's car in the yard. Marta seldom came back during the week. Monday through Wednesday were booked-solid days, so she usually didn't get in till seven or eight. Suzanne opened the back door and softly climbed the steps partway to listen. Yes, it was Elena's voice. What were they doing back at Marta's in the middle of the day?

He could have forgotten something (then why was Elena with him?). They could be having lunch (why wouldn't they eat someplace nearer his office?). They could be having a personal conversation about some problem at the office (with all that laughter and then long silences?).

She motioned Jake to silence as they crept out to his rented car, parked at the curb. "I have the most awful sinking feeling that Elena is doing a number with my best friend's husband."

"Don't jump to conclusions," Jake said, "She'll never forgive you if you're wrong."

"I'll never forgive her if I'm right."

"Of course you will. Down the pike. The thing to do is try to figure out what's really happening. All lawyers are part detective, or want to be."

She sighed. "I was happy a few minutes ago. I really was."

22

Elena

Elena noticed it the third week she was working there, the way Jim looked at her, how often he looked. She was surprised and not surprised. She was used to men looking at her with that kind of interest, but she had never paid much attention to him before. He was the old guy upstairs in the house where she hadn't wanted to move. Marta was always giving her little hints about life and education and the future that were really depressing. Their son, Adam, was a pain in the ass, covering everything she had been supposed to do and never did. Now he was at NYU studying film, like all the grind-hard kids from high school who thought they were the next Quentin Tarantino. Adam was seven years younger than she was, but he always acted as if he knew everything better.

Jim had been like an uncle, someone you could borrow twenty bucks from or get a ride someplace, the guy who wouldn't tell on you if he caught you smoking on the porch. She doubted she had ever looked at him carefully. He had pale gray-blue eyes like glacial runoff, eyes of tremendous intensity. He was in great shape. He ran every day. He worked out. He kept himself lean.

What she first liked about him was that Jim was no workaholic like her mother, like Rachel, like their nerdy son Adam, like Marta. Jim was a goof-off like her. She had never realized that. He had patients, sure, five on a busy day, sometimes just a couple, but he didn't really give a fuck. Once she grasped that, she loved the job, in spite of the disappointing grungy office over a tropical fish store and next to a bowling alley in Brighton. When she had first seen the office with its beaten-up furniture, two tiny rooms that hadn't been painted since World War II, she had wanted to turn around and flee. Now she understood: he didn't care if the office turned some patients off. He didn't really give a damn. Some days he played on the Internet. They shared cool sites. She began to look at him with deliberate interest, a kind of itch, like who was he really and what was going on with him? He let himself have fun. He liked to take it easy and chill out, even in the office. He had an eye for women, she could tell. She was sure he had girls on the side. Vaguely she remembered something from years before: Rachel had told her about Jim and a student. She could hardly write Rachel in Israel and ask her, but there had been something, she knew it.

She was tired of the gonzos she had met at the restaurant, that she met at the gym. They were either lawyers like her mother or just as bad, buzz saws with penises. Or they were losers like the swimming pool salesman, nothing much going on, just boring. Or kids who had no clue. Jim did not seem to be dying to get his hands on her. What he seemed to want when she came into his office between appointments was to talk with her. To really talk. He talked about how he lost his teaching job. It had been a student and they had been in love, but it hadn't worked out. Her parents pulled her out of school and he got fired. Sure he had kept it from Marta. It was easy. She was so wrapped up in herself and her law practice, she barely noticed what was going on with him.

She told him what really happened at the restaurant, how that guy had grabbed her and she had belted him. She told him about her friend Courtney getting AIDS from a bad needle. She told him about Kevin walking off a cliff when he was stoned, and her swearing off drugs, finally.

His eyes were beautiful, icy, intense. Wintry with all the blaze of winter sun. Sometimes she found her gaze dropping from his, just because of his intensity. She liked it. That intensity felt familiar, felt right. It wasn't until the first time he embraced her, as they were about to leave the office one evening after she had been working there for two months. He slid his arms around her and held her to him. That was all he did for about three minutes, just held her. She could feel his erection, but he did not make a move on her. Finally she pulled his head down and kissed him.

It was as she was kissing him that she understood the power, the compulsion of it: it was how he felt, his body against hers. He was tall like Evan, he was lean like Evan, and the way he held her made her think of Evan, freshly, blindingly. There was that same intensity, the way they talked with each other. Never had she thought she would find it again, a twin soul, her other, her brother. Love struck her like lightning during that first kiss, the way it should, the way it must. She was shocked with love, smoldering.

For two weeks after that all they did when they could snatch a moment was kiss and talk, make out and talk. She was melting. She was dissolving. At night she could not sleep for imagining sex with him. Instead of feeling like a jaded sophisticate, burned out and bored, she felt as if she had become fifteen again. She told him about Evan and Chad, the whole thing. He knew the general story, but from Marta's point of view, the story she had been made to tell in court, how she was just a poor innocent drag-along. How the bad boys had done her in. She told him the way it really was and then the year afterward, when all she could do was lie there for two months and then get up and go through the motions. How Suzanne had ripped her out of her old life, old school, old friends. She was waiting all the time to die. She had collaborated in Chad's death and she had been supposed to die next, but she had chickened out and Evan had been shot because of her, because of her cowardice, getting out of the car and running. That was why the state trooper shot Evan.

Marta had defended her. It was sickening, but her mother and Marta kept telling her she had to keep her mouth shut. She could not tell the truth. The big lie was that she was a weak-willed girl under the influence of two guys who had made her run off with them. They had fed her drugs and forced her into sex with them. They were evil and she was a poor misguided lamb led astray. Chad was the ringleader, Evan was the follower, and she was the victim, blah blah blah. She had hated Marta as she sat in that courtroom. She was underage anyhow. In the eyes of the law she was a child. In her own eyes, she was a guilty old woman who had lived too long and was too scared to die.

Now she was given a second chance, after all these stupid wasted useless empty years. She talked to Jim about wanting to die. He listened, really listened, and then he took the story and made it change. He made her a heroine who had tried to save Evan and Chad. He made her a faithful friend who, when she could not save them, was willing to go with them into the land of shadows, but the police arrived too soon. Chad and Evan died of their own weaknesses, their inner demons. She was only the pretext for their immolation. Now she must find her own way. She was not to blame for the weakness of others, but she needed to believe in her own inner strength.

Jim told her about the death of his daughter, only two months after they got her home from the hospital. His second child. He knew Marta was not to blame but could not help blaming her. Something had obviously gone wrong during the pregnancy, when she had insisted on working until the day her water burst. The girl, Annette, had been fragile, born prematurely. Then she was dead in her crib, sudden infant death syndrome, it was called, as if that explained anything. It just said, your baby died and we don't know why.

Elena and Jim held each other. He seemed afraid to go much further than kissing and stroking her hair and holding her face between his hands. He kept saying he was too old for her. The more he protested, the more fiercely she argued.

She was half wild with desire for him. She told herself it was like poison ivy of the brain. She could think of nothing else. She waited until a Monday afternoon when everybody was out of the house except Beverly and Sylvia. Then Sylvia took Beverly to the speech therapist. Jim was upstairs working on his book. She just went quietly up and put her arms around him as he sat at the computer. She was not wearing a bra or panties, just a loose rayon dress, cut low and slit up one side. When he stood and began to kiss her, she put his hand on her breast. Her breast was burning to be touched. She kneaded his back, pulling his shirt loose from his pants, then slid her grasp down to his firm buttocks. He felt good, lean and sleek and hot under her hands. He was breathing hard now. Yes, she would have him. When they were undressed, she knelt and kissed his penis. "Put it in me. Just do it now. I can't wait any longer."

They made love on the couch in the living room. She groaned and thrust up her hips, feeling him enter her. This was love they were making, something different and new again, something special, something holy. He kept saying, "I love you, I love you, I love you."

She kept saying the same thing. Then she added, "I want to belong to you. I want to be yours."

"I want you to be mine." But when they were showered and dressed, he said, "We must be very careful. If we pay too much attention to each other, one of them will guess. . . . You're on the pill, right?"

He was too cautious, but she could wait.

"I feel out of control with you," she said. "I haven't felt that way in years. Always I've been the one driving the car. I couldn't trust any of them enough to let go."

"I understand," he said, "and your trust honors me. We have to cut through all these roles of control and the fear of it and be vulnerable and open to each other. To be naked."

The next time, she got him to make love on the bed he slept in with Marta. It was obscene to think of them together. Marta had no right to him, for she did not love him. They were always fighting, Elena could hear them in the evenings if she shut off her music and listened. They argued about money, about their son, Adam, about accountants and doctors, about the dishwasher and roof repairs. If they had ever loved each other, it was long, long over. They were just used to living together. They were each other's bad habit. But Jim wanted her as strongly as she wanted him, because they were really one. They were one will, one life, one body. She saw that, even if he didn't; and sometimes, already, he did.

23

Beverly

Beverly liked her new computer. She had resisted using one for years, for she could not see incurring the expense for no good reason. At first she had thought they were a fad, and then she thought she was past learning about them, since technical stuff had never been her strong suit. Now just to learn something new was a reassurance her life was not completely over, that she was still alive upstairs. It was hard. She forgot more easily than she ever had, and concentration was difficult and strenuous. At least the computer opened up rather than closed down her world, shrinking since the night of her stroke.

Even with the large keys to type with, she was slow. The mouse was easier. Suzanne set her up on E-mail and showed her the Internet. She didn't think any of her old friends did E-mail except Lucy, who had taught at CUNY for twenty-five years and had a computer before any of them. She carefully typed out a note on the computer to Lucy at Eighty-fifth Street, asking her if she was on E-mail. Sylvia would mail it for her. Beverly wanted to E-mail somebody. She asked Suzanne at breakfast the next morning. Suzanne printed out a list of the E-mail addresses of politicians.

Later that morning, Beverly composed an E-mail to the President about the problems of Medicare coverage. She wrote about all the people she had seen in the hospital and in the rehab center and what happened to them and how awful it was that people couldn't be covered at home, where they were much better off than in a nursing home—dump, and it was less wasteful of money and resources. She wrote the letter for forty-five minutes. Then she hit "send" and went to bed. She was exhausted. But she was happy.

Now she could send the same letter to the senators from New York and the two from Massachusetts. She would find out the name of the representative for Brookline and send him one too. She was no longer helpless. She would collect useful E-mail addresses and harangue them all. It seemed much more intimate than writing a letter. She felt as if she was going right through their defenses, past their secretaries and assistants, straight into their faces. Tomorrow she would compose a letter on immigration policies. Then welfare. Then minimum wage. Suzanne showed her a site where she could monitor proposed legislation. She would have plenty to tell them all.

She actually had some appetite for supper. Suzanne brought home Chinese takeout. Beverly remembered how she used to eat proficiently with chopsticks. Back in '68, she had a Chinese boyfriend, a Maoist and nutty, but she liked him anyhow. He had beautiful eyes, great bones, and an erection that never died. She sighed, remembering. He had married a Chinese woman who managed a television repair shop. For months, he continued to visit Beverly, but she wasn't comfortable with that. Soon he had a baby boy and they moved to Atlanta, where his wife's family sent him to graduate school.

Now she had to eat with a special fork that could be managed easily. She got so weary sometimes of all the things she could no longer handle, ordinary silverware and cups, ordinary clothes she could no longer fasten. Ordinary stairs. Ordinary public transportation she had used all her life.

But tonight she would not dwell on that. "Letter . . . Rachel?"

She had seen it in the hall when Sylvia was helping her go for her walk. When they had finished supper, Suzanne read it to her. It was full of tourist stuff, this road, that shuk, going to Sarah's Tomb. She and Michael were living in a dormitory near Hebrew University. "We each have a roommate. Mine is from Cincinnati. She is two years older than I am and much prettier, with blond hair halfway down her back. Michael is rooming with a Brit from Coventry. Every day we walk and walk and walk. When we don't walk, we take buses. We are memorizing all the bus routes. You have to know before you get on, because it's push and shove and chaos. I always expect the walls to buckle." Beverly wanted to know what Rachel thought about Israel politically, if she had met any Palestinians yet, how she was getting on with her boyfriend: the real stuff. "Yesterday we visited the Old City again. When we went out the Damascus Gate where there's a row of some kind of palms (I can't tell the different kinds yet) that look like upright feather dusters, we saw this fountain, nothing fancy, and in the basin, already kids were splashing around. It made me feel like joining them, but we're on our best behavior—although nobody else is! I'll have E-mail by the time you get this. Here's my address."

Suzanne gave her Rachel's E-mail address. Now she could ask her all the questions she wanted to. Beverly felt as if she went around grinning now, maybe crookedly, but with honest joy.

A couple of nights a week when Suzanne was actually home all evening, after supper, Suzanne would clear and load the dishwasher while Beverly lay down to nap. Then Beverly would wake in an hour or so, and they would go together to her computer. Suzanne logged her into the *New York Times* on-line. Then AP. Then ABC news. Then the

Washington Post. Beverly's heart was beating hard. She would keep up with news after all. There must be liberal and radical sites. She would find them. Now every morning and noon and night she would dip into some news site and pick up the breaking news. She also discovered there was a huge amount of stroke information on-line. A couple of days later, she stumbled onto a listserv of old radicals, and Suzanne showed her how to subscribe. Now every day she got messages from people all around the country who were politically savvy and experienced. She could get into wonderful arguments and discussions. There was also a stroke support group she joined, although it was sometimes depressing.

She wished she did not tire so quickly. But on-line communication was easy compared to writing a real letter. The phone was her bugaboo. She hated the rare times when she had to answer. She had been hung up on numerous times, because she could not force out a reply quickly enough. But with E-mail, she could take her time reading and comprehending what people wrote and composing and laboriously typing an answer with one hand. Nobody got impatient except her server, who dumped her occasionally, and then she had to reconnect.

She began doing her hand and arm exercises with the same fervent concentration she brought to her speech exercises. Her clumsy left hand was her link to the world. However dimly, she was reconnected. Her old friend Lucy wrote back. Almost every day they E-mailed short or longer notes about their lives. Lucy had broken her hip when she was knocked down by a Rollerblader and had trouble getting around. She had undergone a hip replacement, but it was painful, and she would never walk easily again. Then she heard from her friend Rose, who had written five books on labor history. Lucy had given Rose Beverly's E-mail address. Now she had two friends as well as her correspondence with all the politicians she felt like advising, berating, occasionally praising, and all the old lefties on the listserv with their monikers. Hers was West Side Rosa, for she had always identified with Rosa Luxemburg, and the West Side was her spiritual home.

She was sorry when her eyes got tired or when her back hurt too much for her to continue. She would have loved to get on-line when she woke up and to stay connected all day. It was exciting. It felt right. She was no longer alone in this pale green room when Sylvia went home but was still vitally in the world. She kept finding new subjects to explore: UFOs, archaeology, specific writers.

Her hand and her eyes betrayed her, particularly her hand. She had to stop after around an hour, although she had got much better at making full use of that hour of connection. She lay resting then, sometimes dozing, sometimes just listening to the house around her. She had identified the steps and voices of Elena and Jim. Two or three times a week, Elena sneaked upstairs or they came back from work together. They were going to bed, of course. She smiled slightly. Elena was still her favorite. Beverly liked Jim. He was an attractive man, and Marta didn't pay enough attention to him. Besides, they had only one kid, in college. Lots of men went off on their own then, found someone new. It was human nature. Often enough in her life, what they had found had been her. She could not judge Elena.

Elena knew she knew. Elena came in and sat down one afternoon. "I love him," she said without preamble. "I can't help it."

Beverly nodded. She understood.

"I knew you'd see it my way," Elena said. "Now I have to go back to work. It's a pretty easy job. I'll look in on you tonight."

From then on, Elena took some time each day to sit with her. Beverly had felt bad that Elena did not want to be with her. Now she understood. It wasn't because of her stroke or her distorted face, no, it was just that Elena was having an affair and had to cover it up. Now that Elena knew that Beverly was not going to make a fuss or be judgmental, they were close again. Beverly thought, I am slowly, slowly coming back to life. It isn't the life I had, but it's a great improvement on last month and infinitely superior to the month before that.

Besides, Beverly rather enjoyed knowing something that Suzanne didn't. Suzanne was worrying about something, Beverly could feel it, probably a case. Suzanne might know a lot about the law, but she was no observer of people. Beverly smiled inwardly. She had Elena's confidence, and Suzanne didn't.

| 24

Elena

Monday morning, Elena lay in bed in the room she finally had to herself again, listening to the sounds from upstairs. That was his tread crossing. Then Marta slogged across the floor. It should be herself up there, not that woman who did not adore him, who did not even know him any longer. Elena had intended to move out and had gone as far as answering ads, before changing her mind. It was too convenient to be living in the same house. She could keep an eye on Marta's van and know when she had left. It made arrangements pitifully simple.

She would move when he moved with her, not before. They would leave together. Neither of them belonged here. Nobody really loved her except him, and of course Beverly. The first time Elena had seen her after her stroke, she had to turn away from what looked like the Halloween mask of a witch. Now Beverly just looked a little lopsided, like a candle that had begun to soften before it ran down in wax. Beverly could talk, if a person had patience. Elena had patience, unlike her mother, who was really being a bitch, half the time finishing Beverly's sentences for her. Elena didn't feel she was so damned important she couldn't wait for Beverly to say what she wanted to. Grandma was on her side. She had had plenty of affairs, and sometimes told her stories about men she had known over the years. That was more interesting than when she got into talking about old strikes and bygone demonstrations. It took Beverly about three times longer than normal to tell a story, but often it was a pretty good story when she spat it out. Elena truly enjoyed hearing Beverly's adventures. Too bad those guys were dead and gone or doddering, because some of them sounded cool. Beverly had been way ahead of her time, having a baby by herself without bothering to get married or lie about it; she just wasn't into marriage and never bothered to marry anybody.

Finally she heard Marta leaving at eight. Now Elena waited for Suzanne to clear out. She was teaching, and then she would be off to Framingham to talk to the woman who'd fooled around with the kids. At eight-thirty, Sylvia came up the walk and Suzanne met her at the door for last-minute instructions. Then she was gone.

Elena gave herself another ten minutes, in case Suzanne had forgotten something—although Suzanne never forgot anything unless her hard disk crashed. Her mother kept all her little memos about the world on her computer, so she never forgot a birthday or an anniversary or a holiday. Elena surreptitiously checked her mother's schedule on her computer regularly, so she wouldn't be surprised. Sometimes having a mother who was so well organized had its advantages. There wasn't a spontaneous moment in Suzanne's day.

Then Elena put on her bathrobe and passed quietly through the kitchen. Sylvia was helping Beverly shower. Elena ran up the stairway to the second floor. He had left the kitchen door unlocked and was waiting in the kitchen. She let her robe fall. He pulled her into his arms wordlessly, caressing her through the thin cotton of the brief gown. Then he picked her up and carried her into the bedroom. She fell with a gasp on top of the bedspread and he threw himself on top of her. They were both excited and barely kissed before he thrust into her. He was driving hard. It almost hurt. She liked it. Nothing existed but his weight on her, his hard slender body under her hands, his prick inside her banging and knocking on her womb. She could not stand it. She could not stand for it to end. She could not stand for it to continue. It was too much, too much. When she came, it was as if she'd broken open and molten blood spilled out.

He cried out, almost a scream, when he came. After they had recovered, they lay and talked. She knew much more about him now, about how his father had died of a heart attack when he was way too young, about how his mother had married again to a man he couldn't stand, and moved to Tucson. She knew he was exactly forty-four—two years younger than Marta. Of course he was younger. She should have known that.

She hated weekends now. Suzanne and Marta had been around all day Saturday and Sunday. At least some Saturdays, the two women went shooting at a range, keeping them out of the house for a couple of hours. When Marta went out Saturday night, Jim had to go with her, to some judge's house. They were starved for each other. She had to figure out some way they could meet on weekends. Maybe in the car in the garage? Nothing sounded feasible. She told him he should start having Saturday morning office hours. They had sex at the office sometimes, but it wasn't comfortable. The damned bowling alley made rumbling noises and booms, and they could hear people talking and the drill going in the dentist's office next door. She wondered why anyone would go to such a cheap dingy place. It was a low-rent building with paper-thin walls and an odd smell to it, half musty, half chemical. He deserved a better office. She was sure that potential patients took one look, caught the odor, and fled.

"I know it," he said, "but it's all I can afford. If Marta would only stake me to a better rental, I know I could get more patients."

They showered together and then had a leisurely breakfast. "I don't feel like you're older than me," she was saying over her coffee. "I know you are, but it just doesn't feel that way."

"I don't belong to my wife's generation. I don't have those baby boomer goals," he said, eating cereal with sliced peaches. "I think feminists like my wife are actually a couple of generations behind. They're acting like men did in the fifties. They believe in the corporate dream. They believe in the gray flannel suit. They think happiness lies in achievement."

"I'm not interested in success," she said. "I don't want to be a success, I don't need to be with a success."

"You've come to the right place." He laughed shortly, his mouth twisting. He had such a mobile mouth, long, full, and dangerous. When she stared at his lips, she felt herself growing wet again. She could look at his mouth and feel it on her. He was saying, "She's defending a murderer now, this guy who shot his parents. It's very Oedipal. No wonder she's become hard through and through. She's turning into a suit of armor with no one inside."

"You think my mother's that way?"

"I think they're both so success oriented, they have no inner life. No spiritual values. No sense of their energy or their larger direction. But teaching is different from being a full-time litigator. Suzanne isn't on the battlefield so much, but she's used to a level of adoration from her students no man can ever give her."

"What do you think of her boyfriend?"

"Same type. Ram it through. Get it done. Move on. Search and destroy."

"They never just sit like this talking."

"We're wasting time. That's what they'd say. I'd say we're spending it—spending it very well. Actually I don't like to think of time as something I waste or spend. I think of it as something I experience."

He took off her nightgown again as they sat on the couch in his study. He put his prick into her but they didn't fuck. They just sat there joined. He sucked her nipples. "This feels so real," she said. "I haven't been this alive since . . . you know."

"Say it."

"I haven't been so alive since Chad and Evan died."

"Did they ever fuck you at the same time?"

"No. One did or the other. But once Evan was fucking Chad while he was fucking me. It was awkward. They were way heavy. I didn't like it." She had felt smothered, squashed. It was not a good memory and she shook her head.

"Marta has a gun. I'm not a violent man, Elena. I've found the gentleness in myself."

"I hate guns." She shuddered.

"Poor baby. My baby." Reaching down, he began to play with her clit.

"I never really understood how my mother justifies shooting for pleasure. It seems like something she'd object to in somebody else."

"Marta represents battered women and sometimes she gets threatened. But it's part of her macho image. She says shooting's her sport." He was rubbing her harder now. The energy was gathering in her, upwelling. It felt so strong, him inside her and his hand pushing against her hard. She came with a little shriek. He liked her to make noise. He said it was liberating. This time he had her get on her knees on the floor and he entered from behind.

They dressed for work around ten-thirty, since his first client of the day was due at eleven. She drove in first and he arrived five minutes later. At twelve they had lunch down the block in a place that had light California-type food, big gorgeous salads and sandwiches with avocado and lots of sprouts. "You should go back to school and train as a therapist. It wouldn't take you long. You have a lot of psych credits."

"I have a lot of everything credits. Why get another degree?"

"So we can practice together," he said patiently. "It would be better for both of us. You'd be good at it, I know you would."

She liked the idea of them both being therapists. It felt like a good way to live. To be together at home and together in the office. They could get off a quick one in between clients. Last Thursday, they'd had sex on his couch. It sagged and hurt her back. When they were both therapists, they'd have a nice big clean office, tastefully furnished with a new couch. "Maybe in the fall. I could go back to school part-time and still work for you." She didn't want another woman in her place in the office.

"Unless we throw it all up and run off together . . ." He grinned.

She wished he would not treat it as a joke. Making a change would be difficult for him, but it was what he needed. He was suffocating in his life, he had said that, and she absolutely agreed. She began to think about California again. Once, years ago with Chad and Evan, she had set out for California. Now she was in love again, once again joined utterly with someone she cared for passionately, someone with whom she formed an intense private world of two. Maybe this time they would really go. In a sense, she was still stuck way back there in the middle of the Nevada desert at dawn, where half of her body and soul had been gunned down to lie bleeding in the gray light. Now perhaps after all these years, she could leave that broken body on the ground and move on toward the West and finally cross the last wall of mountains.

"I want to be with you," she said, putting her hands on either side of his face and looking into his pale pale eyes. "I want to be with you today and tomorrow and next week and next year."

"You're my girl," he said. "We belong together. We work."

Nobody else had ever cared so much about her feelings, ever. She could explain how she felt about things, and he'd actually listen and try to help her sort it out, instead of telling her she didn't really feel that way, or shouldn't.

When she came home on Wednesday, Suzanne was waiting for her.

Now what? Suzanne got right to the point. She crossed her arms and stood, somehow impressive in spite of the fact that she was five inches shorter than Elena. "Are you having an affair with Jim?"

"No, I'm working for him. What are you talking about?"

"I had to come back during the day. You two were upstairs."

"Is this your best courtroom cross-examination manner?"

"I take it not answering my question is a yes."

Elena shrugged. "I don't know what you're driving at. We came back here to have lunch and to look at some files of his. He wants me to go back to school to become a therapist. He thinks I'd be good at it. I don't know. What do you think?" Distract her. Usually the idea of Elena going back to school could excite her mother for up to a week.

Suzanne frowned, silent for several minutes. "Much as I would like to believe you, I'm not sure I can. If you haven't yet begun an affair with him, don't. It would be so unfair to Marta. Marta is my best friend. She saved your hide."

"By lying about me. By making me lie about myself and about Evan."

"Was it so much a lie? Did you want to go to a youth detention center for three years? Chad was the one who wanted to kill himself. You had no reason."

"No reason except that my life sucked. Except that you were always trying to make me do what I didn't want to. You were always trying to turn me into somebody I wasn't and then making me feel guilty and shitty if I didn't fulfill your fantasies." She always had that anger within ready to be loosed, but she was also aware that she had thrown a switch and sent her mother along a track other than the one she had been bearing down on. They could always fight to exacerbated raw nerves over Chad's and Evan's deaths.

"Are you really thinking of going back to school?" Suzanne asked.

"Yes. I'd go on working for Jim part-time. He thinks I'd make a good therapist. Wouldn't you like that better than me working in a restaurant?"

"Of course." Suzanne was frowning again. "Elena, I'd be absolutely delighted if you returned to school. If therapy appeals to you, I'd be glad to help. But please, please, don't get involved with my best friend's husband. It won't work out for you. He isn't about to leave Marta. He's more dependent on her than you may realize. Everyone will get hurt and nobody will get what they want, Elena, not even you. Especially not you."

25

Suzanne

Alexa came to see her with Celeste for backup. They went to lunch, but Suzanne ended up barely picking at her food while she defended herself.

Alexa presided, as she always did. She had tremendous presence for a woman scarcely taller than Suzanne, although solid, stocky. Her shoulders were broad for a woman. "It's a terrible throwback, Suzanne, to how it was when I was in school. Freud laid down the law that when women reported sexual abuse, it was their fantasies about Daddy. It took ten years of the women's movement before we had the stuff to prove that sexual abuse of children is shockingly common, not a matter of kiddies making it up out of Oedipal urges."

"I think inventing abuse in the family is rare, and I believe that multiple abuse in an unbearable situation does lead to repression of memories for years." Suzanne gave up and put down her fork. She was not going to get any lunch. "But I think the child care cases are a kind of witch-hunting of our time. Mothers and fathers and the larger society feel guilty about someone else's caretaking. This guilt is turning into persecution."

"You didn't think that woman you represented who murdered her husband was making up the stories about him molesting their daughter," Celeste said. She was looking a little better than she had even a month ago. She had abandoned hope of reconciliation and all her emotion was going into trying to get a good settlement. A little color had come back into her gaunt face. She had touched up her hair to a rich auburn.

"No, I didn't. I have to look at everything on a case-by-case basis. If you could meet Maxine, you'd see a woman I don't think is a liar or an abuser, but a sympathetic caring woman who has been through hell. I've read all the transcripts by now, and I think she was railroaded. I've seen the videotapes, the unedited videotapes—not those snatches the jury saw—and I think I can prove the manipulation that went on between the psychologists, the DA, and those children. Look, with parents and a strong prosecutor and a team of experts all coaching children, I'm convinced a child will produce testimony about almost anything to please. You have to understand that every child began by denying the abuse and continued to do so until persuaded or coerced into a different story."

Alexa was biting her lip, her large hands spread on the table in supplication. "You've gone over to the side of those associations of men who claim feminists made up all repressed memory and sexual abuse in families."

"I have not gone over to the other side. I'm handling the appeal of one specific woman royally abused herself by the justice system. Child abuse is so unsavory that even to be accused of it is a crime in itself. No matter if I win her appeal, understand, Maxine will never, never be free of this. She will never be restored to her previous life and her good name, in spite of what I do!"

Suzanne wished she could show her friends the videotapes she had studied. The psychologists told the children that other children had all testified a certain way and what was wrong with them? You could see the children wavering. Some began to weep. Others produced stories on demand, but fantastic ones of flying witches and the torture and dismemberment of squirrels and kittens and bunnies. It was indeed like the trials of the witches, in which neighbors, lovers, friends, and family testified to seeing the accused turn into a big black dog or fly through the air or dance with the devil. As far as she could tell, it was the prosecution that was dancing with the devil in this case. But her friends would never see those videotapes of the sessions with the children.

Suzanne felt alone as she walked back to her office. She could not make Alexa understand, and now Celeste too was estranged from her. She had only half an hour before her next class, and several phone calls to make. She had won Phoebe's appeal and Phoebe was out of prison and reunited with her daughter—but two years had been lost and their relationship would never be the same. She was trying to help Phoebe find a job, pulling in favors. Libraries did not seem eager to hire someone who had spent two years in prison, even if she had finally won her case on appeal. Phoebe needed a job and soon.

What was sitting on her mind like a big green bullfrog was her suspicion about Elena. Was Elena having an affair with Jim? She did not want to believe it but neither could she lose that fear. Would Elena, who usually scorned middle-aged men, men who were less than physically perfect (but Jim worked out all the time), really choose someone she had known since childhood for an affair? Her mind was working over Elena's statement as she would that of any other witness. She was weighing the evidence and the background of the defendant. For Elena, flirtation was a standard way she dealt with men. She probably flirted without even deciding to. Certainly she flirted with Jake whenever she saw him. He just ignored it. "I understand it's nothing personal," he said with a grin. Perhaps if Elena did not flirt with Jim, it was more meaningful. All Suzanne could do was watch. Her mind worked over the grounds of appeal for Maxine, Phoebe's problems, the lecture she was about to give, and her scrutiny of Elena, all separate but all in process.

Justice was her mistress, and sometimes a cruel one, sometimes capricious. The law was an immense skyscraper built out of medieval timbers, the stones of cathedrals, plywood, masking tape, skulls, dried vines, mud bricks, and library paste. It was far from perfect and she did not have the love of the law many of her colleagues claimed to enjoy. She saw its imperfections and its loopholes and its sinkholes. For her, justice wore a female face, a face of mercy as well as of judgment. The rickety edifice of the law had been built by men, for men, and she was a woman forcing her way in and trying to make it proper housing for women and children. Last year someone from the governor's office had approached her in a preliminary sortie to discover if she had a desire to become a judge in the state system. She had been flattered, tempted, but her answer had been, not yet. She had work to do as a lawyer still.

She had often wished for a wife, and never more than now. Someone to take care of the nurturing, caretaking side of the house, of the lives piled around and against hers. She had never been great at that, and she wasn't doing much of a job of it now. She had envied Marta having Jim home as much as he was at the office, presumably taking care of things at least minimally. For years he had done their grocery shopping and took in and picked up dry cleaning and laundry. He had been available for chauffeur service, back when the kids needed to be taken to lessons, practice, events. Jim and Marta had always seemed to Suzanne to have a fine marriage. Why did she think he was fucking around? Because she knew from a colleague that he had an affair with a student just before he was fired by Simmons. She was inclined to believe that if a man had one affair he'd probably had others.

She sat in her office at home that evening quietly toting up arguments on a legal pad. She would observe. There was absolutely no point saying anything to Marta when she had nothing to report except suspicions that she fervently hoped would prove groundless. She could do irreparable damage. She stood up and walked back to Beverly's room. She had been tempted to ask Sylvia, but she understood at once it was inappropriate. She could not intrude on Sylvia's personal space with such a question. It was not Sylvia's business to monitor the sex lives of the household.

Beverly sat as straight as she could in the armchair. Her good hand fluffed her hair. She had not been able to dye it since her stroke, and it was mostly gray, making Beverly look much older than she had last winter.

"Mother, I'm worried about Elena."

Beverly said nothing. It seemed to Suzanne that she watched more warily. She made no sound, volunteered nothing.

"I'm worried she may be about to get into an affair with Jim. I know that sounds ludicrous, but they're together a great deal. It would be a disaster."

Beverly still did not answer. She seemed to be looking past Suzanne out the window to the street.

"Mother, are you listening? I'm scared Elena may be using the house and her job to launch an affair with Jim, Marta's husband. Do you know about this?"

First Beverly shrugged on one side. Then seeing that would not get her off the hook, she croaked, "Know . . . nothing. Elena . . . good girl."

Suzanne began to wonder if she were suffering from lawyer's paranoia, that state in which if someone near and dear said that it was raining, you wondered if they were lying. You analyzed their motivations. She seemed to be disbelieving everyone around her. It was ridiculous to imagine that Beverly was conscious of the world beyond her bed and the narrow circle of things she could reach, that she would be observing anything clandestine. "Never mind, Mother, it's all right. I'm just being silly." She felt a slippage of guilt for pestering Beverly. She was becoming a petty tyrant, cross-examining everyone.

Beverly hauled herself to her feet and went thudding around her room, pushing herself along in the walker.

Back in her office, Suzanne pressed her face into her hands. Was she becoming a total cynic, as happened to trial lawyers often enough to make it an occupational hazard? She intensely disliked the idea of mounting surveillance over her daughter, of watching her every interaction with Jim, of monitoring her comings and goings. If Elena realized what she was doing, it would further alienate her daughter. But whatever she did, she would not pester Beverly again with her suspicions: it simply was not fair to her mother.

On Friday, she suggested they all have Shabbat dinner together, something that only happened when she was home enough that day to prepare it. She tried to observe Jim and Elena's interactions, but there weren't many to ponder. Jim sat at the big round table in her dining room between Marta and Beverly. Then came Elena. Then herself. Then Jake. Suzanne had decided it was time to include him in family events. Then Marta. She observed no long glances, no meaningful meeting of gazes. They neither avoided each other nor sought each other. She began to wonder if she had been completely mistaken. Everybody ate, drank, and sang, reasonably jolly. Marta seemed in an unusually ebullient mood. Suzanne thought she looked glowing. Marta was a woman who could look incandescently beautiful one day and plain the next. When she was happy, her pink-pale skin lit up from within. Her grayblond hair was loose tonight on her shoulders.

Elena seemed more contained, eating steadily but not saying much. She was especially solicitous of Beverly. Suzanne was pleased that Elena had gotten over her first reaction to her grandmother and was close to her again, protective. She reminded herself to say something to Elena about appreciating the hours she spent amusing Beverly. When Elena was not occupying herself with Beverly, she was obliquely watching Suzanne and Jake together. If Suzanne was trying to figure out her daughter's relationship to Jim, her daughter was observing hers with Jake.

There was not a lot to observe, as Suzanne was occupied with the meal, and Jake was being friendly to all. They were not likely to act physical in public. Each was too conscious of position and audience. Yet she was intensely aware of him beside her. It seemed to her his arm below his T-shirt glowed with sexual heat just inches from her own. His sharp foxy face was relaxed tonight. He seemed to be genuinely enjoying the food and the company.

Beverly flirted a little with Jake, but mainly listened to Elena. Elena did seem interested in this job. Several times during the week, Suzanne had heard Beverly laugh with Sylvia, in the evenings with Elena. Beverly did not laugh with her. Her relationship with her mother had not warmed or softened. She knew it was her fault, because she wasn't around most of the time. She was supporting Beverly financially and physically, but she wasn't giving much personally. Yet she was always exhausted. Their times together drained her. Perhaps they drained her mother also. She just could not seem to work out a way they could communicate easily, that they could be together smoothly, warmly. When she was apart from Beverly, she could imagine affectionate interaction; but when they were face-to-face, old habits ruled. It was bumpy. She felt as if Beverly was always angry with her.

She would love a real Shabbat—a period of rest, of contemplation— she thought as she stared at the flames atop the beeswax candles dancing in the breeze from the open windows. A scent of roses entered from the garden behind the house, old-fashioned sturdy pink climbing roses that bloomed only in the early summer. A time without tasks, responsibilities, worries. To fix her mind on a rose and sit. She did not know if she had ever experienced that kind of peace and probably never would. She imagined going away someplace with Jake. Then she realized how hard it would be for either of them to snatch that time.

She swore to herself she would put effort into trying to improve her relationship with Beverly but knew the week would go by in a rush of depositions, motions, searching of precedents, teaching and seeing students, faculty meetings, and finishing a law review article she had started months before. She would put Jaime to work on running down the citations and then she would knock the rest of it off . . . sometime. Sometime this week.

* * *

She decided even though she knew nothing, it would not be right to keep her suspicions from Marta, who, after all, was the principal victim if something underhanded was going on. She went upstairs at breakfast time for two days running, but Jim was there both times. It was Thursday before she got some time alone with Marta.

Marta immediately seized her hands, squeezing. "I have news. You're never going to guess."

Marta was a partner already, had been for seven years. A better offer? But she was satisfied where she was. She liked a small office and she liked her partners, especially Miles. Something to do with Adam? If Suzanne was wrong, did she have a right to upset Marta? Possibly injure her marriage?

"I went to the gynecologist last week. I haven't been having my periods. . . ."

"I guess menopause could be considered good news, although it usually isn't."

"That's what I thought. But, Suzanne, you're not going to believe this any more than I did. I'm pregnant!"

"Are you serious?"

"Sure as I'm standing here."

"How can you be?"

"It's one of those little miracles, isn't it? Not so little. I'm three months along."

Marta and Jim had tried to get pregnant after the loss of their baby girl. She had been pregnant twice and miscarried twice. Then they had given up, for it was too heartbreaking. "That's wonderful," Suzanne said. "Have you told Jim?"

"No! I won't until my pregnancy is further along. I could still lose the baby, Suzanne. Remember what happened before."

"I still think you should tell him."

"Why?"

Suzanne could hardly say, so he won't consider getting into an affair with Elena. "I think he has a right to know what's going on with you. If you keep it from him, he'll feel you don't trust him, that you're afraid to let him in."

"I don't believe he'll take it that way. Wouldn't he understand I just didn't want him to endure weeks and weeks of uncertainty?"

"Besides," Suzanne said, beginning to seriously consider Marta's situation, "aren't you at least a little scared? You're forty-six. Your son was born twenty years ago. It's not like you're . . . I mean you're not twenty-six now."

"I'm healthy. My ob-gyn lady says I'm in good shape. She thinks I can do it. I'm sure going to try, Suzanne. Besides, my mother was forty-one when she had me. It runs in the family."

Forty-one when she had you and dead now, Suzanne thought but did not say. "Please tell Jim. I think it would be good for both of you to share this, even the waiting."

"I'll think about it." Marta grimaced. "You're the first person I've told. And don't you tell him! I'd kill you."

"I promise. I wouldn't steal your thunder."

"And I promise I'll consider telling him."

"Please, do."

"But Suzanne," Jake said, drawing her name out the way he did when he was teasing or remonstrating with her, so that it had three syllables, "you don't have anything to tell Marta. You don't know one fact."

"True. But I feel like a disloyal friend sitting on my suspicions."

"And how would you like it if you told her and she miscarried?"

Suzanne felt a sharp pain in her gut. "Oh my god . . . If only I could figure out what's happening, whether anything is happening."

"But since you don't know zip, you should keep your mouth shut and don't let on even that you have suspicions."

Sometimes she wondered if his advice was good, or just intended to avoid hassles and yet more complications in her life. "I did speak already with Elena."

"Just chill for a while and let it go. You feel responsible for everything. I want you to fix the weather. It's too humid."

She buried her face in his chest. The hair tickled her cheek, but she did not mind. She wanted to crawl inside him and hide. "If you asked me to fix the weather, I'd probably try. Then I'd fail and feel guilty." She sometimes felt as if the less time they had, the more energy they felt free to spend on each other when they were together. Was it real then? Did that matter? They presented only a certain side to each other, she was sure. She wavered between thinking he was genuinely passionate about her or just an opportunist who wanted to recruit her to his cause and did not mind doing so in bed. Perhaps he was both. She did not even know if she wanted to reach a final conclusion about him. She needed what they had too badly to subject it to her usual level of scrutiny.

"Feel guilty for not spending more time with me."

"Jake, I feel guilty for the time I do spend." She sighed. "So what's happening with your case in California? The one that goes back to that demonstration against logging old-growth redwoods. Will it be dismissed?"

"It doesn't look that way. My lawyer is arguing for a change of venue. The logging of old redwoods is an important industry to most of the people in the town, and they passionately hate us for trying to stop them. The local prosecutor is going after me for everything they can think of: trespassing, resisting arrest, disorderly conduct. Conspiracy to commit an unlawful act and conspiracy to obstruct commerce. The last two are felonies. My lawyer is trying to get the felony indictments reduced to misdemeanors. He thinks I can finally plead guilty to trespassing and get off with a week or two in jail or a stiff fine. It's a matter of them seeing me as the outside agitator who's trying to steal their livelihood away and close them down. We got a lot of press coverage, making them furious."

"It sounds inflated. Do you think they'll bargain down?"

"My lawyer thinks they have to. He wants a change of venue because, as he says, in that town, they'd convict me of wife beating though I'm not married. It's a strange thing, Suzanne, how much you get to care about those trees. The loggers call us tree huggers and think we're weird and spacy. But those trees—they have character. They have a kind of power, a charisma to them it amazes me that anyone near them can't feel. You look at one of them, big as a church spire, and it's been there since the Dark Ages at least, and you can't bear, you just can't bear to think of it being killed and turned into planks. It's like shooting the last great tiger to put its head up on your den wall. You just have to stop it. Once such a tree is gone, it's not like it can be replaced. It's a giant falling—for what? The profit of small men in big companies. I sympathize with the guys who just want to make a living where they live, but tobacco farmers feel the same way—and so do crack dealers. Everybody wants to make it, but you have to look at the larger cost."

"So when do you have to fly back?"

"I don't have to be in court for some of these preliminary arguments. He'll let me know next week."

"It sounds as if it should get to plea bargaining fairly soon." She rested her head on his chest and before she realized it, dozed off from exhaustion.

26

Beverly

Beverly often wished she could say all she wanted to, that she could speak aloud the way she could communicate on-line. It might take her half an hour to type out a paragraph of an E-mail letter, but then it was instantly transmitted and nobody knew she hadn't written it in four minutes. If only she could talk that way too, everything would be so much pleasanter, if she could work out the communication and shape the sounds and gather them up in some cache in her head and then say it all correctly and with reasonable speed, then everyone would listen. Now only Sylvia and Elena were reliably patient. Even Karla just talked to Suzanne about her instead of talking with her. Karla wrote her a letter every week, full of the doings of the twins and Rosella and her husband and his family, news of Suwanda in San Diego, news of her synagogue, her neighborhood. It was humiliating to envy the sister she had always felt superior to.

Much of the time she simply gave up saying what she wanted to, because it was just taking too long to get it out. She could not think of the word she knew she knew. Her mind had mud slides, when everything was swept away in soft muck and buried. She had learned to stop and wait for her brain to clear itself. It was hard. She had always been glib and forceful, verbally. She had depended often enough on her ready brain and tongue to get her out of a jam. Twice she had talked her way out of a rape situation. Several times she had talked a cop out of busting her when she was in a protest, a picket line, a demonstration. She had cajoled men into bed and out of bed. She had talked her way into jobs she wanted and out of tasks she dreaded. It had been her best weapon; as she got older, her only weapon.

She wished she could talk with Jake, Suzanne's boyfriend. He seemed like a real organizer, the genuine thing, and she would have given anything to be able to question him closely about his work. She knew they would understand each other, if only she could speak to him. But he smiled at her when he came in, and then he went on as if she wasn't in the room. He was one of the only people she saw around her who might understand her life and her choices, and she couldn't have a decent conversation with him.

She looked into Elena's face. Her granddaughter was lovely. She never grew tired of looking at her. Her hair was worn unfashionably long, silken, glossy, the rippling pelt of a panther. She had always moved well, since she was a little girl. Beverly did not think Elena had ever gone through an awkward stage. Her skin was like perfect fruit, never a blemish. It was tropical, smooth, inviting. Even that ridiculous stud in her nose had looked good on her, but lately it had disappeared. She pointed to her own nose and tapped it, then pointed to Elena's nose. Elena was terrific at figuring out what she was asking.

"Jim didn't want it there. He's like, it's distracting when we're kissing. And he pointed out what it meant—it was my pact with Chad and Evan. He says it's time to let go of that old trauma and walk on."

Her eyes were commanding and melting at once. Beverly explained to Elena that Elena was the daughter of passion, while her sister Rachel was the daughter of rationality. Patiently Elena heard her out. "But, Grandma, I think Mother did love Sam, at first. She just forgot about him after a while. He wasn't as interesting as a good case or a day in court. Then she let her pride take over when she learned he was bam bam with a client."

"No passion. Fondness."

"Whatever." Elena shrugged. "I think Jim and I should get away from here. I know he's used to it, but it's time for him to leave. It's too easy for him. He needs a challenge. He needs a new world to conquer, you see?"

Beverly nodded crookedly.

"I know that as long as he's around here, he could backslide. All his friends are going to be just shocked out of their chairs when he leaves Marta. Their teeth will drop out. Like I vandalized a public statue, you know? 'Cause their marriage is an institution. This house is like a stupid public crossroads for the legal profession. They're always 'entertaining.' It's gross, really gross."

Beverly nodded again. "Bourgeois. Way it's done."

"Exactly. I could puke. I feel so bad when I see him going through the motions, doing the right thing. It's so sick. He doesn't even like any of those people. It's all for her. Because she wants to be a judge by and by."

"Judge? Hangman."

"Right. It's so phony, it reeks. He isn't like that. He's more like me, emotional, more physical, sort of wanting to plow straight ahead, zoom, at what he wants. He doesn't crush his feelings and pretend they don't exist."

Rachel had said something funny to Beverly, maybe a year ago when she was trying hard to talk Rachel out of studying to be a rabbi. Rachel said, "You don't believe in the Eternal One, but you believe in passion, in Eros. Don't you think that's just as irrational? Why not pick a major deity, anyhow?" Beverly had been startled. Since she was five Rachel had been coming out with statements or questions you just never expected. Her mind worked differently.

Beverly had answered, "I've experienced passionate love. I've never experienced your god. I prefer to stick to what I can feel, what I can know."

Beverly realized that Elena was sitting there expectantly. Beverly had dropped right out of the conversation as if through a trapdoor, into her memories. It was rude and disconcerting, but she could not help it. Her mind would cough up a memory like a fish landed suddenly out of a river onto a bank. To cover up her inattention, she nodded wildly.

"I knew you'd agree."

With what, she wondered. But she probably would agree, whatever it was. She had fallen in love with her granddaughter when Elena was only three. "No! Not right," Elena would say, not shouting but with a totally convinced intensity that Beverly recognized as her own.

"Like it's a second chance for me, finally." Elena leaned forward, her hands twisting on her jeans. One knee stuck through the torn fabric, shiny, pale against the denim. "I never thought I'd really give a shit about a guy again. I mean, yeah, for fun, to pass the time, to buy you dinner, to take you out. But to really feel like you're both in one skin. Like you know where he is at because you're really both in the same place at the same time? I knew you'd get it."

Elena was the center of her life now. Her granddaughter had always been important to her, but now Beverly poured all her love into Elena. She longed to see her as fervently as she had ever waited for a lover. She gazed into her face with as much joy and passion and the underlying pain of anticipated loss. Elena would go off with Jim to California, and she would never see her. It would be a loss as great as the loss of her right hand and her ability to speak clearly. She needed to see Elena daily, she must see her. It was necessary for her survival as well as for her happiness. Elena was life itself, vitality. As Elena felt about Jim, she felt about Elena. She breathed her. She drank her in.

Suzanne was sitting in the same chair after supper as Elena had occupied that afternoon. Suzanne had actually cooked tonight. Beverly had always thought of her daughter as being far more domestic than she was. She had not realized that Suzanne was often not home at suppertime, and when she was, half the time she just picked up takeout. Suzanne suddenly stared at her. "You look different. Your hair."

"Elena." Her granddaughter had gone out and gotten her old hair dye and now her hair was red again. She felt almost human. Elena had used conditioner and brushed it out: now she had her own hair back.

"Mother, I know we haven't been communicating very well."

Beverly turned her face away. Did Suzanne think Beverly was "communicating" terrifically with anybody? Even her speech therapist couldn't always decipher what she was trying to spit out.

"You probably feel I'm not here often enough for you."

Beverly didn't bother answering that one. She just shrugged. As if

Suzanne sitting on her like a mother hen on a recalcitrant egg would help her.

"I wish I could say it's going to improve, but when school starts in the fall, it'll be worse than it is now. But I'm hoping we can work out a way that we do spend time together regularly and we can do better."

"Better . . . than what?"

Suzanne was losing the patient manner she assumed like an apron. "Better than we usually do. Better than we've done since I can remember."

Beverly waved her left hand.

"Mother, you have to believe me when I say I want us to be closer. I have the feeling you're mad at me all the time. What are you angry about? Or am I projecting? Am I completely wrong?"

Beverly shrugged. When Suzanne went on staring at her, she finally said, "My apart . . . ment."

"Your apartment?" Suzanne looked at her blankly. "We had to let that go five months ago."

"Mine." Beverly sought as so often for a simple way to say what she meant. "Friends. You took away."

"I took away your friends?" Suzanne looked baffled. "Mother, you had a stroke. You couldn't live alone in New York. You couldn't shop or cook or take care of yourself."

"Sylvia . . . there."

Suzanne frowned, mulling it over. "You mean, you wanted help to stay there? But it couldn't have worked. I couldn't go on running back and forth all the time. You couldn't pay the rent there, and if I paid your rent, I couldn't pay Sylvia."

Beverly closed her eyes to signify that the conversation was over. There had to have been a way, there had to be a way; but Suzanne had let her apartment go, and now there was no place to return to. She asked her friends on-line and checked rental Web sites about places in New York that she could afford. There seemed to be none. She was stuck here in Suzanne's house where she had no business, no use, no group of friends to sustain her. All her life she had lived involved with others, with causes, with actions, with work, with friends and lovers, enemies and cohorts. She was useless, silent as a phone yanked from its connection. The only connections she had that meant anything were to Sylvia, to Elena, to Mao, who lived mostly in her room, and to her computer and through it and only through it, to the world beyond.

From a large family in Trinidad, Sylvia had sacrificed her own prospects to her younger siblings. She had been bringing them to the States one at a time, setting them up, until sure they could make it here. Now they all sent money back to the parents and grandparents. It seemed archaic to Beverly, although Sylvia was twenty-three years younger than herself: to live in a big multigenerational family and owe your life to them, the way Victorian daughters had been expected to be spinsters and take care of their aged father, giving up their possibilities of marriage and family to him. Sylvia was quite contemporary in other ways. She had a fairly sophisticated analysis of colonialism and, of course, of racism. She seemed unimpressed by U.S. electoral politics, although she had taken out citizenship years before and did conscientiously vote. Her irrationality was the lottery. She played it religiously, full of tales of people who had played a number they had seen in a dream or that had some fateful significance, and then, suddenly, they were rich. A lady she had cleaned for when she first came to the States had just three years ago won a million dollars: Sylvia had seen it in the papers. "And she didn't even need it," Sylvia said, throwing up her hands. "She had a nice house already, her son a doctor, her daughter working for Bell Atlantic. What did she need that for?"

Sylvia kept trying to get her to play the lottery and would not listen when Beverly tried to explain to her how it was a way to milk the poor. "That lady, she had plenty of money, she had two fur coats, and she still played the lottery. And she won. Why not me?"

Sylvia had the patience to wait for her to finish a sentence, even if it took her three or four minutes to get it out. "If I had a will, I'd remember you in it, for being so kind with me. But I'm piss poor. I have a few books and old clothes. I don't even have anything to pawn, if I need cash." That was what she said, although it took her a while, many jerky pauses, and some wrong words before she managed to say it. She wanted Sylvia to know how much she appreciated her care and her attention. She knew from what had happened to some of her older friends, how callous and even cruel some caregivers from agencies could be. She remembered the bruises on her friend Moira's arms and legs before she was put in the nursing home to rot away.

"Your daughter pays for me. Don't worry about it. She's a good child, Beverly. She works real hard. I know you're crazy about your grand-daughter, but I don't see her working so hard. She takes care of herself and she likes to get others to take care of her."

Beverly only smiled. She did not expect Sylvia to appreciate Elena's passion and beauty, but Elena was the brightest spot in her life. She loved being Elena's confidante. It was a drama she followed from day to day, anticipating each new episode of Elena's romance. It was like being young and having a girlfriend who confided. She touched her refurbished hair. Now she looked more like herself. She looked more like the woman she had been. Beverly, she said to the woman in the hand mirror, Beverly: Elena made you reappear. You're almost visible again.

27

Elena

Elena had never felt such a sense of fullness, not even with Evan and Chad. Then she had been a kid, not in control of anything, doomed to serve out her educational sentence of boredom and humiliation. Now her feelings were even more intense, as if during those years of mean-ingless sex, inside she had been growing stronger and waiting, always waiting.

Missing him when they were not together was an ache she carried with her like a bad tooth. He was a fluid environment that surrounded her, in which she lived, in which she floated, in which she swam. Her feelings were not inside her, but she was inside them. They were so large they must carry everything before them. It did not matter what Suzanne suspected or what Marta might do, their love was too big and too strong and too intense to be contained by anyone.

They saw each other every day of the week, except weekends. He told Marta he needed Elena to come upstairs afternoons Monday and Thursday, to act as his secretary on the book project. Marta was actually happy that he wanted a secretary. She thought it was just great they were getting along so well. Elena felt Suzanne watching her when they were together, but Suzanne was in court, Suzanne was at school, Suzanne was even sometimes with that weird little boyfriend of hers. When they were all collected at some meal or event, she and Jim were utterly cool, only watching each other from the corners of their eyes, nothing steamy, no meaningful glances. They cooperated, fitting together without even having to chew it over. It was part of their seamless unity.

Weekends were chancy. Sometimes Marta and Suzanne went shooting. Sometimes Suzanne took Beverly off someplace. Suzanne was making an effort to spend time with Beverly on weekends. Elena knew Beverly found that a dubious blessing but could not say so. Everyone was always telling Beverly what a good daughter Suzanne was to take her in, as if she really had a choice: she could hardly dump her mother in the street. Every day Elena blessed her luck that she had not moved out. She had meant to, but she did not have close friends in Boston where she could crash. Her best friends were in Chicago or New York, places she had lived between college and the present. The people she knew here were kids she had gone to high school with—people she had zero desire to see—and guys from the restaurant. Beverly had turned out to be her best supporter, the only person besides Jim she could confide in—and she could hardly discuss Jim with Jim. Her grandmother had been a slut in her own time and knew a lot about guys. And she was, clearly, totally on Elena's side.

"Sometimes I wonder if I should get pregnant," she said to Beverly. "I mean he has a kid with Marta. Adam, a weasel. I could do better than that without trying."

"Not sure . . . thing."

"You mean, that I could do better?"

"That he . . . like baby."

"Yeah, maybe you're right. That I should wait till he leaves her and we go out to California."

Beverly nodded crookedly but fervently. "Wait."

"But I was thinking it could nudge him along. It's going to take something to get him to move out."

"Better . . . free . . . choice."

"Of course he'd choose me. He loves me. He's crazy for me, Grandma. But he's entrenched. It'll take a little dynamite to blow him loose, don't you see."

"Big bang . . . can hurt . . . you too."

She went out Saturday night with a guy she knew from the restaurant, the red-haired sous-chef who had a crush on her. She had run into him at Chestnut Hill when she was shopping for a new bathing suit at the late summer sales. Jim liked to swim, and last Tuesday, when he didn't have any appointments, they had sneaked off to Walden Pond. They had fucked in the woods on a beach towel. It was exciting. He told her she made him feel twenty years younger.

Jim didn't like her going out with Stan, but she told him it was a good cover. She enjoyed seeing him smoke with jealousy. Stan was just a guy, gangly and adolescent, on Prozac and moody in a totally uninteresting way. He was about as sexy as one of his salads, but he was perfect for going out with on a night she couldn't see Jim. Evenings were generally off-limits for them. Soon they would be living together and this dodging around would end.

It would take them a little while to get on their feet in California, but who cared? She was used to living on the margin, and she'd teach him tricks for getting by on little cash. Soon he would be set up there as a therapist and patients would come to him. She'd get a job in a restaurant or an office, easy. She didn't need much, and he had told her time and again that owning things meant nothing to him. He was living Marta's life, he said. All he needed, he could fit in a backpack and a briefcase, besides her. She was what he really needed. They'd go out to bars to hear music and to movies, and it wouldn't matter who saw them. They would make love whenever they pleased. They would sleep in the same sweet bed. They would wake together and shower together and eat together every morning. They'd live together in a way that would be cool and loose and pretty. She was totally amused that Jim could manage to work up jealousy over Stan, but if he wanted to suffer, good. He should realize that she was attractive to other men, that if he didn't grab her, someone else would. Slinking around and acting like secret agents was amusing at times, but enough! Maybe they would rent a house in Cal-

ifornia where he could use part of it for his office, much nicer than that
hole he had now.

It was easy to be cool and sensible when she wasn't with him, but
when he was there and touching her, her brains boiled dry. She couldn't
think, she could only feel at top decibels. That was love, and she had
known it once, and never since. She was consumed by it as if she were
set on fire from toes to hair. She wondered that people did not turn on
the street and stare at her, astonished. Sometimes she felt like a goddess,
glowing from within, burning white-hot with a passion that must be
palpable to those who came near her. This was hyperreality, this was
what was meant to be.

She liked to keep him on edge. When they rode to work together in
the mornings, on days when they did not take separate cars, she would
put her head in his lap and sometimes she would suck him. Twice he
fucked her on the couch between appointments, with her hand thrust
into her mouth to bite so she wouldn't cry out. Once, the next client
sat in the waiting room just outside. Sometimes she came when they
did these odd quickies in random places, but often she didn't. She did
not care. It was the excitement she craved, the sense that they were out
of control, that they were so besotted with each other that they had to
take wild chances. If she was going to pry him loose from his boring
marriage and his ill-fitting staid life, she had to draw him over the edge,
teach him to relish taking chances, give him back his recklessness and
daring.

"I'm good for you," she said, as they lay on his bed upstairs—the bed
he shared at night with his fat wife. Marta used to be thin, but lately
she had been gaining weight, especially around the middle. She had a
belly. Elena, who observed her carefully, noticed her middle-age spread.
She was letting herself go. "You don't think so, but I give you back what
you've lost over the years."

"You're certainly good for john henry." He put her hand on his prick,
flaccid after their recent fuck.

"I'm good for all of you, Jimmy."

"No one's called me that in years. Not since high school."

"What were you like then?"

He laughed shortly. "I was class president. That meant a lot to me.

I'd have killed for it, but I only had to charm everyone. I was on the track team. I was the second-best pitcher. I played in a stupid garage band, the Lords of Chaos. My girlfriend was voted the prettiest in our class."

"I don't think I would have liked you then."

"I don't think I liked myself. I was putting on an act all the time."

"Same as you were doing when I met you, Jimmy. You'd gone to sleep. Now you're fully awake."

"Not at the moment." He yawned. "I'd love to take a nap. If only we dared take a snooze . . ."

"Some afternoon we will. But I'm not sleepy yet." She rolled over onto him, feeling him harden beneath her. "And neither are you, baby boy."

28

Suzanne

Suzanne had her checkbook and returned checks spread out on her desk. What she had feared but dismissed from possibility was true: she was living far beyond her means. She was spending more than she was making, and she had to transfer money from her investment accounts to cover household expenses.

It was expensive for Rachel to spend this year in Israel, and electricity and food costs had risen to more than double what they had been now that Elena and Beverly were living in the apartment. But it was the cost of Beverly's illness that was bleeding the money away. Sylvia came in five days a week. Medicaid no longer covered the therapists. The medication and the rental on items from the hospital bed to the wheelchair were expensive. In the few months Beverly had been with her, Suzanne's cushion for the year had gone. She had already used up money saved in the last five years. Modifications to the house had cost well over twelve thousand dollars, wiping out an IRA on which she had to pay a stiff penalty. She could see the situation clearly, and it scared her. She would have a modest pension from the university if she hung on until retirement, but the expenditures she was looking at were catastrophic.

She rose from her desk to stand at the bay window, staring. What could she do? Rachel had another year of rabbinical school when she returned. She was going to have to urge Rachel to have a small wedding, which she suspected would disappoint her. She would have to approach Rachel again about waiting till she was back in the States to marry Michael. The airfare to Israel and the hotels would be a major expense in a good year; now, she did not see how she could manage it. Was Elena serious about going back to school? If so, where was that money coming from? Could she cut back Sylvia to four days? Could she get Elena to spend one or two days a week with Beverly? She was going to have to do less pro bono work and more law for money. Her life was crumbling before her, and she did not know how to stop the hemorrhage of money and time. She had a man seriously interested in her for the first time in a decade and a half and she barely had time to fall into bed with him once a week. She would lose him. She would lose herself. What options did she have?

The next night as she clung to Jake, the words burst out of her. "It's not fair, it's not fair!" At once a panic seized her. He would see how selfish she was; he would be turned off by her callousness and cruelty, in even thinking that.

"Of course, nothing is, so whatever you're talking about has to be true. I met today with people from Pittsfield, where GE has been dumping PCBs for years and years. . . ."

But she had to talk to him. She felt choked with unspoken words. Who else could she trust? "My mother. We've never gotten along. We aren't close. And here she is like a great stone that's landed on me. I feel like the ancient mariner, with the dead huge bird, the albatross around his neck. But I didn't shoot my mother. She shot herself."

He drew back to look levelly at her. "You really are upset. How about a drink? Would a nice cognac somebody gave me soothe you a little?"

"I don't want a drink, I want a solution. She went on smoking for years after it was clear how dangerous it was. Well, she wanted to smoke. She's never eaten in a healthy way. She had her energy and she did whatever the hell she pleased. Now I'm stuck with the consequences."

Jake stood looking at her. He grimaced, "So is she, baby. So is she."

Suzanne sighed, deflating. "I know that. It's just that I can't afford all the help she needs. Illness is so unbelievably expensive, it just breaks you. There's no help to be had. It breaks you financially and it breaks you emotionally and it breaks you into exhaustion."

"Would it cost less to put her in a nursing home?"

"It would cost even more. And I can't do it. It's not an option. She's been a strong political woman who spent most of her life trying to make the world more decent. She doesn't deserve terminal storage."

He was pacing. She wished he wouldn't. It distracted her and made her a little edgy. It was part of his superabundant energy. He stopped in front of her and said, "This Pittsfield business, we're going to need your help."

"My help."

"I think it's going to require going to court."

She groaned and turned away. One more thing she was supposed to do, and it would be gratis, of course. A year ago, six months ago, she would not have hesitated in a good cause: now she was stymied. She could end up representing a client like GE because she needed the money to support her mother.

He was frowning. "What bugs me is how long this minor case in California is taking. It keeps getting postponed. Both sides keep making motions and it goes on and on. I have a chance to go to Greenland and I'm going to have to pass it up. They let me come to Boston because it would be a hardship and the court trusts me that far, but I'm not allowed out of the country."

She stared at him. "Why would you want to go to Greenland?"

"I like extreme places," he said. "I like wilderness. Although it isn't quite. The last time I was there, we used an old army installation, from the days of the early warning system. At some point, the place had been evacuated, and they'd never returned. It was like a crime scene—everything abandoned and left as it was. A frying pan on the stove with old grease in it. A girlie magazine open on the john floor. . . . One of the things that drove my last girlfriend crazy was that I'll pick up and go anyplace, Suzanne. I can't resist it."

"What is it you can't resist?" She noticed that his desire for travel did not frighten her. Better adventure with polar bears than with other women.

He turned at last to face her. "My childhood was dull. Dreary. I think my parents never talked to each other except when they were traveling. Maybe I still think traveling is the answer to boredom. Perhaps I'm just not a very imaginative person and I need a change of scene to keep my blood flowing. But I can't stand the idea of places I've never been. And if I've had a good time in a place, I want to go back. It's a permanent itch."

"Maybe a trip with a purpose is for you what an interesting case is for me." It was a relief to think about Jake, even briefly, instead of herself and her life.

Rachel was back to communicating on E-mail. She sent short messages every couple of days, although sometimes she got long-winded and lyrical with endless descriptions of Jerusalem, like a woman with whom Rachel had fallen in love and who also angered her constantly, as faithless lovers will. Jerusalem belonged to too many. You could never have an illusion you had discovered her or even that she was special for you. She was special for everyone. She touched them all into rich madness. For three thousand years poets and prophets and priests and nuts had sung her praises, and they still fought to the death for her.

Rachel seemed so distant, she had an impulse to pick up and go to her. She missed Rachel's positive, level mind and temperament. Of course she could not. Suzanne had a brief interval between summer school and the beginning of classes in the fall. They used to go out on Cape Cod. Then they went up to Maine. Now she was lucky if she got as far as the corner deli. She could not barge off and leave Beverly alone in the house, with Elena working. Elena had been better with her grandmother than Suzanne had ever expected, and she was grateful. Elena spent hours with her grandmother, who seemed more responsive to her than to Suzanne or anyone else, except Sylvia.

"I really, really appreciate your kindness to Beverly," Suzanne said to her daughter. They were both in the kitchen having a quick breakfast. Elena was bound for Jim's office and Suzanne was headed for court.

"It isn't kindness. You don't understand. Nobody does, except maybe Sylvia. Grandma's all there. She's still all there inside."

"Of course I understand—"

"Then why are you always in a hurry with her?"

"I don't think I am. . . ."

Elena laughed sharply. "You can't ever wait for her to finish a sentence."

"I just try to anticipate what she's trying so hard to say."

"She hates that."

"I think you're projecting."

"She told me she hates it."

Suzanne was embarrassed. "Why didn't she tell me?"

Elena shook back her black mane. "You'd finish that sentence too. Some other way."

Suzanne felt as if they had conspired to put her in the wrong. She was trying so hard to make it all work and to carry the load of the house. She had a moment of blind furious exasperation. Her hand clenched on her coffee mug. She had a brief desire to throw it at her daughter, an urge she was ashamed of as soon as she became aware of it. "It's hard for all of us," she said softly.

"How hard is it really for you? You're out of the house most of the time. Sylvia does nine tenths of the work."

"Fine. I'll quit everything and stay home with my mother. Will you get a job that pays enough to support this entire household?"

"I couldn't support a pet dog, and you know it. It always comes down to money with you. Beverly's right!"

"It all comes down to money with everybody, Elena. Food on the table, shelter overhead, Sylvia, her medicine . . ."

"Just don't ever talk that way to Grandma or I'll never, never forgive you."

"Elena, I brought her here. From the time she had her stroke, I flew down to see her every weekend. Obviously I care about her and I'm perfectly willing to sacrifice to make her comfortable. It requires effort from all of us."

Suzanne went off to the bathroom and shut herself in, trembling with frustration and irritation. I'm perfectly willing to sacrifice, huh? What choice do I have? Who asked me what I want, anyhow? I'm sick and tired of being good, but there's no escape from duty, is there? And no use fuming about it. Elena will leave when she wants to, and I'll still be here with Beverly, now and tomorrow and next year. It could go on for twenty years.

She had an acute sense of being in a trap. She stood in the bathroom, not the most spacious room, painted a pale blue, and stared at the white ceiling. She sank onto the cover of the toilet, clutching herself, feeling pecked to death, pulled and stretched to dangerous thinness. Her nerves were hot as overloaded wires. Her brain was a neglected radiator. She did not know what to do with her frustration, her anger, her weariness. There was no one she could hand it off to. She had started out feeling gratitude toward Elena for spending time with Beverly, and she had ended up wanting to break something over her daughter's head.

She ran upstairs to Marta, who was standing in her slip putting on makeup in the bathroom. "Target practice, target practice this Saturday, please, please. If I don't get to shoot something, my head is going to explode. We haven't been going often enough."

Marta looked at her over her shoulder as she carefully darkened her brows and eyelashes, giving her face more definition. "Are we in a crisis?"

Suzanne nodded. "I'm overextended and crazy. I need it. Promise me."

Marta stood finishing her makeup and running over her schedule in her head. "We could steal away for an hour and a half Saturday morning, if we get going early. Ten minutes to get there, ten to get back. We should have a full hour to shoot once we set up."

"There's no way I can pay more of Rachel's expenses," Sam said bluntly. "So you have your mother? I have Stephanie, Jonah, and Emma. An old lady lying in bed doesn't touch what one active kid burns up in piles of cash—a kid who wears out clothes every day and takes fourteen kinds of lessons with all that gear and private school and doctors and dentists up the wazoo. Therapists. Orthodontists. Their clothes cost as much as my suits."

She recognized that voice of Sam's. It was not his negotiating voice. It was his, This is my final offer voice. "I'm getting further in debt with every day. Rachel's year in Israel is not cheap, as you may have noticed. . . ."

"It wasn't my idea she become a rabbi."

"Right. She could always get a restaurant job."

"At least Elena doesn't send me tuition bills every time I turn around."

Saturday morning as Marta and Suzanne stood in front of the shooting table at the rod and gun club they had joined years before, she thought, there's something satisfying about handling the gun, aiming, and then that moment of percussion and destruction—harmless, appeasing to the tension within, punishing only the target and releasing the week's frustration and rage. They had used to go every Saturday, enjoying the incongruity of two feminists shooting together. Gradually they had let the game lapse until they went only once a month or so.

"Why did we stop doing this? It's fun. It's a tremendous release."

"Why?" Marta grinned, taking careful aim. Since they were wearing ear protectors, they talked loudly to hear each other. They were early, and the range was half empty. "Why did we stop going to movies? Why did we stop going for walks in the country? Why did I never get another dog after Archie died?" She got every shot into the target. Marta was a better shot than Suzanne, but Suzanne's clusters were more consistent.

It was Suzanne's turn. "Because we don't have time, only projects and duties and relationships." Soon Marta would have a baby and her time would be even more limited. An elderly invalid downstairs and a new baby upstairs: they would be one crazy overextended household. Suzanne got most of her bullets in the target, missing only twice on that round. "Have you told Jim yet about the baby?"

"Soon. Very soon."

"What are you waiting for? The onset of labor?"

"My doctor's coming back from the Cape and I have an appointment to see her the first Monday after Labor Day. If everything's on schedule, I'll tell him that day." Marta was missing most of her shots.

"The longer you wait, the more he's going to feel out of the loop." She wanted to urge Marta to tell him now, before it was too late, because she had an increasing sense of trouble coming.

Suzanne loved fall. It meant going back to school, as it had in her childhood, and she enjoyed teaching. She looked forward to the new classes, to the new students, and to her research assistant, Jaime, back from the Philippines where he had been visiting relatives. She wanted to get on with the law review article that had been languishing in her computer since February. She was tired of heat and air-conditioning equally, of soft asphalt underfoot, of fading cottons and browning grass and weary leaves on the maples along the street. She was beyond irritation at the kids next door screaming under her window when she was trying to work. She was sick of trying to figure out what to feed her family that wasn't hideously expensive and wouldn't heat up the kitchen.

The first crispness in the air the week after Labor Day perked up her spirits. She began her classes with energy, went shopping with Marta and bought a gray pinstripe suit in the newer cut they were showing, everything longer again. Fortunately, it came in petite, so skirt and jacket would not have to be altered. Marta bought a new gabardine dress, cut loosely. "Think ahead," she said happily. "Four months and counting."

"What did Jim say when you told him?"

"I haven't. . . ."

"Marta, you have to."

"I'm scared." Marta turned away from the mirror of the fitting room.

"What are you scared of?"

"That if I say it to him, I'll lose the baby."

Suzanne's stomach clenched on itself. "Please tell him."

"I will. As soon as my ob lady checks me over."

"I thought that was last Monday?"

"She kicked me over to next Monday."

"Are you sure Jim hasn't noticed something?"

"We haven't been at it much this summer. He's a little depressed about work and his book. I haven't pushed things, since I discovered I'm pregnant. I figure the less that goes on, the calmer it will stay for the little one."

"Marta, you're forty-six. This is going to make an enormous change in both your lives. I really think you better tell Jim, and soon."

Marta shrugged, smoothing down the fabric. "Isn't it funny how we just can't bear to look at woolen things until the weather turns, even though we know damned well it's going to be fall and then winter, just like every other year?"

"Marta, listen to me. You have to promise me you'll tell him. I'm afraid for you. You can't go on keeping this from him. He'll be furious if you don't share the news with him while it's still early enough to do something about it if you both decide you don't want the child."

"Of course we want the child, Suzanne. Didn't we try for three years nonstop?"

"That was ten years ago."

"The years go by so fast, don't they?" Marta took both her hands and squeezed them. "I promise, I'll tell him. I'm seeing the doctor next Monday. Right afterward, if everything's okay and the amniocentesis comes out well, I'll tell him. Okay?

"Promise me you will. Promise! If you don't, Marta, then I will."

"All right! Don't get brutal about it. Next Monday."

Next Saturday morning Marta and she put in close to an hour target shooting, again getting up early to be there when the range opened. Today the canopy that protected the firearms from rain was flapping briskly like a sail over their heads. The wind carried a slight salt tang, coming in from the ocean and carrying a promise of rain that would wash the city air clean.

"We have to do things like this more often. Do you realize we did two things this week that weren't demanded of us? We went shopping and here we are off to target shoot," Marta said, eyeing the target. "We're becoming frivolous. Next we'll turn into ladies who lunch."

"Lunch? What's that? That apple I eat at my desk? The yogurt I gulp down in the car on my way to court?"

"Sometime this fall, we'll do it! We'll meet for lunch, like real ladies do. We'll have a salad apiece and then dessert. We'll dress up and carry shopping bags, even if there's nothing in them but briefs. We'll flirt with the waiter and complain about our husbands and our children. You can complain about Jake."

"We'll never do it," Suzanne said bleakly.

"Oh, but we will, before I'm the size of a cruise ship."

"If you tell Jim."

"I'm telling him Monday, if the news is good. I see the doctor at one."

"Good luck."

"More than that. I want magic."

* * *

When she got home, Suzanne spent some time with Beverly, while running up and downstairs to do her laundry. She felt she was annoying Beverly by zipping in, sitting for half an hour, then running off to move the wet laundry to the dryer and load the next pile of dirty clothes, but this was the time she had. Her time was almost all double-booked. Sheets from three beds, all those towels were a nuisance, but she could not add one more expense. She was going under financially. She had to do the laundry herself now.

"Makes me . . . nervous." Beverly shook her head. "Always in hurry."

"Mother, how does that make us different? You were always in a hurry too. We're both impatient people. I get it from you."

Beverly grinned crookedly. If Suzanne could amuse her, things were always better. That was one way that her mother remained accessible. "Mother, I'd like us to use this time to get closer."

"Laundry time."

"I mean these months. I'd like us to . . . do better with each other. Communicate better." She could see the skepticism in Beverly's eyes. She went on. "Why do you doubt me? Or do you think we just can't do it?"

"Always . . . want each . . . other . . . different."

Suzanne was trying not to guess, not to rush to finish Beverly's sentences for her. Elena's accusation stung. She sat nodding, leaning forward, settling back in the straight chair. "Maybe we can stop doing that and accept each other after fifty years."

"Fifty years!" Beverly repeated, as if appalled or astonished. "So long. You fifty?"

"I will be next spring."

"Goes fast."

"Doesn't it."

"Okay." Beverly lurched forward and patted Suzanne's arm. "Will try."

"No, she hasn't told her husband." Suzanne felt guilty, as if she had betrayed Marta by sharing her secret with Jake. "I keep begging her to." He had been showing her photos of the Fraser River in British Columbia where he had been last year at this time, with whom, she wondered. "It looks like Chinese landscape paintings—steep mountains like monoliths."

"It's a beautiful gorge. Where we were going, the only way across was a sort of hanging cage way above the waters."

Who had he been traveling with? He always said "I," but sometimes she observed another man or a woman in the photos: and in any case, someone was operating the camera. She suffered a throb of envy for the someone who had the freedom and time to pick up and wander off with him.

He lay propped on his elbow. The sun poured in through the slats of the blinds in his new apartment, igniting a stray white hair among the curls on his chest. "Marta had better tell him. Not something she should spring on him. By the way, dear, I'm actually not fat, I'm having contractions, so could you rush me to the hospital?"

"She's superstitious about it. They tried for years to get pregnant after they lost a baby daughter. She kept miscarrying. Then they gave up." She was still wondering who his "we" was.

"How does she know he wants a baby still?"

"I almost think it doesn't matter. She wants it."

"It's his, right?"

"Of course! Marta wouldn't have five minutes a week for an affair. It's Jim I was suspicious of."

"No longer?"

"I've been watching. I still don't understand what was going on upstairs that afternoon, but I haven't seen or heard anything since. A lawyer gets to be suspicious, and maybe my dirty imagination was running away with me."

"Did you ask your mother?"

"She said nothing's going on."

"Well, she's there a lot more than you are. Speaking of time, I need you to meet with the other lawyer who's going to help us on the PCB case. Would you like me to set up an appointment, or do you want to talk to him yourself?"

No, she did not want to play telephone tag with Sid Braun. "I can make it Friday at three or the following Wednesday for a breakfast meeting." She could not say *No* to Jake. It was a good cause, and she wanted him too badly. These times with him were a fix of pleasure, something that sustained her through the rest of the week. A hit of warmth.

"I'll see what we can put together."

She didn't have this Sunday afternoon to spend lying here making love and chatting, and she didn't have Friday at three to waste either, but she had to sacrifice them to Jake. Could she afford him? How could she possibly not try to? At her age and in her situation, having a lover was a luxury whose price had to come out of her flesh, but as long as she could have him, she suspected she would somehow manage. She only wished that he had less of an agenda. But if he were not the activist he was, rushing from court case to bargaining table to meeting to lobbying session, he would want far more than she could give him. If that time came, she did not know what she would do.

"I'd love to take you to British Columbia. A lot is still wilderness. It's gorgeous. We could backpack into some of my favorite places. We wouldn't see another soul for a week. Wouldn't that be paradise?"

Suzanne could not imagine herself backpacking into the wilderness, even the beautiful mountains and waterfalls he had photographed, but it was all moot. He wasn't going there anytime soon, and neither was she.

29

Elena

Elena was always super hot on Mondays, because usually Jim and she did not get a chance to be alone the whole weekend. This Saturday, they had from eight to nine-thirty in the morning: that was it. They almost got caught, because they had expected Marta to be at the range longer. Elena knew they simply could not continue like this. Yes, it made things hot, but it would be ever so much nicer to sleep and wake together, the ultimate couple thing: sleeping twined in the same sweet bed. She had never had that with anyone she loved, just guys who were convenient, whose main virtue was that they were there: not since traveling with Chad and Evan, and then they had slept in sleazy motels or crummy hotels, in the car, beside the car. So many meaningless guys since then, sometimes she couldn't remember what they looked like. She was not sure she would recognize some of them in the street. Far from wanting to spend the entire night with them, she was bored shitless having to deal with them the next morning when all she wanted was strong coffee and to get her blood moving with some aerobics.

That was one thing she had gotten from her mother—that she liked to move, she liked to work out. She had to say that Suzanne kept herself in shape for a woman her age. She had real muscles, unlike cow Marta, who had been gaining weight steadily, visible to Elena's watchful eye. There's someone who needed a workout and wasn't bothering. Elena had only to look at Jim, tight, taut, buff, and then at Marta with her belly pushing on her pants to know they were no longer suited, if ever they had been.

He needed her, he did, or he would die inside. Electric Elena he called her, my soul. Even in her dreams, she was with him. Last night she had dreamed they were making love in a large warm pool, floating together. She had come in her sleep, then wakened alone in the bed, deeply resenting their separation. It had to end. If she contemplated life without him, it was a return to dust and ashes. It was worse than meaningless, it was total nothingness. Love centered her. Love impaled her and held her upright. Loving him made her thrum with energy. She felt as if her touch could heal. When she massaged Beverly's shoulders, Beverly told her it felt wonderful. She knew it was the magic from her love that was giving her holy energy that coursed out from her like light.

She went into Beverly's room to give her breakfast, as she did every Monday. Suzanne had cut back one day on Sylvia this fall. Beverly skipped bathing those mornings, for she did not want Elena's help in the shower. Elena understood her grandma's embarrassment, although truly she would not have minded. Sylvia told her she could have been a nurse. She knew Sylvia meant it kindly, but that was no life. Helping her grandma a couple of times a week was nothing. Spending forty to fifty hours a week doing the same with strangers would drive her up the wall.

She made Beverly scrambled eggs with peppers and hot sauce, one of her specialties. Beverly loved it. "Tired . . . bland food."

"Every Monday, you get my special eggs. Maybe we'll run off to Mexico together, you and me. Hey, Grandma, ever been there?"

Beverly nodded and held up three fingers. Three times.

Elena brushed out Beverly's hair. It looked much better red again, bringing out the green in Beverly's eyes. She loved to fix up Beverly, who totally appreciated the attention. It gave Grandma a lift to know she looked better—more like herself. It was funny the things that gave you that sense of identity. When she was still in high school, she had this tough black studded leather jacket she had got Sam to buy for her birthday. She had worn it winter and summer, when it was far too cold or too hot for the jacket. It had gone west with her into trouble and the death of her friends. When it had been stolen at a party her senior year, she was devastated. Suzanne bought her another, but it was never the same. Years later, she would have the impulse to put on that jacket, her real jacket of which all others were imitations, and feel the loss all over again.

She could hear Jim walking around upstairs. He trotted out for his run, down the front stairs. She would not go upstairs till later. He liked the mornings to himself. He ran, he lifted weights. He caught up on his E-mail and made phone calls and puttered around the Internet. That was fine with her. She was a night person and woke slowly to full alertness. She never put her fine lingerie in with the regular wash. Monday mornings she did her hand laundry, enjoying the spectacle of her salmon, grass green, blue, scarlet, and black bras and panties, camisoles and slips hung on the line. This time she put them outside instead of down the basement. It was a gorgeous day. Summer had come back, warm enough to wear a sundress, her favorite, a dark honey color that set off her skin and eyes. The light was the same color today. She stood outside with her eyes closed, feeling the sun hot and red on her lids. She liked the way her underthings looked, like pennants, flags of pleasure and delight, silk and satin and nylon banners moving languidly in the faint breeze that was like a sigh. After the rain of yesterday, the weather had warmed, humidity and sweet sun from the South.

"Did you like fancy underwear, Grandma?"

"Liked . . . my body."

She helped Beverly into the living room and put on CNN for her. Neither of them had ever been able to get into watching the soaps, although Sylvia had her favorite, *General Hospital*, she watched every day. Elena thought that neither her grandma nor she could enjoy other people's pretend lives, for they both liked real action too much. Soaps were for women who imagined taking lovers but didn't dare, women stuck in fading lives, who knew now they would never be loved the way they dreamed of, the way she was loved. She held herself gently by the elbows as if she might fly apart. Never had she believed, since she was fifteen and her life had cracked like an egg, that she would know love again and be totally, vehemently loved. She walked with that love shining around her.

She was making a simple red dress for herself, a tank top A-line that would come to midthigh and move well. It would be perfect for dancing. She kept trying to get Jim to go dancing with her, but he was afraid to go out in public. "Like, do you think one of her judges is going to be boogying at a club?"

Beverly pointed, grinning. "Only you sew."

"You mean I'm the only one in the family who can."

Beverly nodded. "Never patient." Pointing to herself. "Nor Suzanne."

"I find it relaxing. I don't do anything I don't want to, Grandma. It's sensual sometimes, the feeling of the material, seeing something take shape under my hands."

Jim crossed over them, back from his run, and both women looked up. Beverly smiled at her. "You . . . love him."

"Like crazy."

"Powerful." Beverly shook her head. "Big wind."

Elena wasn't quite sure what her grandmother meant, but she smiled and nodded back. Whatever Beverly meant, Beverly was on her side and wished her well, so it didn't matter if she couldn't exactly understand what the words intended. Big wind, she mulled over, something that tears the roof off. "You mean like a hurricane that blows everything inside out and tears the leaves from the trees and roofs off houses."

Beverly nodded fervently. "All changed."

She made lunch for them, hot dogs she found in the freezer. They were turkey hot dogs but that was better than tofu, anyhow. Didn't people eat real hot dogs any longer? She also found whole wheat buns.

Beverly had no trouble managing a hot dog in a bun, since it was essentially one-handed food. They drank diet soda that Elena went down to the corner to buy, since Suzanne simply wouldn't get it. Elena decided she would get real buns and hot dogs with her own money. If you were going to eat a hot dog, you wanted a real hot dog, not a health food imitation.

After a leisurely lunch, Elena loaded the dishwasher and turned it on. Then she kissed Beverly on the forehead and went upstairs. As she climbed the stairs, already her heart was beating loudly, quickly. She began to feel that warmth building in her groin, liquid heat pooling between her thighs. She liked the way it made her feel. She liked the leisurely morning with Beverly, getting ready, slowly moving toward him. By the time she pushed in the kitchen door, she could have fucked him right away. They kissed with her sitting in his lap feeling his erection against her stomach as she faced him, her thighs on either side of his narrow hips. They used to have lunch together on Mondays. Now they didn't, but it was cool. They had lunch together Tuesday through Friday, and they had the whole afternoon to themselves on Mondays, a treat after the wasteland of the weekend.

His hair was all tousled, the way it got when he was trying to work on his book. She liked to muss his hair, hair almond brown, close to blond, with small patches of gray over both ears, fine and silky. She loved to tangle her hands in it. He wore it too close to his head. He looked much younger when it was messed. He was letting it grow lately, over his collar. His features were so chiseled. She kissed his nose, his forehead, his chin, his cheeks, his eyelids. "I adore you, I adore you."

"I like being adored. Adore me some more." He led her into the bedroom. With a practiced hand, he shucked her clothes, spreading her on the towel he always carefully placed over the wedding ring quilt on his bed. She hated that towel. It represented stealth and secrecy. She needed to be with him all the time, in light as well as in shadow, but she wanted him too badly to argue about it now. He was in a hurry, thrusting into her. The weekend drought stoked up his desire too. He told her he was no longer having sex with Marta, that it had been more than a year, and she believed him. Why would he want to? Getting thick in the waist and with her belly sticking out, obviously she didn't care. He rode hard on her, his balls slapping against her. She tongued his nipple as he rode, making it hard. Then she nipped him lightly. Riding her at a gallop, pounding. Lately she liked it that way. Hard, . Harder, their bodies thumping one on one, so that she felt as if they were rising and being pounded down at one and the same time, a complicated motion like those carnival rides she had loved as a child. And then at last she burst.

They showered together. Then they split a beer, both naked in the heat of the afternoon. She wished they could make love on a blanket in the yard. It must be eighty in the full sun and heat of midafternoon. She told him her wish as they lay on the bed again, just chilling. Relaxed together.

He grinned. "That would give the neighbors a thrill."

"It would give me a thrill."

"I can arrange that, without needing to trot downstairs." Languidly he reached for her, and they began slow, easy, sensuous lovemaking. The towel had fallen to the floor. She noticed that but didn't think he had. Good-bye, towel like a condom, towel like a no trespassing sign. They kissed and kissed, touching each other all over their sleek backs, his chest and her breasts, their bellies and thighs. She plucked a hair from his thigh, causing him to cry out. He bit her neck.

"Vampire!" she moaned.

"I am ze Count Drac-yu-lah . . . I do not drink . . . wine."

Finally he spread her legs and began to eat her, his head buried in her thighs, doing her leisurely, feeling her, tasting her, flicking his tongue. She lay with her eyes closed, concentrating, when she heard something. Someone walking. She froze, but he did not notice. His ears were buried in her flesh. A woman's voice called something. Marta. Elena controlled her reaction. She did not blink or move a muscle. Let Marta find them. Let the secrecy be over. Let the farce end. He was making those funny noises he made when he was eating her, as if she tasted like ice cream, and he heard nothing. Elena controlled her breathing, controlled her desire to bolt. She lay there, waiting.

Marta appeared in the doorway, stopping abruptly as if flash frozen. She stood staring, Elena saw through her lashes. Elena had her lids lowered, her head flung back, as if she were in a trance and could see nothing. Marta made an awful choking sound. Elena was cold through but determined. Let the pretense end. Let the lying stop. Marta was still standing just inside the bedroom staring, transfixed. Elena was beginning to get nervous. She was trying to decide if it was time for her to see Marta and scream. She felt stone cold. How long could Marta just stand there?

Then Marta began to scream herself. "No!" She cried out, "No!" moving now, toward the dresser just inside the door, the chest of drawers with a green bag on top and a pile of books. Jim froze and then leapt from between Elena's legs and knelt on the bed babbling. "Marta, I'm sorry! It doesn't mean anything!" he cried out.

Elena was naked and exposed to Marta. She had to explain quickly. "We love each other. We have to be together. We're going to live together. I wanted him to tell you, but he wasn't ready. . . ." It did not feel victorious but bad. Sickening. Wrong all through.

Jim was mumbling, "Oh my god, oh my god, shit, shit . . ." He hopped off the bed and took a step toward Marta. "Marta, never mind the kid—"

She tried to calm him. "Jim, it's okay. It had to happen. We have to make her understand how we feel about each other."

Marta was fumbling with the green gym bag on the top of the dresser. The books cascaded to the floor. "You bastards! I'm pregnant, you bastards." She was holding something now in both her hands, letting the bag drop with the books. She was clicking something into place. Elena scrambled off the bed in Jim's direction, the bed now between them and Marta, who was holding something out. Elena looked around the room for her clothes. She was not sure where they had fallen. She grabbed the bedspread off the bed and wrapped it around herself. Jim was stepping into his briefs, yanking them on as if it mattered. Then she saw what Marta had in her hand. She stared, disbelieving.

"No," Jim was saying to Marta. He took a step toward her and then backed rapidly away. "Baby, this doesn't mean what you think. It's a mistake! You don't want to do this, Marta. Put down the gun." He climbed back onto the bed, crouching there.

"While I'm working and in court, this is what you do, you bastards." She raised the gun in both hands and shot. Elena threw herself in front of Jim. Marta fired shot after shot. Elena waited for the bullets to tear through her flesh. She had been meant to die in the desert and she had failed then. Now it would be complete. At least she would save her lover.

Jim was shouting over and over, "It didn't mean anything, baby, it didn't mean anything. It was just this once. It was an accident!"

As what he was saying sank in, she drew away from him and sat on the bed, stunned. She felt very cold. Everything seemed too brightly lit in the room and outlined in light. She saw that Marta was aiming way over both their heads. Marta had drilled a neat line of bullet holes in the wall high over the bed. Elena almost smiled, but her face was frozen. Her heart was frozen. She did not think it was beating. "Jim, you don't have to pretend. You don't have to lie about us," she said, but he paid no attention. "Don't be scared. She isn't shooting at us." He would not even look at her. It was as if she had not spoken.

The gun fell and Marta ran from the room, sobbing wildly, crying out something Elena could not understand. Jim was talking now very fast, "It doesn't matter, it doesn't mean anything!" he was shouting and chasing after Marta, leaving Elena on the bed. She got up and grabbed her clothes from the floor, dressing quickly. Jim in his underwear was pleading with Marta in the living room. Carrying her shoes, Elena headed for the kitchen and the back stairs.

It doesn't matter, it doesn't matter if he says it doesn't. Maybe nothing at all mattered in her life. She wished Marta had shot both of them dead. Marta said she was pregnant, she was sure Marta had said that, which meant Jim had been lying and lying to her. She put her hand on the kitchen door and paused. In her head his words repeated themselves over and over again. It doesn't matter. It doesn't mean anything. So it didn't.

30

Beverly

After Elena made them lunch, her granddaughter went upstairs, and Beverly, back to bed. Waking from her postlunch nap, Beverly rolled over to her computer and started composing an E-mail to the *New York Times*, complaining about their coverage of an airline strike. She was trying to think of a word that was escaping her, the way they so often did—like trying to grab a minnow in a bucket—when she heard loud noises from upstairs. Screaming. More screaming. Then the sharp report of shots.

Beverly had heard shots often enough in her life to recognize them. Heard them in the South. Heard them in the streets of her neighborhood. Guns meant trouble. Trouble and blood and somebody hurt. Then she heard even more loud yelling. She called out, "Elena! Elena?"

Beverly struggled out of her chair into her walker and began her slow progress toward the back stairs. Finally she arrived at the bottom and called out again. No one answered, although she could hear someone crying upstairs. It must be Elena. She had to get to her. Marta had a gun upstairs. It was a stupid thing to have around. She hated firearms. Little kids were always getting killed playing with them. They should be banned. She could understand some clerk in a 7-Eleven keeping one under the counter, but in somebody's house? She had fought with Suzanne many times about owning a gun, but Suzanne at least kept hers under lock and key. Nobody else ever saw or handled it, stored in a small safe in her office.

Beverly began laboring up the stairs. It was hard. In fact, it was almost impossible. The walker just wouldn't balance on the narrow back stairs. She was dragging herself up by the railing, pulling the walker after her, thumping. She had to get upstairs to see what had happened. Oh, she could imagine terrible things. She heard yelling but no one answered her calling for Elena.

She had climbed halfway up when she lost her balance. The walker skidded on the edge of the narrow step. She grabbed at the railing and held herself by her good left hand. The walker clattered down. She was lying on the steps holding on by one hand. Her arm ached. She tried to form words more clearly, but she could only shriek in incoherent blurts of sound. Slowly her grip began to slide off the railing. She tried to get her knee up onto the step, but she couldn't. Her leg wasn't strong enough.

She heard steps coming, the door opening. "Help . . . me," she called. Elena appeared at the head of the steps. She was crying and her sundress was on inside out. Beverly tried to speak but she was slipping down the steps and then thumping, banging, step after step hitting her brutally as she went down. Elena came after her, flinging herself down the stairs, grabbing for her. "Grandma! Hold on! I'm coming!"

Their hands touched. Elena tried to grip her but could not get a purchase on her hand. Beverly was hurled from step to step to the bottom where she lay in a heap. Elena ran down and knelt over her. "Grandma. Are you okay?" Elena was gently examining her. "Grandma, where does it hurt?"

Now Marta appeared at the top of the stairs. Her face was swollen and wet. She spoke in a strange numb voice, "What happened?" She came slowly down the steps and leaned over Beverly, touching her carefully. She did not look at Elena. Jim was standing above in his underwear, wringing his hands and calling to Marta, who ignored him.

Marta was gingerly exploring her leg. "Beverly, can you hear me? I think your leg is broken. We mustn't move you." Gently Marta ran her hands over Beverly's back. "I don't think you have a spinal injury, but I'm not a doctor. Listen, don't be afraid, Beverly. I'll call an ambulance." She carefully disengaged herself, never touching Elena or looking at her, and ran back upstairs.

"Grandma, Grandma. Don't die on me! Grandma! I couldn't stand it. Please! Please don't die. It's all my fault. Please!"

She wanted to speak but she couldn't. Elena was cradling her. Beverly could not form words. Her head was roaring. Her back hurt horribly, her legs hurt. One of them was twisted under her. It must be broken, as Marta said. But the worst pain was the one in her head. She recognized it. She remembered it. It was lightning in the brain, the nightmare come again. She was having another stroke.

31

Suzanne

Suzanne canceled her litigation class. Her hands were shaking so badly she had to dictate the note Jaime taped to her office door canceling her hours till further notice. Then he got her car to take her to the hospital, for she did not trust herself to drive. Her mouth kept twisting into a weird crooked smile, a nervous grimace of appeasement, the way a frightened dog will wag his tail. Beverly had been doing so well. She had been walking daily, no matter how awkwardly. She had been involved with acquaintances and causes on the Internet. There had been no warning signs. Beverly seemed to have been steadily improving, pleasing her therapists with her progress. Suzanne had just talked to the agency about cutting back Sylvia to four mornings, since Beverly thought she could manage by herself in the afternoons.

Suzanne went up to the front desk of the hospital, to ask for her mother. Beverly was in surgery. In addition to the stroke, she had broken bones. Suzanne was directed to a lounge, where she found Elena huddled in a chair. "What happened?"

Elena looked at her momentarily, but her eyes immediately slipped away from Suzanne's gaze. "It's all my fault."

"Just tell me what happened."

Elena was silent for several minutes, while Suzanne reminded herself of her vows of patience. Finally Elena in a flat almost inaudible voice told her the story. Halfway through she began to weep uncontrollably. Suzanne was startled, almost frightened. Elena never cried. Elena had stopped crying when she was twelve, and Suzanne had not seen her in tears since. Elena seemed reduced to childhood by her tears, convulsed, out of control. She spat the story out in gulps. Tentatively, Suzanne embraced her, held her as her shoulders shook.

"Marta started screaming, I was screaming, Jim was going on and on to her how she should forgive him and I meant nothing, nothing to him."

"He was scared. And guilty."

"She said she was pregnant. Then she took her gun out of the gym bag on the dresser—"

"Did she shoot Jim?"

"She didn't shoot anyone. She just drilled a row of holes over our heads to scare us." Elena sighed. "She had every right to shoot us, and I wish she had!"

"I'm devoutly glad she didn't." Marta was volatile, but under it, she was a rock. Besides, it was hard for a defense attorney to ignore the consequences of murder. This was a disaster. "It was my fault too. I should have gone to her with my suspicions." She should have confronted Elena more forcefully. She should have backed Jim into a corner. He had always been a little afraid of her. She could have used that on him.

"It's not your fault, Mother. You tried to tell me. You said I'd get hurt. I deserve to get hurt, but Grandma didn't." Quickly, brokenly Elena told her what had happened. "I've killed her. And I love her so much!"

"She's not dead." Suzanne hugged her daughter. "She's not dead and you're alive. I couldn't lose you, and Marta knows that." Marta had been there for her for years and years, before she had married Sam, when Rachel was little, after Sam and she broke up. Marta had helped raise Rachel, certainly. She had been more than an aunt. If she had been raised by her Aunt Karla as much as by Beverly, so Rachel at least had been raised partly by Marta, and Marta had always helped with Elena, when Elena would permit any help.

Suzanne sighed. "It is a mess, that's for sure. Now I'm going to try to find someone I can ask about Beverly. She can't still be in the operating room."

She found a nurse at last who had an answer. "Mrs. Blume's in the recovery room. I can't tell you anything else. You'll have to speak to the doctor, and he's operating. No, you can't see her yet. Come back in an hour. She should be out of recovery by then."

At least Beverly had survived the operation. Suzanne had never felt more helpless. She was not accustomed to total uselessness. She ought to tell Rachel. Not till there was something more definite to report. It was four-thirty here, so it was the middle of the night in Israel. They had been communicating exclusively through E-mail. No reason to worry Rachel until the situation was clear. Clear. What a bland word. Like a shard of glass.

Marta had left a message to call her. She must, although she felt guilty before Marta. Had Marta miscarried? That was the critical question. Instead of going back into the lounge immediately, she sat down in the corridor, in a plastic chair holding her head in her hands as the tears began to seep out.

Why wasn't Jim the one lying in the recovery room? That would have been justice. He was seventeen years older than her daughter, which should have given him some discretion, some pass at wisdom. Suzanne found a quiet corner and called Marta on her cell phone. "Are you all right? I mean as all right as you can be. . . ."

"I didn't lose the baby, if that's what you mean."

"That's what I mean."

"I can't talk long now. Jim and I are having a huge fight. I just want him to get out and leave me alone."

"I'll be there as soon as I can. Beverly's out of the operating room, but she hasn't regained consciousness."

"When you get here, come upstairs—but don't bring Elena, please. I can't deal with her yet."

Is our friendship over? That was what Suzanne most wanted to ask, but how could she bother Marta at a time like this? She would have to move out. She would have to take Elena and move out. She felt desolated. She felt painfully alone. She began to bargain with fate: all right, just let my mother live, let Beverly survive and I will gladly move to any miserable place and not complain, I promise, I promise! And I won't complain about expenses, never again. I will make her happy somehow, I promise. I will make it better!

At five-thirty, Beverly was out of recovery and moved to the intensive care unit. She was not yet conscious. Suzanne was allowed to see her briefly, to speak to her inert body with the tubes threaded through her arm and nose. Beverly looked tiny in the bed, among the apparatus that kept her alive. Her skin was blue-gray. Then Suzanne had to leave, and Elena was allowed to go into the room briefly.

When the nurse told them that they must leave, they went downstairs. The doctor would see them in an hour or so. They were silent, both exhausted with emotion. They decided to go to the cafeteria and sat, both with a cup of bitter coffee on the table, facing each other. Elena would not meet her gaze but pressed her face into her hands.

"I must sound callous, but I half wish she had plugged Jim. I know"—she started to say "you think you love him" and realized how patronizing that sounded—"I know you love him—"

"I did! I can't now. I made him up. He was just a middle-aged married man fucking an employee who was shoved in his face. It was my fault—"

"Don't keep saying that, Elena. He's supposed to know what he's doing. He's a therapist, for pity's sake."

"Mama, you don't even know how to swear, do you?" Elena briefly, bleakly laughed. "Grandma's the last person I ever wanted to hurt. All I can hear in my head is Marta shouting that she's pregnant, and Jim being a complete worm and telling her I didn't mean a thing to him—"

"He was scared, Elena. He didn't necessarily mean what he said."

"But he did. Long after she threw down the gun and ran out of the room, all he could think of was denying what happened, trying to make it go away! He didn't think for one second of how I felt."

"You have to understand, Elena, he's really dependent on Marta—emotionally, economically, socially, every way. He wasn't about to leave her. I tried to tell you that. I've known them for so many years, I know how their marriage works."

"I thought their marriage was over. I didn't think they cared about each other."

"It's hard to judge other people's marriages from the outside—"

"Mother, don't be so rational. I've fucked everything up! Everything!" Elena was clutching herself by the shoulders. "Grandma looks terrible. I've been such a fool, but why does she have to pay for it?"

"It's my fault for agreeing that you take that job. I knew he had a history with young women. I just didn't think he'd come after you."

"Maybe I went after him, Mother. You pretended I was an innocent when I was fifteen. Don't do it now. How could you have prevented me from taking the job? How could you have prevented me from taking him?"

"So we'll all have to share responsibility for what's happened." Suzanne stood. She must go back upstairs to wait for the doctor, who was supposed to make an appearance to talk with them. "The consequences will be with us for a while."

32

Elena

Elena felt deeply ashamed, not because she had been with Jim, although being walked in on that way was totally tacky. She felt ashamed that she had believed passionately in a frail lie. She had believed he did not care about his wife, that their marriage was over and dusty, and that he loved her as strongly, as purely, as devoutly as she loved him. She had made herself believe all those foolish lies, she had been willing to hurt everyone around her, all for a piece of self-hypnosis. She'd been a blind idiot.

When she had thrown herself in front of Jim, she had expected to die. Now it seemed like silly melodrama, but she could not shake that sense of once again having brushed against violent death. When Chad had blown his head open and Evan had been shot, most of her old classmates made it clear they thought she should have died with them. Someone left a note on her locker, IF AT FIRST YOU DON'T SUCCEED . . . and a drawing of a gun with a balloon message BANG!

Elena was impressed with Marta. She knew how to put real fear into them, but she hadn't lost control. Marta had sure scared the shit out of Jim. Elena would never forget the sound of his quavering voice begging for his life, begging for forgiveness. Even when she and Marta were bending over Beverly crumpled at the bottom of the steep back stairs, he was going, "I was depressed. It was a stupid midlife thing. I never meant to hurt you, Marta. She's a kid! That's all." He ignored Beverly. He ignored her.

She had seen herself in a great romance. Now she was just a fool and Beverly was paying the price. She could not stand it if her grandmother died because of her. Chad and Evan had died in the desert and she had not gone with them. If she caused Beverly to die, she did not think she could continue. She had made a mess of her life. She had to go out having done something she could feel good about. She was not used to feeling so small, so mean. Love had been a roaring inside her that drowned out everything else. She had wanted that old intensity so hungrily she had pretended to herself, lied to herself to get it. She had ruined everything for the people around her, out of her need for a lie.

They came back to the house together and Elena shut herself in her room.

"Stay out of Marta's way for now," Suzanne said.

No fucking problem, Elena thought. That was her intention.

"Although you're going to have to have a real conversation with her. But wait until she's ready. I'm going upstairs now."

Elena did not want to lie and listen for Jim passing over her head. She did not put on her usual salsa. Instead she found her old tapes, Judas Priest, that song that she had played again and again after Chad and Evan, "Night Comes Down." She put her Walkman over her ears and spaced out. That music filled with pain and energy and lightning had once felt like reality turned into sound. Mötley Crüe's "Bastard." She kept playing the two songs over and over from fourteen, thirteen years ago. What a loser she was still. If she was not going to die, she needed to change herself. Into what? A pumpkin? She had no idea.

Still she had actually dozed off with the music still thundering in her head when she felt rather than heard the door open, and Suzanne came in. She shut off her music at once and sat up, embarrassed because she had fallen asleep, embarrassed because she had been able to sleep.

Suzanne sat down on the chair in front of the desk, turning it to face her. "She's thrown Jim out."

"For real, or just because she's pissed?"

"I don't know if *she* knows. He doesn't believe it yet either."

"I better find another place to live, fast."

"Elena, you just lost your job. It wasn't much of a job anyhow. Just hold on. We have to work this out, all three of us, and running away won't fix things."

Marta could have killed her. Easily. She kept thinking about that. No more Elena. Zero. When she was younger, she had brooded about death. It seemed like this cool thing, the place where all troubles vanished and everything was quiet. It was the place that gave you peace and made everybody else sorry for you. It was the dark place at the center of the best music, at the center of orgasm when she thought she would die of pleasure. It was the most real of all realities, the ultimate rush, the fire at the core.

After she had been brought back to her mother and school, she had wished many times she had died with Chad and Evan. They were heroes. She was a failure. A coward. But she had not tried to kill herself. At first she felt she wasn't good enough to deserve it, because she had not done it when she had the chance. Other times she remembered Chad's head blown open. She could not want that. Then slowly her life recommenced, the boredom and the tiny pleasures and the minor troubles and anxieties and occasional victories.

She said to her mother, "I have to figure it all out. Why I'm alive."

"Why shouldn't you be alive? Marta didn't really want to hurt you."

"But my life has to have a purpose. Twice now I've faced gunfire and survived." She could not explain to Suzanne the shame she felt. She knew Beverly would understand, but her grandmother was still unconscious.

"Just being you, Elena, is purpose enough."

"Not any longer. You of all people must see it, Mother. I need a reason. I need to find it."

Suzanne would understand by and by. But first she had to understand it herself. She was not sure what she was looking for. She didn't intend to go off and join Mother Teresa's order or start licking lepers. Jim had fooled her, in part because she had wanted so badly to believe in passion, in absolute love. That had been her religion. Now she needed a new one. She needed something real to do with the rest of her twice broken life.

33

Suzanne

Suzanne had to go to Framingham to see Maxine, whose case was approaching the court date to hear her appeal. She needed some points of testimony clarified. She also knew her visit was necessary to keep hope alive for Maxine, for whom prison was an unending nightmare.

Maxine looked gaunt, seemingly thinner each time Suzanne saw her, as if she were wasting away, burning up from some internal fever of despair. She had always been a sharp-featured woman, but now she was frighteningly angular. In the two years since her conviction, she had aged ten years. Suzanne felt if she could not work a judicial miracle for Maxine, then she would simply turn her face to the wall and die inside.

At least sitting in the visitors' room with Maxine was some kind of pretense that her life might return to normal, although the assortment of families scattered around the room and the vending machines trying to squeeze intimacy out of a limited time slot was hardly typical family life. Little kids ran around overexcited and the women tried to read hope from the faces of their boyfriends and husbands, mothers and others.

"What happened to your arm?"

Maxine shrugged and looked over her shoulder to make sure no one was listening. "I got shoved and kicked."

"By a guard?"

"Another inmate. They hate me. They think I did it." Maxine's head drooped on her shoulders. "They can't stand people who abuse children. A lot of these women have children outside, and they worry about them. I understand. But they don't believe I'm innocent any more than that jury did."

"We'll win on appeal. Either this time or the next level. You were railroaded. I know that, and sooner or later, a court will recognize it too."

*   *   *

When Suzanne returned, Elena was reading the help-wanted columns with a Magic Marker in her teeth. The house smelled spicy. "Did you make yourself supper?"

"I made supper for both of us. If you're willing to eat it."

"I'll eat anything," Suzanne said. "Thank you."

"I've been keeping it warm. Beef burritos. That okay?"

"Wonderful." Suzanne never ate Mexican food, so she wasn't completely sure what a burrito was, some kind of chip? It sounded as if it should be a small donkey, but not having to cook was a blessing. She had planned to graze on anything she could find in the refrigerator, probably cold and standing up. She heard voices from upstairs. It sounded like Jim yelling.

"I wonder if she took him back," she mused, listening. She couldn't make out any words, only loud voices.

"No," Elena said. "She's not that stupid. I am, but even I won't take him back. He knocked on the door down here, but I wouldn't let him in."

"No good can come from him," Suzanne said fervently, shoveling the food in. "I want to get to the hospital to check up on Beverly."

"I was there," Elena said. "No change." Elena had been going to the hospital every afternoon, while Suzanne took the evening shift.

They both heard Jim when he left, thumping down the stairs cursing. Then he slammed the outer door. Suzanne decided she had to catch Marta before going to the hospital.

Marta answered the door, but she was on the phone. Even across the room, Suzanne could hear Adam yelling through the receiver. "That is the shittiest stupidest thing I ever heard in my life! Is he crazy? Is she crazy?"

"Your father has had affairs before. I forgave him, but I can't this time."

She could not hear Adam's reply. Apparently his voice had dropped to normal decibels.

"No, I can't continue with him this time. I won't!" Marta said firmly.

Suzanne knew that Adam had his caring side. He was wonderful with small children and animals. He was also a master whiner. Adam was superb at sulking and accomplished at getting his way. He took this situation as a personal affront, but he would get over it. He had always been close to his mother, and he would support her no matter what, Suzanne was sure.

"Adam, you're at school. You're twenty and you can surely survive a divorce now. You can see both of us separately when you come home—"

Another long pause. She could hear Adam yelling but not what he was saying.

"Oh, by the way, I'm pregnant."

Marta put down the phone with a deep, prolonged sigh. She rested her hands on her slightly swollen abdomen. "It's good to see you. How's Beverly?"

Suzanne told her and then added, "Have you really thrown Jim out?"

"Really. And he's furious about it."

"How can he be? You caught him in bed."

"Somehow he makes it my fault that I walked in. He keeps talking about me shooting at them."

"Elena says you didn't shoot at them. She says you carefully aimed over their heads. But what were you thinking of?"

"I just wanted to do something. I wanted to express how much at that moment I wanted to see them both dead and bleeding. I wasn't going to do it. Having a baby in prison is not my idea of the way to start a new life."

Suzanne came over to the chair where Marta was sitting and put her arms around her. "Thank you for your forbearance. Elena's a real pisser in some ways, but she's my daughter, and I love her. I couldn't stand to lose her, Marta."

"I know that." Marta put her hand over Suzanne's, where it rested on her arm. "Jim is going to make trouble. He's trying to fight the divorce."

"But you walked in on them."

"He's got Harvey Saunders. Harvey's a tiger."

"Have you reached the point of thinking of a lawyer?"

"I talked to Miles the first night."

They had all known each other for twenty-odd years, since they had worked in the same law collective over a furniture store in an old Cambridge building. Miles was of medium height, medium build, with sandy hair and light brown eyes. He was the sort of man easily overlooked in a crowd, a class, a party. In fact he had married later than any of them, to an ambitious lawyer who went into politics and was now a state representative from the western suburbs. In court no one ever overlooked him twice. He had a deep persuasive voice, polished when he wanted it to be, full of emotion or dry and trenchant. He was actually a fine singer who loved choral music, but in court, he sang solo, and the jury often listened and was moved. While he usually did criminal law, he had handled difficult divorces before. He would push hard for Marta.

"What were you fighting about earlier?"

"He appeared without any notice and started berating me about threatening him. He's all worked up about the shooting. He seems to have fixated on it as something he can hold over me."

"Marta, it was an easily misunderstood gesture. Harvey can use it."

Marta shook her head slowly. "It wasn't as violent as I wanted to be. I'm too sane to do more than the gesture. But I don't want to see Jim outside court and I'm not ready to see Elena yet. . . ."

At the hospital, she sat by Beverly's bed with her briefcase beside her, working, preparing for tomorrow. As if anybody ever could prepare for tomorrow, because the troubles that were pelting, bruising them all in a rain of bloody earth were nothing she had ever anticipated or for which she had in any way prepared. Every few minutes, she put down her paperwork and took Beverly's limp hand in hers. How cold she felt. That worried her. She chafed the hand, held it to her cheek. Every so often she would address Beverly, in case she could hear.

Jake had called her twice. She had not returned his calls. If she dialed his apartment now, she would surely get his answering machine and be able to leave a message that would alert him to her situation. She could not speak with him. She had not an ounce of emotional energy left for him or anyone else. It was absurd. She had finally met a man who was truly interested in her, and she simply did not have time to see him. Her family had closed over her head, and it was all she could do to teach her classes, meet her students, and try to hold on to her cases that were proceeding inevitably to court.

As it happened, she was there at the right moment. Her mother's eyelids fluttered several times as had happened before. Now, however, her eyes opened a slit and she moaned. "Mother," Suzanne said loudly, unsure if Beverly could hear her. "Mother! I'm here."

Beverly moaned again and Suzanne ran into the hall to tell the nurse. Suzanne could not tell if Beverly knew where she was. Suzanne stood by the side of the bed while the nurse checked her mother over, checking pulse and pressure. Then they made her leave. She thought that unfair, since she desperately wanted to find out what kind of shape Beverly was in.

Still, she and Elena mildly celebrated Beverly's return to the living with a couple of big cookies Elena picked up at the local bakery. Suzanne said, "It makes me nervous, him trying to see you."

"Don't worry. It was stupid. I was stupid. Marta and you were stupid to throw us together. He's a sleaze, Mother."

"Did Beverly know what was going on?"

"Well, of course. She was home all day. She liked to know what was going on. It made her feel more . . . real. Connected. In touch."

"She should have told me."

"And betrayed my confidences? Come on. Grandma's always been on my side."

"Someone truly on your side would've advised you to clear out, and fast."

"Grandma's like me. She likes intense emotions and drama. But I'm going to change. I'm going to be calm and mature. I'm going to be like a rock. That's what I'm going to be when I finally grow up: a boulder."

"Elena, precious, you don't have to go from extreme to extreme."

"Maybe I do, Mother. Then someday I'll end up in the golden happy middle. But maybe I can only get there by banging from one side to the other."

She noticed suddenly that all three cats were lying in a heap on the plush chair, clutching one another in sleep. Some peace accord had been reached. Perhaps they understood that chaos had come and things would never be the same. Mao lay between the two larger orange cats, sleeping soundly. At least someone was benefiting from the troubles that had beset her family.

34

Beverly

Beverly woke to blurred grayness, her head throbbing. Her right leg was in a cast. She touched it tentatively, her bad leg. That at least was better than if it were her left leg. She kept blinking but she could not see well, and then she was too exhausted to cling to the narrow rock shelf of consciousness. She slid off and dark waters closed over her.

Suzanne had been there, she remembered that. A strange nurse, Black but not Sylvia. She could not speak. Again, again. She groaned when she thought of how hard she had worked to regain some speech, and now it was gone. She had slid all the way down the glass mountain and lay in a heap at the bottom, worse than before, because her vision was blurred, so how would she read or see the computer screen?

She desperately needed to know what had happened upstairs, when she had tried to climb the stairs. She must find out if Elena was all right. No one had thought to offer her pen and paper and she could not speak. She felt entirely helpless, imprisoned in isolation. They would not let anyone be with her long. Suzanne came and went, nurses and aides and orderlies. Finally Elena came. Elena's face was blurred but her voice was clear and low pitched. "Grandma. Can you make out what I'm saying?" Elena peered at her, bringing her face close to Beverly's. "Okay, if you can understand me, press your finger into my palm."

She pressed her finger into Elena's warm soft palm. Then she traced a question mark again and again.

"Oh, you want to know what happened, right?" Her Elena, bright and sensitive as always, sat beside the bed and told her everything. Beverly was immensely grateful. Nobody had thought to bring her up-to-date. Elena came every day, as did Suzanne. Beverly slept a great deal, if she could call that dark heavy place "sleep," full of fragments that brushed her mind, perhaps fragments of her mind partly exploded, debris floating loose in her.

Beverly could tell that the nurse had an attitude about Elena, who was always being judged by other women. Beverly fiercely wanted to comfort her, to protect her, to show that nurse her solidarity with Elena, but she could not. She supposed everyone in the hospital knew the story. It was easy to pass judgment on women who took chances: bad women they were labeled for being adventurous. Elena's crime had been falling in love with a man who was leading her on. Married men could be dangerous, because they knew women better than bachelors and they had a lot of practice at manipulating a woman. They knew what to say and how to make you feel sorry for them. She had been in that bed several times herself. A married man had a lot of practice in lying successfully to a woman, in making excuses, in making promises that sounded convincing.

They made her get up and hobble to the bathroom. They had to hold her because of her broken leg. If that leg wasn't stupid, she would never have broken it. Strong bones ran in her family. She had never before broken a bone except when her wrist was snapped in a demonstration, but that was intentional. She had healed fast then. A textile mill strike in South Carolina.

All those flowers. People had really cared then. She had been a heroine to the women of the mill. That had felt stronger than the pain of her wrist. She couldn't even remember the pain, but she could recall vividly the cookies. She had been so young then that eating all those cookies had made her face break out. She could still taste the coconut orange cookies one middle-aged woman had brought her with a big red bow left over from Valentine's Day on top.

She had been strong then for such a small woman. She astonished the male organizers, the way she could hold up in a march or a picket line, the way she could work all day and still have the energy for a good rousing speech at night. She had looked far more delicate than she was, but that too had often been to her advantage. She had been roughed up a few times, beaten, especially in the South. The civil rights days had been dangerous. She had felt real fear days and nights and days and nights.

Lying in the narrow hospital bed, she remembered another narrow bed, upstairs in the house of a Black family in Alabama. There was only one loft room and she had been put in it, while the rest of the Lucases doubled up downstairs. Those nights were hot and still and the air was thick, almost wooly in that loft. The sound of a car pausing outside the house choked conversation at once, could wake her from what passed with them all for sleep.

She could see Leander's face vividly, and his sister Marcella, both with slightly uptilted eyes, a tint of red in their hair and skin, the high cheekbones of southern Blacks with an Indian ancestor. She could hear their voices. Marcella had been jailed for two months after a march and then went on a hunger strike for better conditions, losing a third of her body weight. She turned ashen, her skin lifeless. Their mother was fired from her maid's job and had to start taking in laundry. Yet they shared what they had with her. Mrs. Lucas was always claiming she wasn't hungry when there wasn't enough food to go around. She herself lost seven pounds while she was staying with them. She was closest to Marcella, who was twenty. They lived warily, all of them, doing what they had to but always on edge.

Sure enough, one night the Ku Klux Klan threw a fire bomb. It crashed through the window into the kitchen. They managed to put out the fire, although it cost them one of their only blankets. They had to. The fire department stood around and watched the flames, making jokes about niggers and nigger lovers. Leander had been burned, but not badly. They had treated it with ice and grease. She remembered the dog, but she could not think of his name, barking hysterically at the fire. She remembered the taste of greens with a bit of pig fat in them. Yes, she had eaten pig down South. If they had any meat, that was what they had. She never said a word. She could taste those greens with fatback and onions. Mrs. Lucas made a kind of fry bread when there wasn't much else. She could not have refused to eat what they shared with her, for they honored her with their sharing. It was all they had to give, besides their trust and their friendship.

When Beverly woke next, she did not know where she was, and she thought she was in her room upstairs in their little house, Leander and Marcella and their parents, Mr. and Mrs. Lucas, and Leander's girlfriend, Ella with the corn rows. The brown dog with his tail that would slam on the floor like a metronome. The smell of the laundry cooking on the stove and the scorched smell of the iron. She was convinced she was there in that loft room until she tried to move and her leg would not obey her and everything turned gray. Then she remembered it was thirty-five years since she had seen them. Yet their shotgun house with the ladder going up to the loft where she slept felt far more real to her than anything in the hospital. She felt as if she could extend her hand to touch Marcella or Leander, hug Mama Lucas and be engulfed by her warmth, sit on the rough wooden steps patting their big waggy dog, Sugar. She was still that thirty-something New Yorker with the strawberry hair and her big green eyes and her false air of fragility and her daily inexhaustible strength. She had been closer in age to Mama Lucas than to Marcella, but she felt much younger than Mrs. Lucas, and everybody seemed to think she was younger too. The hard life and poor nutrition aged them early and fast. Somewhere in the wreck of her stroke-wracked body that woman with the reddish hair and the peach complexion still abided. Her real life was not here in this sterile place where she had no identity, but out there, somewhere, where things counted and lives were changed, out there where if she could only summon the strength and the willpower, surely she could break through and once again live—live touching others truly and being touched by them, a woman other people might love, might hate, might admire, but never could ignore. Here she was as invisible as dust on the windowsill, and as unimportant.

35

Elena

Elena was glad when Grandma was transferred from the hospital to the rehab center, where it was a lot less depressing and easier to park.

"Yeah, I'm looking for work," she told her grandma, who was propped up awkwardly in a chair, dumped there like a bag of laundry. "My car needed a brake job, so Suzanne had to pay for it, which made me feel totally shitty. But I'm back to my own wheels again. I'm going to get a fucking job somewhere, somehow."

"Hurt?" Grandma was talking but very slowly, laboriously. Her voice sounded as if it had been squashed. It was much worse than before.

"Sometimes. I get depressed when I think how stupid I was. How I could believe so passionately in such a nasty wimp."

"Want . . . home."

"I'll bet you want to get out of here. But the therapy is helping, isn't it?"

Grandma shrugged. She printed on her pad, 2ND TIME, THEY DON'T TRY.

"But you're trying hard."

Grandma shrugged again. She spoke, "Point?"

"You mean, what's the point? So you can get around again. So you can speak to me."

Grandma printed, ONLY YOU UNDERSTAND.

"That's because, you and me, we love each other better than anybody else loves us, Grandma."

Grandma tapped her hand and tried to smile. Her face was twisted and her smile, a grimace, but Elena understood. It was such a rotten thing that the old woman had to go through all this again. Some of the therapists were good, they worked hard, but Elena could see that the orderlies treated her grandma like a sack of flour. They picked her up and put her here or there, they spoke around her, they touched her roughly and unfeelingly, as if she were a piece of furniture. They did not have the patience to wait while she got together the word or two she meant to speak. Elena made a great point of her own presence, to try to protect Grandma if she could, but she knew the effect was short-lived.

"I can't figure out what I want to do."

"Live," Grandma said.

"Yeah, that's cool and everything—like, neither of us is dead. But I have to figure out what I want to do. I can't go on the way I have been." She waited for Beverly's nod. She could explain to her grandma exactly how she felt, as she never could to anyone else. "So now I have to grow up. Mother's a lawyer. Rachel's going to be a rabbi. But I'm nothing. I was thinking for a while maybe I'd go to law school. . . ."

Grandma managed to shake her head vigorously.

"I know, I know. Big mistake. I could never stand it. Too boring. Too in the head. I know."

Grandma nodded. Made a lunge and patted her hand.

"Well, I'm not going to be a doctor or a nurse. I can't stand these places." Elena waved her hand at the Maalox-green walls, mint-flavored antacids. "I can use a computer, but I don't love them, the way Mother does. I just don't love words that much."

"Colors," Grandma said.

"Yeah, I love color. My eyes sink in. But I'm not cut out to be an artist, Grandma. I don't believe in those framed things on the wall, like they mean that much. I hate museums. I feel trapped and coerced. Like someone is yelling in my ear, Appreciate, Appreciate you shithead, you turkey!"

Grandma giggled. Elena loved her even more then. She could not imagine her mother giggling at that. Rachel certainly wouldn't. They would both want her to appreciate! Where did those voices come from anyhow? Grandma was never her conscience. "Grandma, if you were my age, we'd be girlfriends. We are anyhow."

Grandma brought Elena's hand to her lips and tried to kiss it. She could not control her mouth very well and drooled a little. Elena did not mind, although Grandma looked embarrassed and dabbed at the hand, grimacing again. "Don't be embarrassed. Dogs do the same thing, and I like dogs."

That made Grandma giggle again. "Me, dog?"

"No way. Just nice like one."

"Friends." Grandma waved between them.

"To the end."

How Elena hated the Sunday want ads. It gave her a headache just to weigh the *Globe* help-wanted section in her hands and look at all that fine print. There had to be something she could do. Oh, she could probably get a job as a receptionist for a while. Boring, boring. But her looks would get her that, and she would be ultrapolite. She would kiss ass down to the bone for a job. She just could not stand being stone broke. She could feel the wheels grinding in the house. Her mother had never spoken to her of money in her life. Whatever Elena had asked for, she had gotten unless her mother did not think it was good for her. It was strangely human for her mother to admit to money troubles. Suzanne had never told them they could not afford a school or a trip or some coat, probably because Suzanne always felt guilty, as if she wasn't a good enough mother. Well, she wasn't a great one for sure, although Elena wondered if she would do any better. With Jim, that loser, she had assumed they'd have children. Life was so fucking weird and malignant. She knew for sure that Suzanne had to be really hard up to mention money to her, so she was determined to carry a bit of the load.

Monday morning as she was doing her laundry, she saw Jim hanging around in the backyard by the oak tree, as if to catch her. Yellow leaves all over the ground like fallen light. He didn't go to his office Monday, of course. He looked like a forlorn kid, like a kid who ought to be in school and didn't know what to do with himself. For a moment, watching from behind the curtain in Beverly's room, she felt sorry for him. She felt a moment's tug of pity. She made herself turn away. *It didn't mean anything.* He tried to get into the house and pounded on the door, but she lay low. Marta had changed the locks, giving them new keys to the front door and the grade door in back. She stayed in her room till he finally drove off.

Two police detectives showed up at the house just as she was about to go to a job interview. Jim was trying to cause trouble for Marta about shooting into the wall that day.

"She didn't shoot at us. Understand, she was standing at the foot of the bed and we were in it. Naked. She'd come in to tell her husband she was pregnant, and there he was all over me. But she didn't shoot *at* us. She raised the gun and shot way over our heads. It was like a symbolic act, understand, but she hadn't lost it, and she actually was very careful not to hurt us. Personally I would have drilled both of us if I'd been her. We both deserved it. It wasn't assault. If anything, we assaulted her."

"You don't want to lodge a complaint against her?"

"I'm guilty. She isn't guilty of anything except trusting two people she had every reason to trust—except we weren't worth it." She would come through for Marta: it was the honorable thing to do. It would serve Jim right. What was he trying to pull off anyhow? "We were never in danger and she wasn't even threatening us. It was like setting off firecrackers. No, I wasn't scared. I was just ashamed."

Because she wanted money, wanted it badly, she took the first job she was offered, a receptionist's job at a group of financial analysts and investment counselors who shared a suite of offices off Route 128 in Needham. It was about twenty minutes from the house, and she would be going against traffic coming and going. The pay was ridiculous, but she wouldn't hesitate to quit if she found something better.

"Elena, you didn't have to take a low-level job like that. I can find you something with friends of ours," Suzanne said, dutifully eating the chicken Elena had fried.

"I have to take it. I need to be working. Your friends would be terrified to hire me, for fear I'd fuck their husbands. You know that."

"Maybe around the university I can find something."

"Whatever. I'll quit if something better comes up. Mother, I'm not trained to do a thing. I'm useless. I have classes toward four different majors besides psychology, and I don't know how to do anything a boss with a brain would pay me for."

"Do you want to go back to school?" Suzanne asked helplessly.

"If I do, I'll go in the evening. If you can get me a deal. Not otherwise. And I haven't the faintest goddamn idea what I'd study, anyhow. I seem to have no interest in life beyond fucking everything up."

"Elena, you've been very good since the . . . disaster. I know you don't want to hurt Marta more. I know she doesn't want to hurt you. You've shown real strength. I believe in you now more than I ever did. I want you to know that."

Elena shrugged, not knowing how to respond. It was a compliment for sure, but she had always been poor at receiving compliments on anything besides her looks. That's what she had always been admired for—by men. She was used to her mother trying to guilt trip her, run her life, give her moldy advice, warn her about dire consequences. She was not used to praise. It embarrassed her, and it also made her feel squishy, as if she might snivel. "So how's your boyfriend these days? I haven't seen him around. He didn't bail out, did he?"

Elena was going over her wardrobe, sewing on buttons, catching up an unraveled hem. Monday she started her new job, and she found dealing with her clothes soothing. Then she heard the key in the lock and went into the living room, startled. It was 9:20. It was that young guy, Jaime, who worked as her mother's assistant. "You have a key?" Yeah, he'd been at Passover.

"Sure, for when she needs me to fetch. She needs her other glasses. Appeals court starts at ten-forty today, so I have to hustle."

"You're her errand boy?" Elena gave him a smile with her dig. She had never really spent time with him. He was almost beautiful.

"I'm whatever it takes." He sauntered into Suzanne's office and found her glasses beside her computer. "She hardly ever forgets anything. This is a first." He looked sideways at Elena. "Have you ever watched your mother in action?"

"Mother? No. Why?"

"Aren't you curious? She's good. She told me you're starting your new . . . career . . . Monday, so why not come along with me today?"

"Wouldn't she be pissed if I barged in?"

"She won't even notice. She's focused, Elena, very focused. Why don't you come and watch?"

She was suddenly ashamed that she had so little interest in what her mother did for a living, plus she was also a little intrigued by Jaime. He reeked confidence for a kid two years younger than herself. He had her mother's car and he drove it with assurance. Her mother didn't lend her the car without a big fuss, while here he was acting as if he owned it. For a moment she had a pang of jealousy. Who was this kid that her mother trusted him so much?

"You keep looking at me. Interested in what you see?"

"Mildly," she said with a grin. "I thought you were gay."

"I don't rule anybody out because of age, sex, or race. I'm an equal opportunity fuck. . . . Actually I'm straight. Interested?"

She just smiled. He really was cute. She had never been involved with anyone younger. She would be in control: maybe she would like that for a change. Maybe after she moved out of her mother's house, she would look him up. Men did not tend to forget her, and she doubted if she would forget Jaime.

The building was located on a narrower plaza off the bleak windswept wasteland of City Hall Plaza. The crescent-shaped building that divided this plaza from the street was new, but the courthouse was not. The lobby was shabby, and after they passed through the metal detector and into the old elevator, it only got worse. Cops all around, people shuffling along, suits rushing past. It was a dreary building badly kept up, full of dirty corridors and crowded offices that hadn't been painted for thirty years. It smelled of old smoke and damp boots and decaying paper, seedy upholstery, the stench of anxiety and fear.

However, the courtroom where the appeals were being heard was a different world. This room was clean and well lit. The ceiling was high; blue velvet curtains hung behind the dais, where three big empty black leather chairs faced microphones. Behind the chairs was a bookcase of shiny law books, resplendent on display. The same blue velvet curtains hung on three high narrow windows. The room was wood paneled, with portraits of old guys in black robes hung on both walls. Jaime went up to her mother, who was sitting in the front row of benches outside the dividing waist-high wall. Suzanne took the glasses and shoved them on her nose. She did not even notice Elena. She could spy on her mother without having to explain, for it did not seem that Jaime was going to tip her mother to her presence.

Jaime handed Suzanne a brief, a trial transcript (all things she had often seen around the house since she was a baby), and a yellow pad covered with Suzanne's scrawl. Then he took his seat in the back row with Elena. They sat around for twenty minutes, while Jaime entertained her with commentary on what would happen and pointed out the reporters to her. Then the judges, three old guys wearing black robes just like on TV, came in, and everybody bounced to their feet. A woman intoned, "Hear ye, hear ye" and gave this archaic-sounding announcement of the court being in session for citizens to present their pleas. But she didn't see any ordinary citizens, only defense lawyers and prosecutors, officers of the court and judges. Marta was sitting in the front row of the benches. Some reporters were taking notes, yawning, taking more notes. Jaime told her they weren't usually present, but they had come in because of Maxine's notoriety.

She supposed she expected Perry Mason, but Suzanne stood almost on tiptoe in front of the podium facing the judges and most of what she said Elena could not follow. "Point three in my brief." "On page one hundred and twelve of the transcript." "On the top of page one hundred and eighty-nine." "Point four of my brief." Cases. One of the judges rose at one point and consulted one of the shiny-looking law books in the bookcase that stood between the blue velvet ceiling-to-floor draperies behind the dais. There was no jury. Nobody talked about guilt or innocence. It was weird. One judge looked half asleep. The other was leaning way back in his chair, although he nodded or grunted occasionally. The other was talkative, addressing her mother as Suzanne and quoting case citings. Her mother spoke for fifteen minutes and was interrupted seven or eight times. Suzanne looked so little and cute up there talking fast, taking what they could hand her, that Elena thought for the first time that what her mother did was actually hard, it was a constant battle.

Then she sat down and a woman prosecutor in a gray suit stood at the podium. The judges were very nice to her. Elena took a particular dislike to the one in the middle, who had asked her mother only one question but who seemed to coo over the young prosecutor. The prosecutor might have been his tall thin blond daughter, slightly horsey faced with an accent Elena had heard in the restaurant, that she supposed they learned in prep school—because she doubted anybody naturally spoke that way. The prosecutor was maybe fifteen years younger than her mother. They were being so sweet to her, all of them awake now. They did not ask her the same kind of tough questions they stuck Suzanne with. Elena wanted to kick the judges. Who would ever guess this was supposed to be a hot case? She was convinced, still, that Suzanne had won, because she had been so together, so fierce, so positive. She had answered every hard one they had thrown at her.

"There won't be an opinion for months," Jaime hissed as the prosecutor sat down and the next lawyer came to the podium.

"How do you think it went?"

"Not so good. I know Suzanne's disappointed."

Elena stood. "I'll take the MBTA home."

"Don't you want a ride?"

"Not really. See you." She would tell her mother later that she had sat in, but she felt she had intruded enough. If she could not say that she understood any better what Suzanne did, at least she knew now where it happened. That was something. It gave her a picture in her head.

36

Suzanne

The Friday before Suzanne was finally to argue Maxine's appeal, Miles wanted to see her in his office.

Miles, who was acting as Marta's lawyer, repeated patiently, "He was trying to invoke the domestic abuse statute."

"Bastard!" Suzanne said. "We both worked for that. There's even some language in the statute that Marta wrote. How can he call walking in on your husband humping a younger woman in your bed and reacting, domestic abuse."

"Assault with a dangerous weapon with the aim of doing malicious harm, as between two partners in a domestic arrangement. But Elena saved Marta's ass. She insisted that Marta never intended more than a symbolic act. The row of bullet holes far up the wall proves that, so the prosecutor told Jim he doesn't have a case."

"It's a miracle she didn't lose the baby."

"It looks as if we're out of the woods, at least until he starts bringing it up in the divorce proceedings." Miles rose from behind his desk and went around to the other side, resting his behind on the edge just in front of her. "So, when's your court date on the day care case appeal?"

"Next Thursday. I've been at the rehab center so much, everything else is going to hell. I have to get my act together."

"Marta too. Your lives have been a bad soap opera, Suzanne. Now Jim's determined to make trouble. I want you to keep that in mind and make that daughter of yours understand too. It hasn't to do with custody of Adam, because after all he's twenty, but the unborn girl. . . . Now I have to know from you, Jim doesn't want a divorce. Does Marta, really? What's your take on this. Is she reacting out of spite? Will she regret it after the baby's born?"

"I have to sit down and talk to her."

"No kidding. Well, get on it and tell me. I don't want her to divorce him while she's pregnant with his child unless she's damned sure that's the path she wants to take—not for right now, but for next year and the next two decades."

Driving to school, she thought about the question Miles had posed her. She had not been able to forgive Sam for his infidelity, but their marriage had dried up by then. She had not felt she required a husband strongly enough to have one who preferred another woman. She had been stung, betrayed, with an almost physical sense of despisal. But Marta might still love Jim; she was, after all, bearing his child. If she herself could forgive Elena, perhaps Marta could forgive Jim. She had been with Beverly so much, she had neglected the support she should be offering Marta. They were supposed to be together in court Thursday for Maxine's appeal.

Suzanne gave over the visiting of Beverly to Elena for the weekend to review her brief and once again go over the videotapes of the children's testimony and the records of the two therapists and assistant prosecutor with the children. This was a case she found herself caring about intensely. The more her friends argued with her and colleagues and acquaintances attacked her for taking it on, the more she studied the records, the more determined she was to secure justice for Maxine and get her out of Framingham. Marta told her she'd be present. Marta knew how much Suzanne cared about this case and how controversial it was, so she would lend her moral support.

When they walked into the courtroom Thursday, there was a stir among the court personnel. Marta sighed. "Here I come, the one woman parade. I should have worn red. I think everybody in Boston has heard what happened."

In the car, she had discovered she'd forgotten the glasses that did not slide down her nose and sent Jaime back for them. "Lawyers are terrible gossips."

"Sex and violence. Pregnancy and betrayal. I hate feeling like such a patsy."

The three judges entered and they rose. She began to focus. She ran over the basic arguments in her head. The children's testimony had been rehearsed, coerced, and heavily edited. The defendant had never been permitted to confront her accusers. There was no cross-examination, no chance to test the coherence of the stories. Maxine had not been granted her full rights by law. Further, evidence of the child witnesses had been tainted by the process by which it had been obtained—repeated questioning, which amounted to coaching and suborning of their testimony.

If the conviction was overturned, the state would appeal; if the conviction was not overturned, she would appeal. Either way, it was going to be a long process. She would be living with this uncomfortable case for the next year or two. Well, Maxine had been living with it a lot longer, ever since she had first been accused by the parents of one of the children in her day care center, of sexual abuse of their son.

As the oldest judge Laplaine had a private conversation with the clerk of the court, she mustered her concentration. She owed Maxine that. Distraction was the antithesis of the focus required to win. She had drawn a judge who was new to the district court of appeals, a man in his early sixties from the North Shore who had been a prosecutor before being elevated to the bench. Then there was Judge Corrigan, just turned seventy. Suzanne had pleaded before him several times. He had the reputation of being fair and learned, but with the disconcerting habit of pulling cases from nowhere. Suzanne had never been caught unprepared, but she knew Marta had once been slapped with a defeat because Judge Corrigan cited a case Marta had never heard of and could not argue. The oldest and chief justice was Laplaine, a little deaf, fair if he followed you but known to space out. Sometimes he dozed with his eyes open. Other times he was sharp, the most conservative of the three, although she did not know how that would affect this case. He was strict in his interpretations. He had given her a hard time with Phoebe, but in the end she had won.

At her cue, Suzanne rose. She had her fifteen minutes. "Good morning. May it please the court, I am Suzanne Blume representing Maxine Rodriguez. I'd like to reserve three minutes for rebuttal. . . ."

Suzanne and Marta sat at a corner table in a seafood restaurant in Faneuil Hall. They both ordered broiled salmon, a salad, and a glass of Evian water.

"So, how do you think it went?" she asked Marta.

"I thought Corrigan was with you. I saw him nod once. He didn't hit you with one of his obscure case citations. He seemed interested." Marta frowned, considering.

"I wasn't sure about Laplaine. I couldn't tell if he was even listening until he asked that question about my interpretation of the rules of evidence. I felt he was iffy. What did you think about the new guy, Beamer?"

"I can't read him yet. I've never argued before him. He was a tough prosecutor and I thought he might be leaning to their side." Marta rubbed her eyes. "It always takes a while to figure out a new judge. Yes, he was a prosecutor, but some judges with that background are harder on prosecutors who haven't done a sterling job. Until Beamer has a track record, how can we read him?"

"Well, we'll find out in a few months. They're considering the appeal, but they're not letting Maxine out in the meantime. I was hoping she could recover her health." Suzanne sighed. "Do you think I did a decent job for her?"

"I thought you were superb. It's partly political, you know. The AG put his weight behind this case."

She considered Marta's answer and her stomach clenched. Marta did not think she had won. What could she have done differently? Had she not been prepared enough? She did not know how much more prison time Maxine could endure. Had her life gotten in the way of her case?

Marta was saying, "I was surprised to see Elena in court."

"*Elena?* Are you sure?"

"You didn't notice? She was sitting with Jaime in back."

"How strange. I'll have to ask her tonight. Marta, we have to talk about what happened." Suzanne propped her chin into her cupped hand. "I don't know where to start. You're my best friend. Elena I love dearly as you know, but she has this talent for creating dangerous messy dramas."

Marta groaned. She pulled at her gray-blond hair that was always elegant, like the color of furniture in Beverly's apartment in the fifties—Hollywood oak, she thought it had been called. Bleached oak, just that silvery ash blond. "Jim is older and is supposed to know better."

"Marta, don't you really think I should take Elena and clear out?"

"I don't want Jim to fuck up my life more than he has. And I don't want anybody downstairs but you. While I'm not ready to forgive and forget, I feel less angry with Elena because of how she dealt with the police. That saved me a lot of grief, and I appreciate it."

"Elena's not seeing him, you know. She's not even talking with him. She's bitterly disillusioned."

"Good. Let's hope it stays that way."

"The worst thing is, Marta, I suspected this maybe two months ago and I confronted Elena. She persuaded me I was crazy. I kept watching them together and I couldn't see any sign that something might be going on."

"I never caught on myself. But it's nice to know I wasn't abnormally dense."

They both picked at their food. Then they walked together, slowly. It was a clear sunny day, one of those cool glassy days of October in Boston. The sky seemed infinite over them. The air was fresh and almost squeaked in the lungs. Only her life, she thought, was full of disorder and murky with the odor of unsolved problems. Suzanne took Marta's arm. "So how are you feeling about being pregnant?"

"Am I still cool with it? Well, I admit I had second thoughts right afterward—"

"It's late but not impossible to do something about it. It still seems to be a pretty risky business, having a baby at our age."

"No! She's my baby. I've always wanted a daughter. I still do."

Suzanne nodded, tightening her grip on Marta's arm. The baby who had died had been a girl. Then came the miscarriages. "But do you really want to raise this baby alone?"

"Oh, he'll insist on visitation. Besides, I won't be alone. I have you. Don't I?"

"Of course. But you don't feel the baby needs two parents?"

"Yes. You and me. Plus Adam. He'll shape up and come through. He's just dazed and pouting for the minute. Jim will make demands. It isn't as if I'm trying to keep him away from the baby. But I don't want to go through my life having a husband who prefers other women to me. The business of making love in our bed was more than I can stomach. I could forgive him once, but this was too close to home."

"Forgive him once?"

"Do you imagine I never knew why he was fired? I just thought it was better for everybody if I pretended I didn't. I thought he'd learned a lesson. I thought it was a onetime aberration. Now I wonder how many more there were I never knew about. I wonder about the receptionist before Elena. I wonder about his patients, but I don't lie awake wondering, and if I stay married to him, I will."

"I know. When I discovered Sam was having that affair, I just couldn't recover from it. I kept thinking, well, if he would rather be with her, why are we together? I kept being haunted by images of them in bed together. I kept listening to everything he said and wanting to cross-examine him. Oh, so you say you went to the dentist. Exactly what time was your appointment? Well, a filling shouldn't take more than half an hour. . . ."

"We're going to be on short rations. Babies are expensive. Adam will be in school for years yet. Maybe we should take in roomers. Oh, Adam's coming home this weekend."

"He sounded martyred on the phone."

"Well, he's going to have to put his bony shoulder to the family wheel. We're all in deep shit, and he's going to have to help rather than suffer at the top of his lungs." Marta sounded cheerful, in spite of her words. "I hope you win this case."

"I have to. If they don't overturn the conviction, I think it'll kill Maxine. That really scares me."

"You did the best you could for her under frankly impossible circumstances."

"You don't think we have a prayer, do you? I have to start preparing for the SJC." The Supreme Judicial Court: the highest court in the state. But would Maxine hold out that long?

37

Beverly

Beverly's words beat around in her head like birds trapped in a house, banging themselves on the windows, able to perceive where they wanted to go but trapped by an invisible barrier. She could not think of a damned thing to look forward to. She would be lucky if she could drag herself around in a walker again. She knew how slow and painful and partial was the recovery from a stroke like hers. She had enjoyed certain things after her first stroke: being with Elena, E-mail, playing around on the Internet, and chatting to the degree she had been able to with Sylvia. Those had been her pleasures. She did not think she would be talking again soon. Sylvia had gone off to another job. Elena would probably leave now, to get away from Marta's hostility. Her vision was too blurry to read a computer screen, although she could more or less see faces. She could distinguish between the bored nurses and orderlies and the truly nasty ones, and the couple of nice young women who tried to make contact.

She was worried about her darling. Elena was unnaturally quiet and broody. Every day she came to the rehab center to sit with her. Elena felt guilty about the fall, and Beverly had not managed to persuade her that to take responsibility for an accident was silly, unnecessary. It was like coming around a corner and bumping into an oncoming truck.

She did not believe in sulking, so she tried, to the degree she was able, to convey good spirits. But when she was alone, she wept. Sometimes she thought she would choke to death from her tears and the way they made her nose and sinuses block up. It would have been perfect if she had never wakened from that coma, just slid from sleep into death and vanished.

Her friend Dave had died in a coma. He had been struck by a scab's truck on a picket line and never regained consciousness. He had left a living will, and for once, the doctors respected it—probably because there was no money in his family. The union was picking up the tab, but there were times it paid to be poor. She knew he would have wanted to go out the way he did, a light turned off, not to be kept like a big turnip in a hospital bed.

Dave and she had gone out for Chinese-Cuban. He loved black beans. When he was younger, his hair was black like those beans, like Elena's. Glossy hair, his complexion ruddy, always a little weathered, and those gray eyes: they went right through her. Was it after the garbage strike? No, it had been a demonstration. Something about welfare. He'd had a scar on his right hand, crossing the back of it, dark red and slightly raised. For some reason, she had never asked him how he got it. She remembered the feel of that scar when she was touching his hand, when he was caressing her. They had never really had an affair, just gone to bed a couple of times. He was no great shakes in bed. Too much in a hurry. It was one item on a list. Too bad. He had been gorgeous to look at. She had gone to bed with him twice, no, three times, each time hoping it would be better, that he would be more involved, more sensual, less abrupt. Then she had decided it was pointless, and that they would just stay friends, which they had, until the end. She was glad he could not see her as she was now. She refused to look at herself in the hand mirror they gave her. That was not her face. Her hair was growing out gray again.

When she thought of her face, she thought of herself when she had been at her peak. For her that had come on the late side, say thirty to forty. Everyone had thought she was younger than she was, but when she had truly been younger, she had not had the confidence, the knowledge of men, to do much with her looks. No, her glory days had been in her thirties and early forties. She had worn a red rinse in her hair. Red hair, green eyes. Suzanne should tint her hair red. She would look much more interesting, but Suzanne had never listened to her when she tried to tell her how to capitalize on her features, how to present herself, how to dress and walk and smile. She had done her best to pass on tips to her daughter, although her hard-won know-how had been rejected every time. It was sad. Suzanne just refused to learn from Beverly, when if she had taken a little advice, she could have had so much more fun. A man like Victor would have gone off anyhow, but she could have kept Sam on the hook far longer if she had known how to play him. Suzanne just shut down whenever Beverly tried to pass on a few good words. If Beverly knew anything, it was men.

Whatever she tried to give her child, Suzanne never seemed to want. Instead she felt as if Suzanne wished she was more like her sister Karla, a homebody, a lump, a *balebusteh*, a grade school teacher with sentimental left politics, rife with superstition. It was her own fault for leaving Suzanne so often with Karla, but it had been out of the question to take her little girl into some of the dangerous situations where she was working as an organizer, particularly in the South. Those Klansmen didn't care if they shot or burned a child instead of an adult. Perhaps they liked it better. She could not understand them, those men so driven by hate and malice and pride, so ready to maim and kill in the name of their skin. More than once she had thought she would die there, in the

South. She had one of the lawyers with the civil rights movement draw up a will for her. She had little to leave, but she wanted it clear that Karla was to be Suzanne's guardian. Once during a march, she had looked up and realized she was in the bead of a man with a rifle standing on an overpass. Then for some reason he laughed instead and did not shoot her. Later she heard he had shot someone else, a young man from Chicago. They never caught him. They usually didn't.

How could she have lived her life so near the edge, so fully, so passionately, and be stuck now in a bed with no more ability to communicate than a worm or a cauliflower? Her voice had been her weapon, her tool. She had been valued by others for her ability to marshal the right words and say them passionately in a ringing voice. Her voice had never been called shrill, a full womanly voice that carried into a crowd. Without her voice, she was indeed crippled. Soon she would not remember what her own voice had sounded like, low pitched and rich in quality that men had compared to honey.

When the doctors or the nurses discussed her, they emphasized it was her second stroke, as if that proved she was careless, in a category of those easily dismissed. Maybe they tried hard with the first-stroke victims, but if it happened again, it was no longer worth their trouble. There was something dismissive in the label. Second-time loser. Second time around. Secondhand. They used to call imperfect merchandise seconds. She was certainly imperfect merchandise.

She wanted out of the rehab center, but going back to Suzanne's was not hugely attractive. Her own life had been demolished, like an old tenement where people had lived for generations and raised their families and faced their troubles. Now it was a parking lot. Now she was parked in this bed. She could taste her despair. It was bitter tea in her mouth.

38

Suzanne

Suzanne read Rachel's E-mail with an increasing sense of separation, physical and mental. Suzanne had been told about a certain kind of rapture, a form of temporary infatuation, that came over people in Jerusalem. She was accustomed to a high level of intimacy with Rachel, and she missed it. They were inhabiting different universes at the moment. Each of them regarded the other's preoccupations as intrusions. Worse than tangential. Irrelevant.

Dear Mom,

Now I know where the old legend of the streets of gold comes from: here. In the late afternoon, the streets near the Old City seem to be made of old gold. Sometimes they seem almost edible to me, like peanut brittle. It seems a pity to walk on them, yet people have for thousands of years.

Sometimes I feel drunk with breathing (and sometimes just plain sick because of the smog from the cars and trucks that gathers in the bowl of the city). But when the exhaust doesn't get to me, the scents make me giddy.

Jerusalem smells of pine, or maybe it's cedar, and of rosemary. When I think how you and Marta used to try to keep one pitiful pot of rosemary going all winter in the kitchen window, it makes me giggle. Here it grows like a weed. They use it for ground covers on hills. They use it for hedges, the way we use privet. Also their gardens are full of lavender. What we cherish as prize little specimens grow everywhere here fiercely as poison ivy in Massachusetts.

We were sitting on a hill near the kibbutz where Michael's friend lives, and I realized we were sitting on thyme. It was all over the ground there. I don't know if they planted it or if it grows wild, but truly, here even the weeds are holy and wonderful. I really do have a desire to kiss the ground sometimes, like some people do when they get off the plane. Wherever we go, I feel the past walking with us, shining through the present, so that at times, everything seems lit from within.

As for us, I think we will be married in late November or early December. We have to decide with the rebbe next week what would be convenient for him, and then I can give you the date. You should make reservations at once, then. It will be early enough in December so you won't run into all the Christians coming for their holidays.

How was she going to make Rachel understand she could not afford flying to Israel herself, let alone with anybody else in the family? She would have to disappoint her daughter, who was never demanding, never surly. She felt rotten, but she also felt trapped. She was plunging headfirst into debt, and there were more expenses coming. She would have to sit down and figure out her situation exactly. Maybe it wasn't as bad as she thought.

Rachel's next E-mail was less ecstatic.

I am really shocked at both Elena and Marta. I can understand Marta better. After all, pregnancy makes some women's tempers short. How is she now? Is she really going to divorce Jim? I am writing her separately. Marta has always been like a really close aunt to me, and I can't even remember a time she was not there, even before we lived together. I know she will be a good mother to her baby, but I also remember how hard you told me it was for you to raise Elena alone. I am worried for Marta and she is always in my thoughts and prayers.

Elena will never cease to amaze me, what she decides to give herself to, what she pursues, and what she flees from. She is my own sister, but I think there is something perverse in her which leads her on dangerous paths and into darkness of her own making. I understand that she didn't know that Marta was expecting, but she certainly knew Jim was married. What did she hope would happen? How did she justify it to herself? I try to imagine, and I can't.

I am less surprised at him. He has always had a wandering eye, and he used to put his arms around me more than I was comfortable with. He always seemed like an old man to me. I mean, he was my "uncle." Everyone has uncles who are just a little too familiar, so I didn't see it as a big problem. Like relatives who insist on kissing you on the mouth when you don't know them that well. Michael's family are big kissers. It's hard for me to get used to, but I resist showing discomfort. It's my fault for being too stiff and formal with people.

This is a great place to work on being overly formal and distant, because everybody talks to you as if they were family and had the right to yell at you and criticize you to your face and give you advice. Everyone from the guy behind the counter in the coffee bar to the cab driver who took us from the airport the very first day to the woman who cuts my hair, off of Ben Yehuda near Cat's Corner where all the kids hang out. She is planning my wedding for me, without my desire or input. At least she thinks she is. She has cut my hair all differently. I will have a picture taken to send you. We don't have a new camera yet, since Michael's was stolen. I wonder if we should ask for a camera as an early wedding present, as we could sure use one here, hint, hint. Maybe I should ask Dad, what do you think?

Suzanne sat at her desk going over bills. Money was still hemorrhaging. She had to find a way to cut costs; she had to find a way to make more money. Of course the simplest solution would be to leave the university and go back into private practice full-time, but if she did that, she would have no time at all for her daughters, her mother, Jake, her life. Herself. She had lived that way when she was younger. About to turn fifty, she found it unappealing. Stick your head in the buzz saw. The total unreflective life.

Still, she would have to cut back on pro bono work. What a choice. Be good to your mother or be useful to the people who really need your help with the courts and the law. It should not be a choice anyone had to make. It was unfair. People got old. People had strokes, heart attacks, developed cancers. It should not come as such a financial shock to a family. Something was wrong with the whole system of health delivery when taking care of a family member could bankrupt you in a few years. She did not know what to do. Everything she was earning, she was spending, and her savings were eroding at a frightening rate. When her savings were gone and her investments cashed in, she would have no cushion for disaster and trouble; and where would the money come from then for Beverly's care? She could complain to no one except to Jake, when he was around, since she hardly felt she could dump on Marta, and it seemed tactless to complain to Karla. Would Rosella step in if something went wrong with Karla? When something went wrong. Rosella's family's financial resources were meager, but Karla was already living with her.

Costs. Okay, drop the rod and gun club. She wasn't going to be shooting with Marta. Cut back to basic cable. She never had time to watch movies anyhow. Less takeout? But who would do the cooking? If she was to litigate more lucrative cases, she would not have time to make even the few meals she did. Elena was going to have to pick up some of the slack. Less dry cleaning, somehow, but she had to be absolutely neat and polished for court.

It was clear that she could not fly to Israel for Rachel's wedding. Maybe Rachel and Michael could wait till they got home. Rachel would be incredibly disappointed, but to fly over would cost several thousand just for herself. She did not know when Beverly would be back home. She did not know what kind of care Beverly would need. Suzanne plunged her face into her hands and sighed. She felt run over. She got up and went into the living room.

"Elena," she said, standing over the couch. Then she thought better of their positions and took a seat in the armchair.

Elena opened her eyes. "I'm trying to learn to meditate."

"Really?" Suzanne tried not to sound skeptical. "Does it help?"

"Sometimes. I should take a class. Marta should learn to meditate."

"I think we should stay off the subject of Marta."

Elena stretched with feral grace, arching her back. Elena had never gone through an awkward age, as Rachel and she herself had—sometimes she wondered if she had ever grown out of it.

"Elena, we have money problems. We're spending much faster than we're earning. We have to cut costs. Beverly's condition is bankrupting me."

"Just don't let Grandma catch on to that."

"I have no intention of speaking to her about the situation. You and I have to solve it."

Elena seemed fascinated by the idea of cooking. "I used to see the cooks whip up dishes at the restaurant. I used to think like I could be a chef, except it's so sweaty and they all have mad dog tempers and throw knives around the kitchen. Besides, I don't want to go back to working in a restaurant. Too many drugs around. Too much nightlife."

"Well, cooking for you, me, and Beverly won't take chef's school."

"You have to let me cook the way I like it. No tofu. No turkey burgers. And at least sometimes I get to make things hot."

"If you cook, you choose what we eat. Agreed."

"I can do it." Elena looked pleased with herself. "I'll take over the grocery shopping too."

"That would truly help." Suzanne had expected a fraught conversation, that Elena would feel martyred and coerced. Finally she said that.

"No." Elena propped her head on her knuckles. "It's kind of sweet that you need me. You've always been so supercompetent, I never felt useful. That's why I didn't mind taking care of Grandma on Mondays. Besides, I love her. I like the way we have to manage together. I'm talented at living on shit and air. I've had a lot of practice. I never did like taking money from you once I was out of college, so a lot of time I was getting by on hope. I can cut our food bills in half. Now that I'm working, I can kick in something toward the electric and phone bills."

It proved much harder to talk to Rachel. The phone call had to be set up by E-mail in advance, because of the time difference.

"Mother, I'm not going to be married three or four times, so if you miss the first, you can't catch the next showing."

"Couldn't you wait till you get back to the States? It's only till May."

"You're just trying to get me to put my wedding off. You tried that when I was home."

"Rachel, my back is to the wall financially. I'm spending more than I'm making. If I borrow money to go to Israel for your wedding, I don't see how I can ever pay it back—and Beverly is going to be living here soon, more dependent on me than ever."

"It won't feel like I'm really married if you aren't there, Mother. It won't feel right."

"Then please wait till you come home, because I don't have the money to go there."

"I'm not going to put off the marriage. It's time for us to get married. I'll never in my life meet anyone else I want to marry. Michael and I, we're two of a kind. We're soul mates. He's my *chassen*, my intended, my *bashert*. I won't take a chance on losing him, on things coming apart."

"Couldn't you put it off for a few months?"

"It's complicated enough. We have to go before the rabbinical court and prove we're Jews and single and so on. It's a formality, but we have to do it to get a marriage license. We're trying to get an appointment soon. It's like a dream, to be married here. Whenever I think of my wedding, which is going to be so beautiful, I want to share it with you. There'll be dancing, Mother, and local wine and great food and friends we've made here that I want you to meet. We're writing vows in Hebrew."

"Rachel, I want to be there. I want desperately to be there. But I can't see my way out of this hole. All I see are the walls of increasing debt around me."

"You'll be in our prayers, Mother. You, Grandma, Marta, . . . and Elena."

Oh, great, Suzanne thought, but she rebuked herself. Religious attention was what Rachel had to offer. "Thank you. We'll get through all this somehow." Her words felt like sawdust in her mouth.

She was lecturing her Feminist Legal Theory class. "As a woman, empathy is one of your strengths. As a lawyer, it can destroy you. Empathize with the victim, and you've lost your momentum as a defense attorney, whose role is defined as speaking for the client and giving him the best defense possible.

"As a lawyer, you're trained at arguing, you're practiced at making points, you're good at turning an argument back on a person, picking holes in stories, cross-examining.

"As a mother or a lover or a wife, these skills and habits are dangerous and undesirable. They can and will destroy personal relationships. Don't think being a lawyer won't change you. It already has. You don't think the same way, you don't talk the same way. You will not act the same way."

As she spoke, she flashed back to the last year with Sam. All her lawyerly observational skills had gone into cracking the facade of their marriage until she proved that he was having an affair, until she knew almost as much about that affair as Sam did. Smart? Maybe. Painful? Absolutely.

Out to California for another damned postponement of this stupid trial. It just goes on and on and on. My lawyer will die of old age before they drop the charges or we finally go to trial. I expected to be flying to Ethiopia, but the court won't allow me out of the country. This is killing me by inches. I'm one of those travelers who are very moved by Africa, and I've never been to Ethiopia. I'm supposed to be useful around water issues, but will I ever get there? I know it's the lumber interests that are screwing me, but what good does it do to know that? Anyhow, at least I'll see you in a couple of weeks. Change of venue refused. Preliminary motions go on. Both sides jockeying for some arcane advantage.

A 10:00 P.M. phone call. "It's not so bad," he said, "this occasionality. Is it so bad? After all, do you want a husband demanding you do the laundry, pay the bills, rub his neck, have supper on the table?"

"No." She didn't even have to think about it. "Like you, I was married once. It was a mess. I don't have time." She loved the sound of his voice in her ear. She closed her eyes when she spoke to him on the phone, lying in bed. "My marriage to Sam died of neglect, like a forgotten goldfish."

"I suppose I have time for a wife who'd stay home, but she'd tire of me fast. I had a live-in girlfriend in Berkeley. While I was in China, she took up with her tae kwon do teacher. She saw me about as often as you do, except for sleeping time. Women who have children want a father for them. Women who don't, want to have them. Everybody wants a person who's there—and as you have observed, I'm with you only now and then. But you're the same way."

"Things are a little easier with Elena helping. I'm getting the advantage of her guilt. She's working now. She's trying. She cooks four nights a week, which is all I'm generally able to eat with her."

"Is she a good cook?"

"I wouldn't go that far. But I'm not about to complain. Food made for me is good. Food I have to prepare is bad."

His dry chuckle in her ear. "The strange thing is, you really are good in the kitchen."

"In another life."

He was silent for a moment, and then his voice was ironically dreamy. "Maybe we'll both retire at sixty-five or seventy and sit and stare at each other and the TV. . . . I'll be honest with you. There are times that sounds like paradise."

"I understand. But my fantasy is listening to music. My music, not Elena's. Symphonies, not rock."

"You can sit with your Beethoven and I'll watch my Forty-Niners and we'll nod at each other in bliss."

"Do you really think so?" She opened her eyes, cocking her head.

"Naw, I'll die of a heart attack in some Norwegian airport, like Trondheim. And you'll get shot by the husband of one of your clients."

"Or maybe we'll both just spontaneously combust."

"Soon, I hope. In the meantime, I'm stuck out here with this stupid petty trial."

Suzanne poured coffee for Marta, who was drumming her hands on Suzanne's kitchen table. When Marta came downstairs for the first time since that damned Monday, Elena got up from the table at once. "Stay," Marta said authoritatively, and Elena sat.

Now all three of them sat there glumly. "It was a courtesy call I suppose," Marta said. "To let me know he's going on what's his name's talk show. To try to get me to show up and make a worse fool of myself."

"Why is he doing this?" Suzanne asked. "You're the wronged party."

"His line is that I'm the author of the domestic violence bill—as if a couple of sentences I contributed make me the author. Miles's wife must be really pissed. It was her bill. But never mind, the idea is that I wrote the domestic violence bill and then I got a gun and tried to kill my husband and his girlfriend."

"I repeat my question, why is he doing this?"

"He's furious I threw him out. He's furious at having to be on his own. In his mind, I really did wrong him by walking in. It's revenge."

"What does Miles say?" Suzanne glanced over at Elena, who was sitting very small in her chair and saying absolutely nothing.

"He says I should start wearing maternity clothes on all occasions."

"He has a point."

"Bullshit. I hate maternity clothes."

"They're supposed to be better than they were twenty years ago."

Marta giggled, sounding twenty years younger. "That's called spacing your children, right? One in college and one in the oven."

Suzanne spent a moment trying to decide how she would feel if she were pregnant instead of experiencing irregularity in her periods and an occasional hot flash. Would she be glad? No, terrified. She had daughters, and two were quite enough. Often it felt like two more than she could manage. She had been at most a passable mother, mostly defined in negatives. Not abusive. Not violent. Not hostile. Not crazy. Just too busy to give everything they needed. With a checkbook instead of a jar of cookies and an open kitchen door. She was of the generation who had children because they felt they had to but didn't always know what to do with them once they had them; who were guilty before their children because they dared to have lives and careers and goals of their own. A transitional generation going forward while looking backward. She was vehemently glad she was passing the age when getting pregnant was a possibility. She had done her bit for the population explosion, and loving and trying to give her best to her daughters was hard enough, sometimes impossible.

Elena finally spoke. "What do you want me to do? I'd go on the show and say how ashamed I am and contradict what he says. Would that help?"

"I'll ask Miles. It might."

Suzanne was lecturing. "You may find increasingly as you practice litigation, that you find in yourself a conflict between your own sense of right and wrong, and your role as a litigator. Now the usual way of dealing with this conflict is to say, I am a hired gun. If the gun thinks too much about how it's being used, it will not be a useful gun. But many lawyers find that they can't make that neat and clean a distinction between their morality and their practice. The exercise I am going to give you today is not a test. There is no right answer, no correct citation. It is an exercise that if it works, will cause you to think about the interplay between your values and your role as a lawyer. You are going to have to think about what you really believe justice to be. It will be a case out of domestic law. Not all of you will receive the same case. It's a matter of chance which of four cases you'll draw. Count yourself off one to four aloud starting in the last row on the right-hand side and working toward me. When you get up to leave, you will find that my assistant has placed four piles at the back of the room. Take a case from your number. You have the weekend to consider how you would argue your case. Two out of the four cases I've chosen are custody cases, among the most hairy in the practice of a lawyer who specializes in domestic law. One is the case of a woman who went after her rapist and shot him. The fourth is a case of environmental law, which pits community safety against jobs. You will write up your argument and what you will be trying to accomplish."

Suzanne met the new client at her office at the university. The dean let her use her university office that way from time to time, as long as she didn't do it too often. Bud Hiller was close to sixty, thin and rigid as a broomstick, large bland features that gave nothing away. He would be a terrific poker player. His voice was pitched a little too loud. Fortunately, her office was reasonably soundproofed by the rows of law books on the walls. He had been through three lawyers on this case, suits and countersuits between the heirs to a chain of outlet stores. The sons and daughters were suing one another for control. They all claimed fraud and even that this one or that one had abused their senile father before his death. It was a busy heap of maggots, reeking of money. Three lawyers had made good fees off this case; it looked as if she would be the fourth.

It was not a case she wanted. She contained herself, listening, questioning him, taking careful notes with Jaime backing her up. Bud Hiller had inquired coldly who Jaime was upon entering her office, but now it was as if Jaime were a cat on a chair. Jaime was a good note taker; he brought the same careful intelligence to all aspects of being a student he would bring to his law career. His beauty was deceptive. He looked languid, graceful, decorative. His mind was spun steel. Meticulous. Wary. Capable of great speed and ruthlessness. She had met his parents, his African-American father and his Filipina mother. By the time Jaime was her age, he would be fat, bald, and far more powerful than she ever would be. She had great faith in him.

Hiller orated on, his injuries, the stinginess of his dead father, the perfidy of his siblings and their spouses, how his previous lawyers had failed him and his just cause. She listened, she took notes, and she thought how she would love to show him the door, but this case leaked money through all its flimsy seams. She had come to a financial crossroads where she must take cases that would pay her bills instead of cases that excited her legally or ethically. She was still the litigator she had always been. She could find a new angle to use. She began to plot her strategy in getting Bud his money and doing his siblings out of theirs.

Jake was still stuck out on the West Coast. She had begun to miss him. Communicating by E-mail and phone worked to a degree, but she missed his presence, his warmth. She did not realize how thoroughly she missed him until she woke Friday night from a dream of his body, found herself wet and steaming with menopausal heat and simple outrageous desire. It was startling to her that she could want him so strongly. She sat at her computer late Saturday night trying to explain why she was feeling especially down and even a little guilty about decisions being forced upon her.

When I went into the law collective after clerking for Judge Fairweather for a year, I had all sorts of notions of defending the unjustly accused, the poor, the marginalized. But we always made a certain amount of our money on drug dealers, fences, bookies—sleaze. We defended the poor and the persecuted, but we also successfully defended the greedy, the dangerous, and the depraved. That's how it goes when you're in criminal practice. You defend criminals, at least part of the time. . . . So when I joined the faculty, one great source of relief and joy was that I took only cases I wanted to take. Cases that were interesting, challenging, and cases where the defendant had right but no money. Now here I am doing what I consider sleaze cases again—because once again I need the money. It depresses me. I wake up in the middle of the night and I feel the stink of it.

Sunday morning, she had a reply.

Look, sometimes I'm required to make jolly with people who are giving us money. For some of them, it's conscience money. For others, it's almost in the nature of a bribe. Give us enough money and we'll look the other way. With seventy major polluters to choose from, we won't go after them. And we don't. It's never spoken about, but it's the way the world runs. On grease. We all make a certain number of compromises for the sake of survival, for the sake of effectiveness.

In academia, I've been faced with few such problems. Guys on foot-ball scholarships don't take law. I've had students try to get me to change grades through threats and promises and histrionics, but I've never seriously been tempted to do so. I hear it's worse when you teach undergraduates—they have a consumer mentality. I paid for this class, so I'm entitled to an A. In law school, we have them more properly intimidated.

This guy and his family are all sharks. The only good thing I can see in the case is that the others are at least as bad as Buddy Boy. You have the feeling if any of them could push a button and cause the others to cease to exist, there'd be no hesitation. But at least he hired me and not a hit man.

As she read his messages, typed on his laptop from motels, she felt a twinge of guilt because it was her nature when involved with a man to try to take care of him: in this case, to make sure that Jake dealt with his stress, made the changes the doctors demanded, ate more sensibly, got enough sleep. But when she only saw a man three or four times a month, she could scarcely monitor his food and exercise and sleep habits. She tried to push it out of her mind, and shortly she succeeded. She had enough to worry about.

39

Elena

Elena could not say she liked her job, but she liked having a job. It felt normal to get into her aging Honda and drive off at the same time most people were heading for work, feeling like a real person instead of a character in a soap opera. She had lunch alone in the building cafeteria or in a restaurant nearby. This was a neighborhood where there were more places to eat at noon than in the evening, for it was ringed with high-tech firms and places like hers that handled money or practiced law for corporations or consulted with them.

It was boring sitting there out front on display saying the same thing over and over again, Good day, Black, Lincoln and Worthington, how may I help you? Mr. Laslau is in a meeting at the moment. May I take your number? Mr. Rowe is out of the office at the moment. May I take your number? Mr. Lincoln's line is busy. Will you hold? Receiving packages from UPS, FedEx, Airborne, the post office. Handing over outgoing mail and parcels. Telling people where to sit and serving them coffee. She was a waitress, but one who never got a tip.

She observed that the different analysts and advisers liked to keep their clients waiting different periods of time. There were the five-minute guys, the ten-minute guys (most common), and the fifteen-to-twenty-minute masters like Mr. Lincoln. Naked power, she thought. She wondered how much of her own life had been spent waiting for those who saw no reason to deal with her promptly.

Sometimes one of the guys asked her to photocopy something. Making coffee was also part of her pitiful job. Mostly she sat on display behind the teak counter, answered the phone, and greeted whoever came through the double doors. Already two of the analysts were hitting on her, but she sloughed them off. She just smiled and passed everything off as a joke. "Oh, Mr. Laslau, you know I can't do that! What a sense of humor." She sounded like an idiot, but she must not let herself care.

She must smile and smile and smile until she thought her face must be sprayed with that strange hair lacquer reminiscent of bug spray one of the secretaries was always using in the women's room. Elena never did more to her hair than get it trimmed to even it up when it started to look ragged, wash it every other day, and once a week use a conditioner. She loved her hair and took comfort in it. She had always resisted cutting it short the way all her friends wore theirs, for she liked retreating behind that sleek black curtain. She liked the weight and heft.

She saw friends from the restaurant more often than she had since she'd been fired, but she could not spend much time with them. They worked late; she had to get up early. The women at Black, Lincoln and Worthington didn't attract her. They seemed slight and vacuous. She had made friends with one of the technicians at the rehab clinic, Cindy, recently divorced. They took to going out together Saturdays to the movies, to a club, to a rock concert. Cindy was a year older, chunky but cute, blond, curvy, and savvy with a great capacity for remembering jokes. Elena never remembered anything but punch lines. She envied people who could hold a crowd with a story.

She spent a lot of time going over the affair with Jim. She was sure she had seduced Jim. She was convinced she had thought of him sexually first, then put out some musk he could not resist. He had not loved her; she had loved him. That was her crime. She had made him come to her. Perhaps she had never forgiven Marta for making her lie in court about Evan and Chad, but she knew Marta had done all that to protect her. Why had she held a grudge so long for something done to keep her out of worse trouble? Because she pushed her own guilt off on Marta, that was why.

She tried to talk to Cindy. Cindy thought she was being mushy and mystical. "So you got involved with a married man? Most men are married. I did that back in college. Everybody does it once. It's only fatal if you keep doing it."

"I think I just bring terrible trouble down."

"On yourself mostly, sounds like."

"Not exactly . . . So are you in the mood for Mexican? Or Thai?"

She had been working at Black, Lincoln and Worthington for exactly three weeks. Her probationary period would end next Friday. Monday as she came into work, she was told to report to Mr. Lincoln. "Miss Blume, I'm afraid we're going to have to let you go."

"But I've always been on time. I come back from my breaks early. I've greeted everyone the way I was told—"

"Miss Blume, it's nothing personal. But you're at the front door of our company."

She saw Sunday's *Globe* lying on his desk. In the Metro section, there was a column about the so-called scandal around Marta, Jim, and domestic violence. Photos of all three of them, including a really stupid one of her with her eyes half shut, were printed with the column.

"Is there anything wrong with my work?" she asked.

"We just feel you haven't really fit in . . ."

She was still on probation. No severance pay, no notice needed. She came in at five to nine on Monday, and by nine-twenty she was back in the parking lot. So much for Black, Lincoln and Worthington. She was unemployed again. And notorious.

Suzanne sat at the table, frowning. "I'm just trying to see if we have a case."

"Mother, enough with law and courts. I'm not going to sue them. It's a crappy job." Elena was waiting to see if her mother liked the Creole chicken.

"You don't want them to take you back?"

"No. They'd resent it and me. I don't have any friends there."

Suzanne frowned, eating absentmindedly, glass of water at the ready. "Maybe they could use you at Earthworks."

"Mother! Haven't you learned anything?"

Suzanne looked blank for a moment. "Oh, Jake is hardly ever there. And if he wanted a young girlfriend, the place is crawling with interns in their twenties. Besides, I think you learned something—I'd like to think so."

"So would I. Do you like the chicken?"

More water. "It's delightful."

"It's too hot for you."

"No, it's fine. . . . I should learn to eat hotter food. It's supposed to be good for you."

Nothing further was said about Elena's going to work for Earthworks. She wished she had saved the Sunday paper. She should have asked Mr. Lincoln for his, since obviously he had finished reading it. She found a couple of possibilities in the daily paper and spent the next morning finding out that each of them had heard of her also. Her picture in the paper hadn't helped her job prospects.

One of the guys at the old restaurant told her Natalie's was looking for a hostess. She wished she could stay out of the late-night restaurant workers' scene, but maybe Natalie's wouldn't mind if she was momentarily notorious. She called up and got an interview. There really was a Natalie, who would be meeting her at 3:00 P.M. Friday in her restaurant at the base of Beacon Hill.

Natalie was about fifty, as short as Suzanne but much heavier, crammed into a pants suit. She had cropped blond hair and smoked constantly. "Yeah, I saw your picture in the paper. What happened, you get canned for that?"

Elena was truthful, figuring she had nothing to lose. Natalie hired her on the spot. "Report for work starting tomorrow. In fact, if you could start tonight?"

"I could be back by five, dressed for work."

"Do it." Natalie dismissed her, going back to her accounts.

Well, at least she didn't have to take money from her mother, and she had a job that paid better than Black, Lincoln and Worthington. Almost anything would, short of baby-sitting. It was a familiar scene, and she fit right in even if half the waiters were younger than she was. Robby, the headwaiter, was the person she had most to please, as Natalie did not pay much attention to the waiting staff unless something went wrong. She spent her time on the menus, on lining up specialty events, on advertising and publicity. Robby was exactly Elena's age and quickly figured out they were the same sign, Aries. Robby was thin, good-looking in an edgy, slightly overpolished way, gay, with ambitions to be an actor. Two of the other waiting staff were would-be filmmakers. They had one poet and one photographer and an ex-model, whose career had lasted six months. It was a typical restaurant scene, and after work, most of them went out together to the bars frequented by other late-nighters. Yes, it was comfortable, it was a scene she slipped into like an old pair of pants. Nonetheless, if she didn't want to spend the rest of her life doing restaurant work, she had to scramble. But in which direction? Up? Sideways? Just not in the same tired circles.

Whenever she was sitting still for a moment, whenever she was in the tub, she no longer fantasized about Jim or any other guy. She tried to imagine herself in various lives. It was a mental trying-on, the way she might try on dresses in a boutique—except with an undercurrent of desperation. She had to choose one of these; she had to try on the right one and plunk down money and time to possess it. She needed to become something real. She had the feeling that then she would be protected from herself, from the wild flight into obsession, from the stupid risk that brought down the roof. But only if the choice she made was the right one. In middle school, they had had a book of short stories. One of them, "The Lady or the Tiger," she remembered. Two doors, with something behind them, happiness or death. Well, she had already loosed the tiger. Lady Luck had to be behind the next door she opened. Had to be.

40

Beverly

Beverly lay in the bed in the room she had been given in Suzanne's house, rolling from side to side as she had been taught. She faithfully performed the range-of-motion exercises, but she no longer believed in them or anything except her own great fatigue with all of this futile fussing. The doctors had told her that her leg was healing nicely, as if that mattered. Her brain, that had always served her so well, would not heal. The neat sweet connection between mind and body she had always taken for granted was broken. Parts of her body obeyed her still; parts obeyed fitfully, like her voice; parts were dead to her, like her right hand. She had a distant lost foot at the end of the broken leg. Once it had belonged to her. No more.

She had to plot carefully how to get up. Moving herself from the bed to her wheelchair required every bit of concentration she could muster. When she was finally in the wheelchair, she trembled with fatigue and had to rest before she could wheel herself to the bathroom. Then she must transfer again, to the toilet. Long after she had used it, she sat there resting. She had finally mastered transferring herself to the chair in the shower. The liquid soap hung on an old belt where she could reach it. Her greatest difficulty lay in getting the water just right. Elena had made marks with nail polish where she should turn the two dials for a good mix, but sometimes the water was hotter than other days. Then one morning she slipped, losing her balance. Suzanne heard her fall and acted terrified, then dragged her to the doctor to be tested all over again.

Every movement had to be planned like a military campaign. Every movement had to be calculated and performed with intense concentration. Otherwise she would fall. Otherwise she could break bones. Otherwise she might bang her head and have another seizure. It was boring to think hard about how to soap herself, how to rinse herself. Drying her body was a tricky undertaking. She was still trying to carry that out when she heard someone in the kitchen. The day had begun for the rest of them. Usually it was Suzanne, because Elena had an evening job and slept late. Now Beverly would have breakfast in bed, because by this time she was exhausted and had to rest. The effort of showering and drying wore her out. Suzanne brought food in on a tray.

After her oatmeal, toast, juice, and coffee, she promptly fell asleep. When she woke, the house was quiet. The phone's ringing had awakened her. She did not move, although there was an extension within reach of her arm. Trying to answer the phone and make herself understood was an agony she would never go through again. It was humiliating. Besides, someone had answered it already, Elena or the answering machine.

She must get up and put clothes on. She rang her bell. Rang it again. It would be much faster if Elena helped her. The physical therapist was coming at ten-thirty, so she had to be out of bed and decent. Had she done the exercises she was supposed to do? She remembered doing them, but sometimes she got confused and thought she had done some task that she had really last done the day before. The days blurred into one another, melting into a featureless lump like melted wax. She slept so much that half the day was gone into unconsciousness, and the rest was disjointed into uneven segments by her napping.

"Oh, it was just somebody from the restaurant, wanting a ride tonight." Elena helped her dress. These days all Beverly ever wore were sweats that closed with Velcro. Anything else was too difficult to get on or off, except for two caftans Elena had bought her. She liked those best. She had always had contempt for people her age who slopped around in sweats, but now she was one of them. At least the caftans hinted that she had once been a woman. She especially liked the green one with glints of gold embroidery that Elena had bought from her first restaurant paycheck.

The physical therapist was about thirty. She had too much forehead, going up and up over her thick brows, making her eyes appear small. They were like round blue dots behind her glasses, like the eyes children drew. She smelled of mints and more lightly of sweat. Today they did a lot of arm and shoulder exercises, the therapist moving the arm for her, placing a hand on her elbow and taking her hand in the therapist's own. Lifting the arm up over her head, then slowly down. Then the same slow dance out to the side. Moving the fingers of the dead hand. Moving the thumb. Before her second stroke, she had begun to have some feeling in that hand, but it was gone—like almost everything else she had cherished.

All but one. Elena. She missed Sylvia, their constant discussions of the news and society in general. She had asked if Sylvia could not come back at least sometimes, but Suzanne had learned she had another full-time job. If she were still a normal person, she could have called Sylvia and chatted. After the physical therapist left, not to be back till Thursday (she came twice a week), Beverly once again slipped down into the sleep of exhaustion. When Elena woke her for lunch, she had been dreaming. She had been a fugitive, running through abandoned buildings with the footsteps of the red squad behind her. They were after her. They were going to beat her. She was running for her life.

Her heart was still pounding in her chest when Elena woke her, repeating, "Grandma, Grandma. Lunchtime."

She insisted on getting out of bed (she was still dressed) to have her lunch. "Next week, you'll get that cast off," Elena said as she maneuvered the wheelchair into the kitchen. "Won't you be glad to see the last of that?"

"It . . . ches."

"I broke my wrist once."

Beverly nodded wildly, crookedly, holding up her good left arm. Meaning she had done so herself: had her wrist broken.

"I remember the itching under the cast. How was your therapy?"

Beverly shrugged on her left side. "Wha?" Pointing.

"Oh, the soup. Hot and sour Chinese. And mu shu pork. After all, neither Suzanne nor Rachel is here, right? So we can sneak us some pig meat."

Beverly grinned.

"I figure if I roll the pancakes up for you, you can eat them one-handed."

Beverly nodded. "Good to me." It came out more like Goo tommy, but Elena understood and nodded back.

"I try, Grandma, I try. You know, Jim and I haven't said one word to each other since that Monday."

"Pig."

"I don't want to talk to him. He hangs around at odd moments waiting for me, but I don't let him catch me. I have nothing to say to him that isn't obscene."

"Big pig."

"You think talking about pork made me think of him?" Elena chuckled. "I'll hide the trash away at the bottom of the bag, and Suzanne will never guess we were wicked. Okay, finish off your soup and I'll start rolling pancakes."

Beverly had been astonished when Marta had shown up with Suzanne to take her back in the van. She had assumed that Suzanne and Elena would have moved into an apartment somewhere. No, it was back to the same apartment in Brookline with Marta upstairs, and Marta and Suzanne apparently still best friends. If only she could speak well enough to ask, but two-word sentences were all she could manage. That didn't make for an effective interrogation procedure, especially when she was prying for the delicate, the uncomfortable, the stuff Suzanne would rather leave unsaid. Elena too seemed to accept the situation. All the women were still living here, and only the man was gone. Elena told her that Marta had thrown Jim out, and that he was furious about it. Beverly thought he ought to be grateful she hadn't shot lower.

She no longer considered Jim worthy of Elena. He had shown himself to be a coward, throwing Elena aside to protect himself. Her good hand fluttered on the table. There was so much she wanted to say to Elena, so much she wanted to teach her, to share with her, and the effort of sputtering out two words exhausted her resources. She touched Elena's hand. "Sweet," she burst out. "You."

"Yeah, sweet like a rattlesnake. I've learned something, believe me." Beverly shook her head.

"Yes, Grandma. I went after him." Elena sighed. "Never mind. I'm doing fine. I don't think I'm cut out to inspire a grand passion in some guy."

Beverly disagreed with wild head shaking. Then she printed on a pad *J?*

Elena looked at her blankly.

Beverly laboriously printed JAKE TRIAL?

Elena looked blank. "He's still out in California. You'll have to ask Suzanne. I didn't know you'd gotten to be friends with him."

They hadn't, because she couldn't talk with him. She understood his situation and how badly things might go for him in court. If the lumber interests owned the judge, as it seemed they did, then he could really be screwed. She didn't think Suzanne had grasped how vulnerable he was to the conspiracy charge. He hadn't taken his defense seriously because he thought it was a minor case, but she had seen organizers railroaded for twenty years just for doing what he had done. It was hopeless. Before her second stroke, she had thought about E-mailing him, but she had not gotten around to it before she could no longer use the computer. She liked him, his presence, his energy, his political strength. Suzanne had made a good choice this time, but he was in bigger trouble than he seemed to understand, unless the judicial system had changed more than she thought it had.

Elena had cleared the table and made them both espresso. "Now what would you like? Would you like me to cut up a pear?"

Beverly shook her head no.

"Maybe later. Those Bosc pears I got are pretty good. I pick out fruit better than Suzanne does."

Beverly nodded.

"But what would you like, Grandma?"

Beverly decided to risk telling the truth. "To die." She held Elena's gaze with her own, never wavering. "To die!"

41

Suzanne

Suzanne came abruptly awake. It was 2:00 A.M. and the phone was ringing. She did not pick it up. She had endured middle-of-the-night phone calls from clients before, and it was best to answer them the next day, unless they had just been busted. Those kinds of phone calls had mostly ceased when she became an academic instead of a full-time lawyer. She sat up in bed, listening while her heart pounded from the sudden jolt into consciousness and the adrenaline slowly receded in her veins. She was especially annoyed because she was getting so little sleep these days. Only after Beverly fell asleep in the evening, did she get to her briefs, her classes, her own work.

"Mother! Mother!" It was Rachel, although it did not sound like her.

"Rachel?" She grabbed at the receiver on the combination answering machine and phone that sat beside her bed. "Are you hurt?" Bombing was the first thing she thought of.

"I'm so humiliated!" Rachel began to sob bitterly.

"What's wrong?" She turned on the bedside light and sat up, mounding the pillows behind her and disturbing the two orange cats, who had been sleeping, one pressed against her right thigh and one against her left.

Rachel was sobbing, and at first Suzanne could not make out what she was saying. It had to do with her marriage, she could tell that much. Patiently she waited for coherence.

"We started it a month ago. That was when your ketubah finally arrived and the letters from our rabbis. So we got our court date."

"Court date? Who's your lawyer?"

"A rabbinical court, Mother, the Beit Hadin. We were supposed to be proving we're Jewish and single. There's an enormous amount of paperwork, but we had everything, we thought. We had two witnesses from school to testify we each were Jewish and single. One of them was my friend Zipporah, and they wouldn't accept her because she was female. I didn't even bother telling you about that. So we got another court date. Another three weeks."

"Women aren't witnesses?"

"Apparently it's a matter of luck. Remember, this is an Orthodox court. Things are so weird here, they assume everybody who practices the religion is Orthodox. Like there's only one flavor and it's walnut. It's pure luck which rabbis you get. How much fuss they decide to make. But this time was worse. When they got to me and I explained I was studying to be a rabbi, Mother, it was as if I said I was a prostitute. They were furious. It was awful, Mother, awful! They were so nasty you wouldn't believe it, what they said to me. So I walked out."

"You can get married at home, sweetheart. Really, it'd be better for all of us."

"Well, we're not getting married at all, so you don't have to worry about it!" Rachel began to sob all over again.

"But, Rachel, you can get married here. So it was a nice gesture to marry in Israel, but you'll be just as married if you do it in Brookline or Philadelphia. And you'll have your choice of a dozen rabbis."

"Michael was furious at me for walking out. He didn't understand why I couldn't keep my mouth shut and put up with it. Well, he's a man, and Orthodoxy is made for him. I just got furious that he couldn't understand how insulted I was and how ashamed. So we had a huge fight. It started in Koresh Street, and went on all the way home on the bus, although we shut up then because other people started to butt in. We went at it when we got back, and we broke up and that's all there is to it!"

"Rachel, it was a devastating experience for you. But you love each other. You'll come back from this."

"Never! I saw a side of Michael I'd never seen. A side that thinks that a woman is less of a Jew than a man, no matter what he says, no matter what he pretends. I cannot be married to that. I can't!"

"Rachel, don't make up your mind about him yet. Give yourself a little cooling off time. Give him some space and take some yourself."

"Not likely," Rachel said, far more soberly. "I don't think I can forget that he didn't back me up and he just wanted me to shut up and let those old men pour shame on my head."

"Then don't forget. But maybe you can forgive. Or maybe at least you can begin communicating again." Why am I arguing so hard on his behalf? Suzanne wondered. I scarcely know him and I wasn't crazy about him in the first place. But Rachel really seemed to love him and to want to be with him.

Rachel sighed heavily, and for a moment the lines between them were silent, both of them hearing only each other's breathing and the echoey metallic sound of the connection. "I'll talk to you tomorrow, Mother."

"Rachel? If you could call before two A.M. our time? It would really help, sweetheart. And try not to be so upset. I'm sure everything is going to turn out all right, somehow."

"I'm sorry, I didn't think about the time, Mama."

"Don't worry, dear. And try to call Aunt Karla too. She will want to know what's happening. I know she was planning to go over for your wedding. She already bought tickets."

Suzanne found the task of helping Beverly shower and dress uncomfortable. She had a deep feeling she should not see her mother's naked body, more a sense of impropriety than squeamishness, for the actual sight of Beverly's withered flesh produced mostly compassion. Beverly had always been vain and careful about who saw her in various states. Suzanne knew she had seen her mother naked when she had been a little girl, but she doubted she had seen her that way since she was twelve—and Beverly, around thirty-five and stunning. It was humiliating to Beverly, who kept her head averted and would not meet her gaze. She was almost pouting. "Water . . . not . . . hot." It actually sounded like wa-ah naw haw, but in the context was clear.

"I'll make it hotter. The last time, it was too hot for you. Maybe I should get one of those bath thermometers?"

"Silly."

"I want to get the shower right for you. You enjoy it if I get it right."

Suzanne knew there wasn't much Beverly did enjoy these days.

Beverly nodded. She pointed at the shower gel that smelled of a combination of rose and lavender. "Nice."

Suzanne was glad she had done something right. Elena and she had to make up for the lack of help—for the bills simply mounted higher and higher. Suzanne did not think that Beverly complained as much with Elena, but she was hard put to please her mother—as it always had been and apparently always would be. "Mother, I want to do everything right for you, but it seems I never please you."

Beverly actually smiled. "Wash back. Gently."

Carefully, slowly, Suzanne ran the washcloth over Beverly's back. Every knob of her spine stood out like wooden beads on a child's necklace. She had owned such a necklace herself, of orange wooden beads. Beverly had brought it back from Copenhagen, when she had gone to a conference with European union officials. She had been angry with her mother for not taking her. They were so often angry with each other. What a waste of time and energy.

Rachel called next in the morning. She was calmer, more elegiac. "I was so in love with Jerusalem. Now I want to run home. Now this isn't home any longer, but a foreign country."

"Ah, dearest, as with most infatuations and disillusionment, the truth is somewhere in between."

"I know, Mother. I'm not about to run away. I just have to digest all this. . . . I've been so good. When I go into Mea Shearim or the Old City, no matter how warm it is, I wear long skirts and blouses with sleeves. I go bundled up the way I used to in New York when I was going to visit Grandma or Aunt Karla, the way you put on layers in spite of the heat because of men in the street. Here it's because they throw things at you." Rachel sniffled, but her voice was clear and resonant. "I was so respectful of their weird ideas. So meek and obedient to rules I not only don't believe in, but intensely despise."

"But Michael didn't make the culture of the Orthodox."

"Michael can go fuck himself!"

Suzanne shook her head. It was extraordinary for Rachel to use profane language. "You're still angry with him," she said mildly.

"I've never in my life been so conscious of being a feminist. I feel like a one-woman parade through Jerusalem. It's schizophrenic here. I meet such strong wonderful capable women, and in the eyes of their religion, they don't count. I don't count."

"I support you whatever you decide," Suzanne intoned, realizing how often in the more recent years of her daughters' lives, she had used that phrase. "You have to sit down with Michael and try to reach an understanding, even if it's that you aren't suited to each other."

Rachel blew out her breath, sounding for a moment like Elena. "You can say that again."

When Suzanne did grab a moment to call Karla from her office while she ate a yogurt and thumbed through a speech Jaime had updated for her, Karla already knew. "It's so sad for her, it's heartbreaking. She's such a good girl, and never deserved such shame and trouble. If I could fly over there, I would."

"Can you get your money back on the tickets?"

"The travel agent says they're refundable, minus a service fee. So what can I do?"

Over long-distance, they sighed and commiserated.

Rachel was back to E-mail, which signaled to Suzanne that her daughter was slowly recovering. Rachel told her more details of the battle in rabbinical court. She reported comments of her fellow students and teachers.

I had coffee with Michael in a café this afternoon, but we could not agree. I think I never understood how strong a grip traditional Judaism has on him, as opposed to newer ways. I think he only got into Reconstructionist rabbinical school because he was turned down by the Conservatives in New York and his parents didn't want him to go to LA. I don't hate him any longer, but I know he is not my bashert. Both Elena and I seem to have mistaken something small for something grand. I feel diminished, if you know what I mean. I am calmer, but I feel I am less. I think, Mother, you saw that tightness and rigidity in Michael even the few times you were with him, but I was blinded. I wanted too much for him to be the way I wished he was, and so I did not let myself know Michael as he is. That was an injustice to him too. I cry a lot still, but I am getting clearer. Today I managed to thank the Eternal One for showing me the real Michael before it was too late.

The cast was finally off, but Beverly had regained little mobility. Without Sylvia or anyone filling in as primary caretaker, it was up to Elena and Suzanne to do most of what needed to be done for Beverly. One or another of the agency employees came in three mornings a week, but otherwise they were on their own with her. Elena took the whole day shift on Monday and Tuesday, when the restaurant was closed. Otherwise she took over at one and stayed with Beverly until four, when she had to leave for work. Suzanne got home as quickly as she could, but there were days when Beverly had to remain alone from four until seven. None of them liked that, but there was nothing Suzanne could do. Weekends she took over.

Suzanne was back to making supper or bringing home takeout Wednesday through Sunday, as Elena ate at the restaurant with the staff from four-thirty to five-fifteen. Home meals had to be something easy for Beverly to eat, as she hated needing help with her food. If Suzanne cut the fish into bite-size pieces before she brought it to the table, Beverly found that acceptable, but not if Suzanne tried to cut the food on her plate. Tonight it was a fish and potato stew she had cooked from scratch—a fast scratch. She was learning entrées that took no more than twenty minutes to cook, or she just couldn't manage. Beverly seemed to find the soup satisfactory, although Suzanne knew it probably tasted bland to her. Then they hobbled together back into the bedroom.

"Mother, this is what I want. We've wasted so much of our lives arguing, disagreeing, trying to make the other more like ourselves. It's hard to break old habits, but maybe we could begin to be gentler and more loving with each other?"

"Loving . . ." Beverly repeated. She lay back on the propped-up pillows, exhausted from the bath but relaxed. There was a scent of the shower gel about her, instead of the musty smell that often clung to her crippled body. "Love me?"

"Yes, I love you. In spite of how badly we've gotten along. In spite of never feeling I please you. You're my origin, my source, my first family.

You were the earliest image of beauty I had. Your face. Of course I love you."

"Then . . . help me . . . die." It took Beverly almost two minutes to get the phrase out, her face knotted with the effort.

Suzanne stared at her mother. "Help you to die?"

"Tired . . . Useless . . . Ready."

"Mother, you're not close to death. You could live for years. I don't think you're in great pain. Haven't we made you feel welcome?"

"Can't do . . . any . . . thing."

"You're bored."

Beverly slowly nodded, her head lolling to one side. "Never . . . before use . . . less."

"You've worked so hard all your life, why do you have to be working? What do you think you have to be accomplishing?"

Beverly shook her finger at Suzanne, pointing.

"You mean I'm the same way."

Beverly nodded. "Tired."

Suzanne looked at her mother, trying to understand. "Everything is difficult for you. Eating. Going to the toilet. Dressing. Bathing. Speaking."

"Tired."

"So you really wish you could die?"

"Now. Soon. Help me."

Suzanne did not reply as she went off to her room, warm tears sliding down her cheeks. Elena stayed that night with her new boyfriend, Sean. Suzanne did not get to speak to her privately until Saturday morning, when she motioned Elena into her office and shut the door.

"Beverly said something really disturbing to me the night before last. She said she wanted to die. She was serious, Elena. She said she wanted help to die."

Elena nodded, slinging herself sideways across a chair with arms. "She's been saying that to me for about a month, Mom. I've been thinking about it a lot. I don't know what to do. But it's mean, it's cruel to ignore her."

They met each other's gaze. "You know, it would be considered murder," Suzanne said. "Mostly people don't get convicted, but sometimes they do. Prosecutors always try to get a conviction. I'm not convinced we need another criminal case in this family. And I'm not convinced she has a right to ask this of us. She's not in enormous pain. She could live for years."

"If she wants our help, we have to give it to her, Mother," Elena said. "Can't you see that? We're the people who love her most in the world."

"I keep thinking, maybe I haven't done enough to make her feel welcome. To make her comfortable."

"Mother, I've spent much more time with her than you have. She can't be comfortable. She hasn't got a life. I understand. Can't you?"

"I'm trying, dear. But no, I can't understand, really. All she has to do is stay with us and let us take care of her."

"All she can be is a good vegetable."

Suzanne stared at her daughter, wondering how Elena could talk so calmly about what was after all murder or being an accomplice to self-murder of someone she loved. How could Elena sit there so placidly staring back at her?

I need you out here. I know it's a terrible time for you but things are going badly. I've called twice, but keep getting your answering machine. I am being tried, crudely and unfairly. My lawyer can't believe what's happening. I think you could help. The organization would be glad to pay your way out here, and I think we can raise your fee. But things are going to hell. It's a hanging judge, George Epson, who represents the lumber interests. He'd like to send all of us up, but particularly me. He denies every motion by my counsel and agrees to every objection of the prosecutor.

I can't come out right now. My mother is much worse. I don't know what to do. I can't get away right now. But I know some really good lawyers out there and I will get on trying to find out who can join your case. I hate to let you down, but things are very very hairy here.

She felt guilty refusing Jake, but she could not stretch herself any thinner; more than that, she felt as if she was already failing her mother and her daughters and her clients. She could not go out to California to help Jake, no matter how much she might want to. There just wasn't enough of her. What she could do was find him a really good California lawyer to join in the case, right away.

She saw her doctor the next day, her annual checkup twice postponed. Dr. Rose frowned at her. "Your blood pressure is one sixty-five over ninety. Sky high."

"I've always had low blood pressure," she said reproachfully. "Could you take it again?"

"I've taken it twice. I want you to buy a little monitor and record it yourself six times a day or whenever you think of it, and keep a log for me."

"Dr. Rose, this must be an aberration."

"Take it seriously. Some women's blood pressure does shoot up around menopause. Your mother has had two strokes. If you don't want to have one yourself, you're going to have to bring that blood pressure down. Frankly, you're exhausted. You're undergoing more stress than your body can handle. Something has to go."

Jake called. "The trial is going badly. I can tell. Come out. Please."

"I can't, Jake. Things with my mother are in crisis. I've leaned on my colleagues to cover for me so many times this school year, I can't ask more favors, and my mother requires intensive caretaking right now. Her deterioration is increasing rapidly."

"Suzanne, I'm facing the possibility of prison."

"Surely they can't give you more than a short sentence, and you can appeal immediately. You should be able to stay out while the appeal is going on."

"I don't think it's going to work out that way."

She wanted to weep with frustration. She felt like a rope in a tug-of-war. She was fraying and everybody else was falling down.

42

Elena

Elena started going out with Sean, she suspected, because she wanted to put some guy between herself and Jim, and Sean was the biggest body she could find. Six feet four and beefy, he had boxed for a time but given it up to become a cook. He went to school and worked his way up through lesser restaurants. Now he was the dessert and pastry chef at Natalie's. He had a bit of a drinking problem, she thought, but he was neither violent nor abusive. He just got quieter. He touched her as if she were the most delicate pastry. Sex with him was occasional and low key, all she felt she could handle at the moment. He was, like her friend Cindy, someone to pass time with, someone caring and never dangerous to her.

The restaurant was a scene she understood, but it too was only passing time. She got on with most of the crowd who worked at Natalie's. One of the cooks disliked her and never passed up a chance to call her a slut. One waitress, slumming from Bennington, was snotty, but otherwise, they were all types she was comfortable with. Her gentle romance with Sean was common knowledge and gave her a little status. Time slid forward. The weather crispened, then grew permanently chilly. One Friday night, it snowed, briefly, more a promise than an event. By the next morning, no trace remained on the streets or on the lawns of her mother's neighborhood, that would never feel truly hers.

She considered moving in with Sean but decided that was more than their fragile link could endure. By spring, she would find an apartment, a roommate, somewhere she wanted to live. She would still see Grandma regularly. Her California dreams had evaporated with her feelings for Jim. Here she belonged, by the cold gray North Atlantic of winter. Often in the mornings now, ice skimmed the puddles. It snowed again and this time it stayed, thatching the grass, turning everything ghostly. That night, after they hung out in a late-night bar, she walked on the Common with Robby, the headwaiter, his current lover Tom, Sean, and Cassie, one of the waitresses. They crunched the new snow. Then Tom, Cassie, and she lay down and made angels. It felt blissful lying in the clean snow that gleamed in the darkness with the fresh flakes falling on her face like little kisses. Robby stood grinning at them. "My, what sweet children. The only snow I like I get from my dealer."

"Ah, but this is free," Tom said, but he got up and dusted himself off. Robby had a gift for making people feel silly when he chose. He was the connection in the restaurant, the man who could get what anyone wanted. Elena, who had not touched drugs in five years, avoided that side of him. She kept herself on a strict two-beer limit. Everyone teased her, but she was Robby's age and had a couple of years on them—except Sean and the kitchen staff.

The talk show she ended up going on with Jim was local, since this case was purely a Massachusetts scandal. She wasn't sure why she'd decided to do it, except maybe as some kind of revenge. She wanted the world to see what kind of a jerk he'd really been. She had never heard of the loudmouth who ran it, but apparently he had been a columnist in the *Herald* for centuries. The audience was gross, whooped up and out to witness bloodletting, but she kept her cool. Jim's line was all about how Marta had written the domestic violence bill that they were all living under, and yet she had not hesitated to grab a gun and try to shoot him.

"First of all, she didn't try to shoot us. She goes to the range regularly and my mother, who's her best friend, says she's a good shot. She shot way over our heads. It was a statement, like, she was really"—she paused for a usable word, for the first several that came to her had *shit* in them—"angry with us. It was like this theatrical gesture."

"Didn't you feel in danger?" Joe, the talk show guy, asked, leaning forward. She could tell he thought she was cute.

"Never. She was aiming way over our heads. That's why the police laughed this off. He's here because the police wouldn't do anything. It was like setting off firecrackers, if you see what I mean?" She gave him a melting look.

"She could have killed us," Jim said. "She shot off a whole round."

"You'd have to stand on a stepladder to get in the way," Elena said and was rewarded by a laugh from the audience.

"Isn't it unusual, don't you think, for a girlfriend to be defending the wife?"

"I was a . . . a fool. An idiot. A bitch, to get involved with him. He told me their marriage was over. He said he hadn't touched her in two years. And meanwhile, she was pregnant. I'm so ashamed."

"She kept it from me!" Jim said. "She never told me."

"That she got herself pregnant?" Elena waved her hand. "She must have, since you never touched her, right?"

"How do I know it's mine? I don't remember dragging you off to bed, screaming and protesting. If I remember right, you came on to me."

"So we're both stupid and unfaithful creeps? As for the baby, try a DNA test if you aren't sure," Elena said. "But you're sure. You don't even have a candidate because she was too busy supporting you to see anyone else. I've always admired Marta, and I think I was trying to be her." That was total bullshit, but she figured it would go over, being the kind of mushy psychologizing she could see the host eating up. She was scared of Jim, in a way, scared of how he had fooled her. Scared she could be sucked back in. Scared she wanted passionate consuming love so badly she made it up out of pasteboard.

It was ugly. Jim accused her of being brainwashed and out to get him because he had stopped seeing her. Everything got twisted around, but she kept her cool. She could tell the host was disappointed that she couldn't be shaken. Soon he let them go and called in the next set of fools, two sisters who were fucking each other's husbands.

She confided in Beverly. "I've been thinking about this summer, thinking about it a lot. And the one thing I've come up with is that I liked working in his office. I like therapy."

Beverly printed on the pad, WORK THERAPIST OFC?

"No. I want to be a therapist."

"Why?" Beverly said in that strangled voice that sounded as if it were ripped from her throat.

Elena shrugged. "I think I'd be better at it than he is, for one thing. I'd be better than the shrinks I was sent to after, you know, Evan and Chad. I know a lot about the dark side of people, how you get into things, how you get obsessed. I think I could help, partly because I've been so fucked up myself. And if I did something that was right for other people, I'd hate myself less."

Beverly printed, WHY HATE SELF? WONDERFUL. GOOD TO ME.

"Then you're the only one I'm any good for. Or who thinks I'm good for anything at all."

YR. MOTHER LOVES. NO GOOD SHOWING.

"Yeah, I feel like she does, maybe for the first time since I was a little girl."

"Lots ways . . . do good," Beverly laboriously mouthed. She pointed to her chest. "Did good . . . for people."

"Grandma, I'm not about to become a union organizer."

Beverly shrugged.

"I guess I want a profession. When I meet people, they always say, And what do you do? What I should answer is, I fuck around and I fuck up."

Beverly shook her head and then winced.

"Come on, lazy. It's time for you to walk."

With the cast off, Beverly was supposed to walk every day, but she was always putting it off because it hurt and it exhausted her. Elena took it on herself to make sure that Beverly took at least a short walk. With the pavement icy, they walked to and fro in the house, or else Elena would take Beverly to a mall. "You want to go to the Chestnut Hill Mall today?"

Beverly shook her head no. "Crowded."

It was getting close to Christmas. Grandma was right. "Okay. We'll take a stroll in lovely *casa nuestra*. Sounds like *cosa nostra*, doesn't it?" Elena ran into the living room and put on one of her favorite disks lately, Juan Luis Guerra. Then she bopped back into Beverly's bedroom and offered her arm. Helped her grandma out of bed. They began walking in time to the music, which she turned up superloud. Beverly liked the music, loosely nodding her head in time as they made their difficult deliberate way out of the bedroom, across the kitchen, and into the living room and then around the living room and back. They turned into a parade, because all three cats followed them as they promenaded. Going half time to the music, stepping along. It made Elena feel good.

While Grandma was napping, Elena did her laundry and got out the yellow pages to start calling colleges and universities in the area about graduate training in becoming a therapist. She felt very competent and focused as she asked questions about the programs and requested their catalogs and registration forms. Was she trying to show Jim that she wasn't just a bimbo? Was she trying to impress her mother? Was she trying to work off guilt? It didn't matter, she could see nowhere else to go.

She did not know if she believed she would do this thing, go back to college where she had often felt ill at ease, get a graduate degree—she who had taken five and a half years to get a B.A. She had majored in psychology finally because it was the easiest for her, except for Spanish. She had begun taking Spanish at Boston Latin as soon as she could, continued in Brookline, continued in every college. She had always pushed herself to learn it so well that she hoped eventually to be mistaken for a native Spanish speaker.

Now she had a new fantasy. She could see herself in a comfortable office warm and welcoming, not like Jim's at all. She would have her own assistant, taking calls and booking appointments and billing insurance companies. She would wear glasses on the job, just clear glasses to make herself look serious. Large important-looking glasses. She would wear her hair caught back and dress in suits, like Suzanne. Suits said that the wearer shouldn't be trifled with. Her mother went to court in suits. Jim dressed too casually. She would not. She would let the clients know she was on the job and serious about it, and she would advertise that she offered therapy in Spanish.

She was lying on the couch in the living room with MTV on just for the company, eating taco chips and drinking diet soda. She could see herself in her office. She could see the office, the desk with a slate top. She would not space out the way Jim confessed he did when a client bored him. She would sit perfectly still except for taking notes. Everything about her would convey intense unwavering attention, what a person wanted who came to see a therapist.

Beverly's bell rang. Elena sighed but got up at once. She had been enjoying her vision. She felt almost as if standing up might let it slip out of her. It was a fantasy she felt good about, and she did not want it to escape. But Beverly was calling. She helped her up and Beverly went to the bathroom while Elena ran downstairs and moved her wash to the dryer. Then she got Beverly settled in bed again.

She could see that her grandmother was working herself up to say something. Sometimes it took Beverly several minutes to get a sentence all lined up before she tried to spit it out. Elena passed the time thinking about Sean. He was good to her. Why couldn't she be in love with him? No, better that she wasn't, for whenever she truly fell in love, she fell off the edge. It was a disaster. Better to feel affectionate toward him and enjoy the occasional sex. Normally she wanted more and hotter, but she was still a casualty of the sex wars, and gentle and occasional was just fine for now. She saw him standing at the window of his North End apartment, doing his morning exercises, a combination of aerobics and tai chi. She had begun learning to do the tai chi with him. For serious exercise, she preferred to go to the gym.

Beverly was speaking now. "Need your help."

"Sure, Grandma. Anything."

"Mean it?"

"Don't you know me yet? What do you want me to do for you?"

"Want die!"

"Grandma, things are better now. You're home. You're getting some benefits from the therapy."

"No use. No point. Want die."

"What exactly do you mean, you want to die?" Elena asked slowly.

"Want pills. Kill me."

"You want to kill yourself? No way. I've been down this road before. Grandma, when you kill yourself, you're really dead. Meat."

"Not child. Know. Want . . . die."

"Grandma, it's not that bad. Are you in a lot of pain?"

Beverly glared at her. Her lips thinned. "Want die."

"Are you asking me to help?"

Beverly nodded again, again.

"Grandma, I love you. But I can't do that. I know what a mess it is. Believe me, I know. I'd miss you too much. Mother would miss you."

"No use."

"You mean, it's no use my arguing with you, or your life is no use?"

"Both."

"Your life is plenty of use. You listen to me. We talk. We spend time

together. It means something to me. It must mean something to you."
Elena took Beverly's hand. Her own felt cold to her, as if the warmth
had drained out of her body when her grandma started talking about
death and dying. Yes, she was scared. She did not want to hear this. She
had to make Beverly stop.

"Love you. Want die. Now."

43

Beverly

Beverly had been exactly twenty-nine, yes, when Suzanne caught
German measles. That was before kids were routinely vaccinated. Did
they even have a vaccine that long ago? Suzanne had been seven, a
skinny little girl, too skinny, with reddish hair, big green watery eyes.
Was she wearing glasses yet? No, they sent her home from school with
a note that she needed glasses that same year, afterward. Suzanne got
dreadfully sick, and then she caught pneumonia and was taken to the
hospital. The doctor was not encouraging. He asked to speak to the
father. "There is no father," Beverly said. She was furious that he was
trying to go over her head. He thought her daughter was going to die.

She had held Suzanne's superheated hand. Her daughter was burning
up. Delirious. Tossing in the bed like a fish dying on a dock. Then
Beverly had thought secretly to herself, guiltily, that perhaps she should
not have had a daughter. It would be terrible if Suzanne died, terrible,
but at the same time, it would be easier. She was always having to think
about what to do with Suzanne when she went away. She had felt she
would not be complete as a woman if she did not have a child, but now
she wondered. A child seemed to eat money sometimes. There was always something that needed attention, that needed fixing, that had to
be replaced or provided.

But when Suzanne was restored to her, thinner than ever, pale and
slight as a sheet of paper, she had wept, holding her daughter and feeling
that nothing could be as precious. How could she have imagined life

without her little one? Then the next day, she hauled off and swatted Suzanne when she spilled her soup all over the table. A clumsy child, there was no getting around it. A little ballet dancer she wasn't. Two left feet and two left hands. There was something intractable in Suzanne from the moment she could sit up and say Mama, intractable and lumpy. Suzanne would sit glowering, making herself dense and immovable.

She had felt guilty about her temper, but Suzanne had a temper of her own. From the time Suzanne was eleven, they'd had screaming matches. They would both stand their ground and shriek at each other. "You will!" "I won't!" Her daughter was as stubborn and willful as she was. They were a match, everyone said that. It used to infuriate her, how Karla could get Suzanne to do almost anything, how Suzanne would do the dishes without being asked at her aunt's, how Suzanne would pick up after herself. At home, she was a little pig.

How had they got off on the wrong foot with each other so quickly, so unremittingly? Two strong wills striking metal against metal. Yet as an adult, Suzanne often seemed phlegmatic. Her daughter appeared to be encased in protocol, duty, busy-ness, the make-work of the law. It felt to her as if Suzanne had gone into the law in order to retreat from her, from their hectic and never affluent life together. The law was Suzanne's shell she carried on her back.

Beverly stirred in the bed, trying vainly to find a comfortable position. Her body was sore all the time. She should try to get up, climb into her wheelchair, roll into the living room. She did not feel like it, so much effort for so little gain. There was nothing on television. It was hard for her to use the computer, for her vision was still blurred. Suzanne had bought her a big expensive monitor that she could read, but it took too much work for her to get to it. With the big monitor, she could no longer use the laptop in bed. Now it sat on the makeshift desk. She stared at it across the room and imagined sending E-mail messages to all the people she used to communicate with. Half of them probably thought she was dead. Wasn't she?

She could see it clearly now, with so much empty time to contemplate her life: she should never have had a child. She was not cut out to be a mother. She had never really wanted to be responsible for another person, to have to explain her decisions and justify them, to have to drag that other through her life clunking behind. She had never wanted to marry. She had understood from adolescence on that being the legal property of a man was a bad idea for her, that simply having another body always there, someone for whose meals, clothing, bills, and opinions she was responsible, would be death itself. She would hate him. He would be a large pole to which she would be tethered. Why hadn't she applied that to children? When she had discovered herself pregnant, she had been delighted, as if it were some kind of accomplishment. She had felt very adult and competent and full of fantasies about her own child.

Her friends were shocked. Women did not just go and have babies by themselves in 1950. If they got pregnant and could not afford to fly to Puerto Rico for an abortion, then they went off to have the baby in a "home" like a women's prison, and the baby was taken away and adopted.

She had been so proud. So confident. Was it only that she enjoyed shocking the people around her, even the most political men and women who thought of themselves as socially advanced and free thinking? Had she been acting in a little private play of her own, the bold heroine, the new woman in her cute maternity outfits Karla sewed for her? Karla had been behind her all the way. Beverly had entertained visions of herself with a miniature version by the hand, a little red-curled Beverly, a brave curly-headed little boy, a darling radical Shirley Temple marching along with her on parades and picket lines.

As soon as she was home from the hospital with a squalling baby, she had intimations she had made a terrible error. Everyone said she was so brave, but here she was in a little apartment in Brooklyn down the block from Karla, and stuck, penned up with a voracious creature with a voice like a steam whistle and one demand after another. She never finished having to fix something for or around the baby. The creature never seemed to sleep more than a couple of hours at a stretch. Karla had endured two miscarriages and was glad to take the baby when Beverly could not stand being stuck with her another hour. It had seemed to her even then that the tiny red-faced Suzanne glared at her balefully, reproaching her for her secret regrets.

She finally dragged herself into the wheelchair and rolled over to the computer. Then she sat there idle in front of it. Elena had made the screen background dark red for her. It was cheerful. But who did she really want to talk to, and what did she really have to say? Labor organizing was useful but sometimes so depressing. You just got people a wage they could live on and raise their families in decency, and then the fucking owners moved the factories where they could get kids to work for fifty cents an hour. Your people were all out of work and back in poverty, stuck in dead-end jobs they could not live on. The more you liked the people, the more you respected and admired them, the worse it was for you. She had tried to affect the economic and political life of her country for half a century, and sometimes she had succeeded and sometimes she had failed, but it was over. She could not push anymore.

It seemed to her she could always smell her own body like decay, like something old and rotten left too long in the garbage pail in the kitchen. If she were really as strong as she had always thought herself to be, she would just swallow her own tongue. She would find some way to kill herself. Drag a radio into the bathroom and prop it in the shower stall, but she could not bring herself to do that. Suppose she did something wrong and ended up alive but paralyzed?

After her first stroke, she had tried hard, she had tried and tried. She had fought to get her strength back, to speak clearly, to move, to walk, to care for herself, believing she could recover. She had expected she would be herself, her own person again. She no longer believed any of that. What had been Beverly Blume was gone forever. Less than half herself was left, and that was dwindling. The caretakers provided by the service spoke to her as if she were feebleminded, a large floppy retarded child. None were like Sylvia, and she could not succeed in creating relationships with any of them. It was not the same women who came, and the way they spoke at her was like a performance on automatic pilot. They did not engage. They did their job.

Suzanne was walking her to and fro tonight. It was so boring. Suzanne was doing a good job walking her along, but Beverly could tell her mind was elsewhere. Suzanne had always been able to do that since she was a little girl, to be sitting one place but be mentally miles away. It had always annoyed Beverly. She would be talking to her daughter and then realize it was like talking to the radio: Suzanne hadn't heard one word she had uttered.

"What . . . think about?" Beverly demanded.

"What? Oh, Maxine's case. I was going over the arguments I'll use before the Supreme Judicial Court."

"What arguments?"

Unintentionally, Suzanne speeded up her pace, hauling Beverly along as she talked. Beverly forgot to listen after a while. It was all legal stuff. At least she had Suzanne's attention. She asked, "Marry him, you?"

"Who?" Suzanne stopped cold.

Beverly laughed. "More . . . one?"

"Jake, you mean? No. Why should I?"

Beverly shrugged. "Did . . . Sam."

"Marrying Sam was a big mistake, you know that. It's not that tight a relationship. It's fine the way it is. I can barely manage that."

"Leave you . . . set up."

"Marriage wouldn't set me up. You didn't think it would set you up, did you? Why foist it on me? Besides, I haven't the time for it."

Beverly jabbed her thumb at her chest. "Burden!"

"No, you aren't."

Beverly made a derisive noise.

"You're my mother."

Suzanne was such a wimp, unable to admit what a nuisance Beverly had made of herself by having two strokes and landing on her. Beverly could feel the money burning up. She noticed how they were trying to economize. They thought she couldn't see how her care was costing more and more. Beverly shook her head. Denial, the young ones called it. Beverly called it willful blindness. Of course she was a burden to her daughter. She was a burden to herself. What a mess life was at the end, never resolved, never cleanly finished, never coming to a proper satisfying conclusion, a final resonant chord of completion.

Beverly plopped herself down in a kitchen chair and pointed at the other. Enough of this pointless staggering back and forth from the bedroom to the living room and back like a gerbil on a treadmill. For this she should struggle on? She dragged a pad over and began to print. NOTHING LIVE FOR. USING UP RESOURCES. PAIN. CAN'T DO ANYTHING MATTERS. TIRED. TIRED. TIRED.

"Mother, what do you want?"

HELP ME DIE. PLEASE PLEASE PLEASE.

"Murder you."

PEACE! HELP ME.

Suzanne looked into her eyes, staring and staring. It was the longest and most intense stare they had ever exchanged, at least since Suzanne was twelve or thirteen. Mostly they had avoided this kind of piercing scrutiny of each other, avoided offering themselves to it out of dread, a need for privacy, even out of delicacy. Now they stared and stared at each other.

"How long have you been thinking about . . . wanting to die?"

3 MONTHS, Beverly wrote. EVERY DAY. EVERY NIGHT.

"You've been talking to Elena about this."

Beverly nodded. She printed carefully, NEED BOTH HELP. SOON. VERY SOON.

Suzanne was frowning. She did not look convinced. Inside Beverly's mind, arguments chased themselves, tumbling over one another like puppies but trapped, mute. To get them out, that was the difficulty. She could only beg. Stare. Plead with her eyes. Help me. A last favor. Give me peace.

44

Elena

"Now he's back on the talk show circuit with this father-right thing," Marta said. "How can anyone take him seriously? Warmed-over Bly."

Pudgy Miles was frowning. "He got in some licks. And judges, mostly men, mostly fathers, are going to like his line. The world is full of men who screwed up their marriages and imagine they want their kids." He turned to Elena, sitting scrunched up in a chair, trying to make herself small and preferably invisible. "Now I need to be sure I can trust you as a witness."

Elena blinked, insulted as if he had slapped her. "I know I was wrong and I want to try to make up some of it to Marta. We were worms."

"You're going to have to do better than that if you want to convince a judge that Marta is the injured party. He's contesting the divorce, so we're at war."

Miles was the beige man, she thought: beige hair, beige skin, beige mind. No one had ever caught his eye across a room and clicked. However, she could hardly say her capacity for instant ignition had won her a lot of prizes. Maybe it was better to be beige or gray. His mind was nasty and sharp-edged enough.

"One thing we want to show is that you're easily influenced by a man you're involved with. That he was the active party."

"Easily influenced. You're not talking about Chad and Evan. You're not going to bring that up!"

"Those records are sealed, since you were a juvenile, but I can have you mention it if I ask the right question. I need your cooperation. I'm telling you how I want to play it."

"I'm the weak little slut who can be pushed around by any man. But Chad and Evan didn't push me around. I was happy with them. Death just seemed like another bigger orgasm or the biggest high of them all. And I wanted Jim at least as much as he wanted me. I thought I wanted him anyhow." She looked briefly at Marta. "I thought I knew who he was. I made him up."

"He's plausible," Marta said. "I believed everything he said for years."

"We need to establish Jim's guilt, so we need to establish your relative innocence," Miles said patiently. "I need your cooperation or I won't use you."

"I've been down this road before. . . ." She sighed. "It's always a story, isn't it? Never the truth."

Miles gave her a steady stare that said he did think it was the truth: that she was an impressionable idiot. Marta was waiting patiently.

"I'll do whatever it takes. I'll say whatever I have to," she said.

"I appreciate what you're trying to do," Marta said. "Understand that I want to forgive you. It's healthier for both of us."

Elena stood at the window looking out while they worked on their line of argument together. Boston was locked in the grip of a glacier. It had snowed and frozen over and snowed and frozen over. Sidewalks were lined with cliffs of dirty ice. On every street battles were waged over parking places. If someone had chipped out a place, it was theirs, by the unwritten law of the city. They might place a trash can or an old chair in it to mark possession, but if anyone moved that trash can or chair and took the place, it was often more than a war of words that would follow. She wondered if anyone had ever been killed in one of these battles. She asked Miles. He frowned and went silent for a few minutes. Then he said, "Almost. Dorchester District Court, 1994. William Procton parked in the place cleared by the defendant Edmund Little. Edmund Little shot William Procton in the thigh. The jury would not convict him of anything more than simple assault. I don't know if he actually served time. Basically, the jury thought Little was justified."

Elena did not know if she were pleased or depressed that Rachel wasn't getting married after all. She had hoped they would all go to Israel, which sounded like a great trip, especially in the winter. She was shocked when Rachel called her. A first. "How could I have been so mistaken about Michael?"

"How could I have been so mistaken about Jim? I made a much worse botch of things. At least you didn't get married. If the rabbinical court hadn't insulted you, you'd be marrying him and then you'd be stuck. Then you'd find out what he's really like."

A long silence while the satellite connection burbled and clanked to itself. "You're right." Rachel couldn't help sounding surprised that Elena had been able to offer her some insight. "I'm trying to be satisfied with that."

"I'm just sorry we didn't all get to go and visit you," Elena said.

Rachel said. "Mother's been poor-mouthing me for months. Are you really eating cat food and sprouted potatoes?"

"Every night," Elena said. "But I eat at the restaurant."

"I thought you were fired?"

"Different restaurant."

Rachel didn't ask anything more about her job: who but another restaurant worker would? "It's so beautiful here. It actually snowed in Jerusalem yesterday. It was like crystal and gold. Glittering."

"I'm going back to school. But don't tell Mother yet. Please."

"Why? What could you be studying that she would object to? Let's see, theological school. Studying to be an Episcopal priest. . . ."

"You can do all the religion for the family. No, I just don't want her getting excited and telling me what a great idea it is, so that I get contrary and don't do it. I want it to be my idea, and I don't want to tell her until I'm taking classes."

"You know, she really wants to be supportive. You think she's trying to butt in, when she's just wanting to make it easier for you."

"It's better if I do it myself, at least till I'm launched and I know it's working. Believe me, it'll be better that way." Elena switched gears. "Anyhow, don't you think you might get back with Michael?"

"Are you going to get back with Jim?"

"But that was stupidity. Just gross. Marta's pregnant! I wouldn't be in the same room, believe me. He tries to corner me, but I won't let him. With Michael, I met him. He isn't married to someone else. He's just young."

"Well, I'm the same age he is, and I'm not going to take his insensitivity. I don't even think he'll be a good rabbi."

"What do I know. He seemed, you know, like he cared about you."

"Well, it was an act. I should think you'd understand that."

Elena shrugged, realizing Rachel could not see her. "I'm an expert on being fooled. Being fooled and fucking up. I can just pretend a man is the way I want him to be and ignore anything that shows me how wrong I am."

"Me too, apparently. Must be genetic."

She did not tell Rachel about Sean. Her sister would be shocked that she had taken up with another man so quickly, never understanding how Sean protected her. She had loved Jim, and she knew that weakness lay inside her like a virus in abeyance, ready to swarm into her blood again if she gave it a chance. She suspected Jim knew that too, and that was why he had not stopped stalking her, waiting for her. Not lately, for he had seen her twice with Sean. Sean's bulk made him impossible to ignore. She also neglected to mention Sean because her relationship with him, while pleasant, did not occupy much of her mind or emotions. Sean was damaged and could give a limited amount. He had wounds she did not push to explore. She simply made do with him and the time passed and took her out of danger.

He drank two or three beers to every one of hers, getting quieter and more withdrawn. She did not try to monitor his drinking after the first couple of times. He did not want her to take care of him. He was on his own lonesome road. She spent more time trying to figure out Robby, because he ran the waiting staff and she had to suit him to keep the job.

She could hostess and go to school, that was her plan. He was quirky, mercurial, sometimes kind and sometimes sarcastic, demanding. She stepped around him carefully, learning to tell when she came into work what kind of mood he was in and pace herself accordingly. He gave her more leeway because they were the same age born on adjacent days. He also liked her style, as he remarked. He told her she moved well. Sometimes when they went to a different bar, they danced. He was fun to dance with. Sean would not dance, saying he'd feel like a performing bear. Going out with the kids passed the time. Sometimes when she thought back to the summer, she imagined she had succumbed to a high dangerous fever that had burned her up and left her debilitated, and that she was still slowly recovering.

45

Suzanne and Beverly

Suzanne thought Rachel, in trying to act cheerful, sounded so miserable, she ended up urging her to get back together with Michael. She could tell that rejecting that suggestion made Rachel feel better. Rachel had made a Mizrachi friend, Nava, a young woman with Moroccan parents. She was invited to the older sister's henna party. Suzanne worried that the wedding preparations would upset Rachel. Perhaps it was too exotic to make her jealous. The henna party was all women, with hours of eating and giggling and dancing. Rachel wrote that she was sending photos. If Rachel was depressed by the wedding, her E-mail did not reflect it. Karla kept insisting they would get back together, but Suzanne was doubtful. If Rachel felt that Michael was in essential disagreement with her about something as important as her religion and her role as a rabbi, they would not reconcile. The rift had hurt Rachel and shaken her confidence.

Suzanne understood how the quarrel could cause Rachel to doubt her ability to command love. She had been down that betrayal road herself. She had been slow to suspect Sam, because even Victor, whom everyone had expected to be constantly running around, had seemed satisfied with her until she got pregnant. She had begun to suspect Sam when stories and schedules did not jibe. She had been shocked at the deceit as much as at the infidelity. She had been told a hundred times that she just didn't understand temptation. It was her nature to fall in love rarely, to put her practice and her daughters before any man, and to have too much trouble trusting the love of one man ever to consider another on the side. She had no time for complications. She could still find buried in the bottom of her brain a hot core of anger, a seed she had never let grow but had never rooted out. It was there, radioactive but unacted upon—that old painful sense of betrayal she called upon in defending many of her women clients.

Sam had phoned her the week before, wanting to discuss Marta's divorce and the situation with Elena. She had referred him to Miles, who surely could handle Sam and deal with his curiosity. Marta and Sam had never gotten along. She wasn't about to say one word to him that might come back to haunt Marta or give him satisfaction. Sometimes she was fond of Sam, but she did not entirely trust him where Marta was concerned. They had old grudges they hadn't aired or relinquished. Years ago, she had resolved never to be caught between them.

Suzanne had to muster all her patience, never considerable, to have a real conversation with Beverly. Beverly was sitting up in bed, while Suzanne sat in a desk chair dragged up beside the bed.

Beverly wrote, BETTER GAVE YOU KARLA FULL TIME.

Instead of denying the suggestion to avoid a fight, Suzanne pondered what Beverly had written. "Maybe so," she said. "It was hard going back and forth. You had such different ideas about everything. With Karla, I went to shul. With Karla, I was supposed to be interested in food and to like to learn to cook. Eating was good. With you, any mention of religion set you off. You didn't want to observe Jewish holidays, so if I didn't spend them with Karla, I didn't get any holidays. You were bored with food. Grab some takeout. Have a snack. You never ate much and you hated to cook."

Beverly shook back her hair, struggling to speak. "Karla . . . fat."

"I didn't think that was so bad. Her house smelled like cinnamon and garlic and onions and rendering chicken fat. Her chairs were easy to sit in. She spoiled me, you said, and certainly she made me feel like something precious. But I couldn't want to be her. She was a third grade teacher. I already knew that wasn't enough to be."

Beverly carefully printed, I MADE YOU SNOB?

"Let's just say you had higher ambitions for me. Security wasn't your goal, and you didn't want it to be mine."

"So not . . . all bad."

"Of course not. But you two sure were a contrast. You were glamorous. You were a flirt—"

Beverly laughed, waving her hand as if to bat at a fly.

"You were always coming and going. You had boyfriends. If you entered a room, everyone knew it. You had politics. You took chances. But Karla was kinder. Gentler. And she was more . . . affectionate."

SHOULD NOT HAD KID.

Suzanne knew she should disagree politely, but she could not, for she had often thought the same thing. When she was little, how often she had wished that Karla were her mother and Beverly her aunt. She had felt guilty for that wish, but she had not been able to keep herself from confiding it to Karla—who had been very, very pleased. She would have said that the two sisters were at war over her, except that her mother seemed rather satisfied to leave her to Karla at least half the time. "Well, I suppose I had two mothers. That must be twice as good as one. Basically, you know, you were flat out, the way I live now. I barely have time for anybody, and you were the same way. We're alike in that. You gave first place to your work, because it was important to you—"

"Im . . . portant . . . others."

"Likewise for me. Besides, she let me down too. When I came back from college, I'd been replaced. She was crazy about Suwanda—she'd just adopted her—and suddenly I was no longer the golden girl. But you and I are more alike than you realize in how we deal with things. You had Karla take care of me, and I get Elena to help and the agency."

Beverly nodded. She let her head loll back on the pillow. "Tired."

Suzanne started to rise. "I'll let you rest then."

Beverly stopped her with a hand on her arm. "Must talk."

Suzanne took her seat again. "Sure. What's on your mind?"

"You know. Want die."

"Yeah. You want to die." She looked hard at her mother. "You're asking me to commit murder, you understand that, Mother."

Beverly shrugged. "Do . . . careful."

"I teach the law. I am an officer of the court. We've already had one notorious case touching this family."

Tears rolled out of Beverly's eyes. "No . . . go on. No."

"What am I supposed to do?" Suzanne asked out loud.

"Pills."

"What kind of pills?"

Beverly gestured toward the bookcase she had been using as a dresser. "Top . . . shelf."

Suzanne went to the bookcase. She saw only socks and stockings and mittens. A jar of oversize safety pins. "What am I looking for?"

"Print . . . out."

She found a sheaf of papers under the socks, downloaded from the Internet, from last July before Beverly's second stroke. It consisted of descriptions of various ways for terminally ill people to end their lives. "But you're not terminally ill."

Beverly had been writing on her pad. NO END. WORSE THAN TERMINAL. On a second sheet she continued printing, LITTLE ME LEFT. ALL I VALUE GONE. BURDEN. THIS NOT LIFE!

Beverly felt exhausted and frustrated. To say something simple, almost simpleminded, took all her strength. Why couldn't she make Suzanne understand? There had to be a way to get through to her. Her thoughts raced in her head, although sometimes a word or a phrase eluded her and she had to make do with some equivalent, but what came out of her mouth was crude and jerky. It was not what she wanted to say, but a brief headline version. Everything became a summary, a synopsis, a piece torn from her meaning. It wasn't enough to sustain her interest just to eat, shit, and sleep. She was trapped in this broken mind and partly paralyzed body. She was tired of it, tired to death. If only she could make them feel what she felt. But how? "Why you . . . make . . . me stay?"

"Is it that bad here?"

Beverly nodded fervently. She longed to tell Suzanne it wasn't anything wrong she was doing. This was not Beverly's life, rather Suzanne's she was squatting in the middle of, out of place, unable to communicate, unable to act.

"Would you be happier in some kind of facility?"

"No! No!" That was living death: to be stored with the other dysfunctional to be minimally tended by underpaid staff who had no idea who she had been and did not care. "On steps . . . disappointed."

Suzanne pondered for a moment. "Are you talking about this summer?"

Beverly nodded. "Bad day."

"It sure was."

"Marta free. Elena okay." She hated to hear herself talk. It was humiliating to sound like a two-year-old or someone who had only begun to learn English. Every time she opened her mouth, she cringed. She printed, NOW TIME HELP ME!

"We're trying to help you. Elena and I and the aides who come in make sure you walk every day. We try to give you what you need, Mother, even if you don't think we succeed."

She glared. How could Suzanne so stubbornly refuse to understand? She felt taken advantage of. Because she could barely argue her case, Suzanne could pretend she did not know what Beverly wanted. "Help . . . die. Only help . . . want."

Suzanne was silent for a long time. Beverly waited her out, staring. Did her daughter really think she would forget what she wanted so passionately, that she would change her mind, that she would drop the subject? Fat chance. She would not let Suzanne forget what had to be done. She would hound her daughter until she got her way. She had to communicate her desperation, even though she felt like a toddler in a high chair banging a spoon. "Only . . . thing . . . want." She hit her good hand against her chest. God, she was skinny and flabby. Her own body disgusted her. It was not the body she had nourished and cared for, the vehicle of her will and her pleasure. "Die!"

Suzanne began to weep. Beverly wished she could hit her. How dare her daughter sit and weep because of what she wanted and desperately needed? As if the whole family wouldn't be much better off with her out of the house. How dare Suzanne assume she was not aware how much her illness was costing—she'd asked the aides what they were paid and multiplied that by two—and for what? Boredom and pain and disgust. She glared at her daughter, who looked up, saw her, and began to cry harder. This is a big help, Beverly thought, a great big help, as if crying made anything different. She was never a weeper. Karla was. Since they'd been little girls, she had wept at anything: you only had to tell her a dog had been run over or a bird had hit a window, and she was off. In the movies, she was always blubbering. Sometimes Beverly had refused to sit with her. In fact, Suzanne had been the same way, but Beverly had shamed it out of her, making her more stoical, stronger. It was undignified to be constantly spouting tears. Women who relied on crying to get their way should be ashamed. Never had she used tears as a weapon, and she was immune to them. Suzanne could blubber all night, but Beverly would not alter one jot of her intent.

Suzanne felt despair like a cold rock in her abdomen. Beverly was not going to relent. She was not going to stop sitting there like a furious owl glaring and repeating in that low cracked voice that she wanted to die. She could just see explaining to Beverly's doctors that her mother was bent on suicide, except that Beverly was far too helpless to commit suicide. Suzanne would be responsible for killing her.

Suzanne had fought legal battles for twenty-five years, but never had she killed anything larger than an earwig. She had lived her life nonviolently. She could not even imagine helping her mother die. She still had in her lap the sheaf of papers Beverly had insisted she take from the shelf. Obviously Beverly had been contemplating suicide even before her second stroke. Obviously she was not about to change her mind, no matter what Suzanne argued. She felt trapped. Whatever she did would bring an avalanche of guilt down on her. She would be buried in guilt whether she refused to help her mother die, or whether she was coerced into killing her. How could she live with either choice?

She waved the papers. "I'll read this and get back to you." How ridiculous that sounded, as if it were a brief on which she was offering an opinion.

"Help . . . me."

"I'll do what I can, Mother. I'll do what I can."

Beverly reached out with her good hand and grasped Suzanne's wrist, hard. Suzanne was surprised how much strength Beverly could muster.

Her mother's gaze never wavered from hers. She seemed determined not to blink. "Must, Suze, must."

Suze: what her mother had called her when she was a little girl, and Beverly was actually pleased with her. She was not so much touched as briefly amused. "You're a crafty old manipulator, Beverly. You won't give up, will you?"

"No."

"I'll read the material and consider very seriously what I can do. Now, let go of my arm, Mother." She then bent down and kissed her on the forehead.

Beverly held on for another minute and then let go. "Tomorrow."

"Yes, tomorrow we'll talk again. That's a promise."

Suzanne turned out the lights and went into her office. What her mother had given her did not exactly seem like bedroom reading. She sat down at her desk to read the directions for ending her mother's life. She wished that she drank whisky, but the strongest thing she ever consumed was sherry, at the dean's socials. She didn't even have any of that handy. There were times it was a real pity she was not a drinking woman.

As she was reading, she got a call from a California lawyer who owed her a favor. She had talked him into helping on Jake's case. "It's bad. The judge has just given instructions to the jury that practically preclude anything but a guilty verdict including the conspiracy charge, which is the real killer. I think there're plenty of grounds for appeal, but since I came in late, I won't know till I see the complete court transcripts."

"There's really a chance Jake could go to prison?"

"I'd say the odds are on it."

46

Elena

Elena listened to her mother going on about this case in Florida where the guy got a suspended sentence for helping his wife die and this case where a guy got fifteen years house arrest. Then there was a case in North Carolina where a son was convicted of first-degree murder, in spite of the fact that his father was dying and begging him to end his suffering. Now she was talking about something called Cruzan.

"It's a crap game," Suzanne said, putting down her notes. "There is no state in which the law recognizes the right of a family member to help someone die, even when they have begged for it and are in terrible pain." Suzanne rose and began pacing, not frantically but almost to Elena's eyes with a mechanical precision, turning each time on her heel. "For exactly the same act, juries have repeatedly let the defendant go free while other juries have sent people to prison for life. The standard defense is the kind of temporary insanity plea. Everybody knows it's patently untrue, but the juries will often seize on it to justify what happened. And in *Washington v. Glucksberg*, the Supreme Court opinion, written by Rehnquist, made a strong distinction between withholding medical treatment and affirmatively giving someone medication that could kill, thus overturning the decisions maintaining the right to die from the Second and Ninth Circuit Courts."

"So a lot of these guys took a gun and snuffed the one they loved. But we're talking about pills," Elena said. "If we do it right, there's no murder investigation. Come on, Mother, we should be able to help her."

Suzanne sat down again to the pages of notes she had brought with her to this little meeting in her home office with the door shut. "You're convinced we should do this?"

"Mother, she's been begging me for two months before she ever asked you. I can't refuse her, just to protect my own neck. I love Grandma."

"I love her too—"

"But you have a lot of history. She was always there for me. She never judged me. I owe her this."

"The fact that I have history with her makes it even more complicated. How do we know we haven't made her feel guilty for being dependent on us?"

"She does feel guilty for being dependent. Wouldn't you?"

"Then we're failing. How do we know we're not subtly encouraging this for our own convenience?"

"I suppose because, according to you, we could both go to prison for life."

"But don't you sometimes feel imprisoned now? Don't you wish you didn't have to rush back here to sit with her? To help her to the bathroom. To change bedpans or sheets when she doesn't make it to the bathroom in time. To help her bathe. To help her eat. To take her to the doctors and the therapists. Doesn't that get to you?"

"Yeah, sometimes. Sometimes not. I have more patience than you do."

"The cats have more patience than I do. But don't you see, Elena, we have motive. How can we be sure it's not our own convenience we're acting on?"

"Because she's been asking and asking again. She's in despair. She hates her life now, Mother. Can't you understand that, can't you try to see this from her point of view, just this once?"

Suzanne sighed. "I hate suicide. I can't help it. When I think you almost killed yourself when you were fifteen—"

"Come on, Mother, that's ancient. It was never my idea. It's one thing Marta was right about. Chad wanted to die, he was so bullshit at his father. He was just ripped. He didn't want the life his father was making him live. He felt he'd rather die than go to military school. I was just fucking bored."

"I know you don't like my starting with the legal aspects, but that's how I come at it. I can divide our research into several parts—"

"Research?" Elena heard her voice rise in a spiral.

Suzanne looked at her in surprise. "Yes, research. First, the law. Second, available methods, pros and cons, and of those methods, determine which are actually practical for Beverly and for us. Then, once we have chosen a method, if we both decide it is advisable to proceed, how to do it."

Elena laughed dryly. "Here we are, working together, Mother. For perhaps the first time."

"Is it really? I guess it is." Suzanne lay back in her desk chair and closed her eyes for a moment. "I wish it was less grim."

"Why should it be grim? We're working to release her. It's the best present we could give her. We have to do it for her, Mother. We both promised."

"Yes, we did, Elena, we must be out of our minds." Suzanne raised her hand wearily to forestall a reaction. "One of the thorniest points is that she is not dying, she is not in unbearable pain. She simply feels helpless and hopeless and she wants to be done with a struggle she's losing. Okay. Now the practical." Her mother brought out the sheaf of papers Elena recognized as Grandma's printout.

Elena stood. "I'll take over this part. I'll do the . . . research."

Her mother looked at her with raised eyebrows. "Are you sure you want to? It's rather dull library stuff."

"You think I can't do it because it's too intellectual for me?"

"Never. Of course you can. I'm a little surprised you're volunteering."

She knew very well her mother did not believe in her ability to dig up information on suicide methods but could not say so. She smiled. Mother was sometimes ridiculously easy to manipulate. Elena wanted to figure it out. She was pretty good at scouting out drugs, and she had connections for getting them without leaving a paper trail. "It's a job I'm more than willing to take on." She trusted herself more than Suzanne's scruples in the situation.

Suddenly Suzanne crumpled. She sat at her desk with her head in her hands, weeping. Sobs wracked her. Elena was terrified for a moment. Suzanne never cried. She moved slowly toward her mother, hoping it would end as spontaneously as it had begun. Then awkwardly, tentatively, she put her arm around Suzanne and patted her back, feeling somewhat like a person afraid of horses attempting to quiet one.

Suzanne got herself back under control. When she could speak, she said softly, "It's hard to explain. But all this means giving up. Giving up the fantasy that someday she and I would understand each other, would

... have a better way of being together. ... Don't be upset, Elena, it's just an old daydream of mine."

"At least the two of us are doing better, Mother, don't you think? That's something neither of us expected, right? At least we have that."

There were lots of nice ways of saying what they were talking about, ways people had invented to discuss a person offing themselves with words like tongs. One of Elena's favorites was "self-deliverance," which sounded like having a baby on your own. If she was amused by the language that went around death on tiptoe, she was matter-of-fact about gathering information. Chad had been sloppy in planning his own death. He had taken Evan with him, without Evan's desire, simply because Chad had been out of control. If he had truly wanted to kill himself and only himself, the solution would have been to take the gun, lock himself in his room at home and use it, or walk into the desert alone and put the gun to his head. But he had not wanted to die alone. He had wanted company in his dying, for them to be with him and for them to die with him. For so many years, she had felt guilty that she had not shot herself or been shot. She had not been able to protect Evan. She had failed him. But she did not feel guilty toward Chad. Finally after all these years, she found in the core of herself a certain amount of anger and a certain amount of pity. Sometimes anger dominated and sometimes pity, but the guilt for not dying with them was utterly wiped. Evan had died because of Chad's gun, not because of her.

She went off to the public library and began to look for books on suicide, which proved irrelevant—endless statistics and stupid generalizations. Psychological profiles. Pontificating. Then she tried poison. That was more useful, although most ways sounded too painful.

In a big bookstore, she found a couple of books that were actually about helping people to die, or people offing themselves. She stood by the shelf reading them for a while before she decided the one to buy. She bought a couple of random books so that the bookstore employee would be less likely to remember her: an Italian cookbook and a book about all the various current psychological therapies. That she might actually read. The clerk was maybe twenty-two and paid no attention. She gave him cash.

She carried home her three books and sat down to read case histories of suicides, *Let Me Die Before I Wake*. Most of the people seemed to have cancer, but Grandma had the same right to decide she didn't want to live. Grandma wanted to do it neatly. She hadn't asked about Mother's gun, which was a blessing. Elena could still see Chad with his head blasted open and the brains and blood spilling out. Shooting a person turned them into garbage.

She sat up on her bed with the pillows piled up behind her and read the book with a yellow transparent marking pen, just as if she were back in college and studying for her finals. She was methodical. It was very important to her to do this right, to learn what was needed to help Grandma and prove herself to her mother and, most importantly, to herself. It mattered a lot that she not fuck up. Her new image of herself as the competent therapist went with the careful note taking, the figuring of the exact amounts of whatever drugs she could buy that were necessary for a sure lethal dose.

After the restaurant closed Friday night, she went out to the late-hours bar with the gang and took a seat next to Robby, watching for a good opportunity to talk when no one else was listening. Robby mostly dealt cocaine, crack, heroin, and marijuana, but he boasted he could provide anything. Finally her chance came. "Robby, I need some stuff."

"I'm listening."

She did not dare ask him to get it all at once. It would be too weird. She would ask for part of it and then in a week or so, request more. "I'd love to have some Nembutals or Amytals or . . ." She went down her list. "And maybe some Darvon or Demerol or codeine?"

"Either/or, or both."

"Like I'd want both, but I'll take what I can get."

"It's going to cost you." What he never would ask was why she wanted it. Presumably to get high, to get low, to get out of it.

"If you want to fly, you got to pay. When can you have it?"

"Next Friday."

"Give me a ballpark figure and I'll have the bills."

When Elena reported back to her mother, she was pleased to tell her not only that she had figured out what to use—drugs and dosage—but that she had lined up the first delivery for the next night. What she needed was cash in fifties. Robby liked fifties. "Neither too big nor too small," he had said in his deep liquid voice. "Just right."

Friday night she gave Robby the money and she got the pills in two vitamin bottles. "The vitamin C is the Nembutal. The B complex is the codeine."

Instead of putting them in her purse, she put them in the pocket of her black silk pants. The bulge would not show under her mandarin-collared tunic of deep red and gold. It felt safer to keep them with her than to leave them in her purse in Natalie's office. Every time she felt them bump against her, she felt proud of herself. Grandma's deliverance. How happy she would be. It wasn't enough, but it was a start.

She waited till she was at Sean's, to count them in the bathroom. She needed thirty Nembutal. Robby had sold her ten. He'd been more generous with the codeine.

Her mother was waiting for her Saturday morning. "Beverly's asleep. Did you get it?"

Elena produced first one bottle with a flourish and then the other. She felt like a magician. "It's part of what she needs."

Her mother looked at the bottles but did not touch them. "That's it?"

"What did you expect, a guillotine?"

Suzanne ran her fingers through her short thick hair. "I don't know, I don't know!"

"It's not like you to be so indecisive."

"I never murdered my mother before."

"Come on, don't be melodramatic. Don't you believe she has a right to decide when to give up her life? When to die with dignity, while she still can?"

"I believe it—in the abstract."

"Well, I'm exhausted. We'll talk it over with Grandma tomorrow in the morning when she's got it together. Now I'm going to bed." Elena was a little miffed that her mother did not appreciate what she had done, but Grandma would.

"Can you get the rest?" Suzanne asked, wringing her hands. "This much won't do it, if I understand you correctly."

"Next week I'll get more. And the week after I'll get the last installment. I can't ask for it all at once. The guy I'm dealing with would be too suspicious."

When it came to the third time she asked, he was leery. "You've been doing a lot of those. Got a habit? Or are you dealing them?"

"I'm doing them with two friends who are in town for a while. I'm not addicted. We've just been into it lately. I don't do it when I have to work. Have I seemed off to you?"

"Guess not." But she noticed him watching her, and she was extra careful with everyone that night and the rest of the week. The price went up. He was testing her. Well, after this batch, she would tell him her friends had left and she was no longer interested. She'd buy some weed just to fool him.

On Saturday he finally sold her the last of what they needed. She did not spend that night at Sean's. She just told him she was feeling a little queasy, something she'd eaten. Sean hadn't seen the transactions in the cloakroom. Robby never talked about his customers. She drove home cautiously, not even running a yellow. When she had actually shut the front door behind her and entered the house with the pills still in her pants pocket, she felt an immense relief. It was all there, everything Grandma needed. She had done it.

47

Beverly

Beverly wanted to keep the two bottles on top of her chest of drawers, where she could gaze on them, eyes no matter how blurry fixed on her deliverance. Suzanne objected. "The aides can see them there. It's important that they not be aware you have the pills. Elena could get into trouble."

Beverly had a project. She was an actress playing her last role. She was persuading the caretakers that she was weaker than she was. She faked apparent sleep even oftener than she lapsed into that druggy stupefaction that overwhelmed her frequently. She saw no reason to perform exercises that were unpleasant and pretended she could no longer do them. Two of the aides told Suzanne Beverly was getting worse and should see her doctor. Suzanne made an appointment for the last week in February. They would do tests to determine if she had undergone another small stroke or if she were suffering from some other complication. Beverly was determined not to endure more tests. That was the deadline, three weeks away.

She felt weirdly expectant and cheerful. Knowing that it would all end soon made everything more bearable, like the pain in her leg that had no feeling. It was impossible the leg should hurt, but it did. The doctor called it phantom pain. Well, he should feel it, then he'd know what a phantom it wasn't. The pain in her head that came and went and came back again. The pain in her back from lying in bed too much, from sitting up in bed, from lying in awkward positions because half her body was dead wood. The pain in her bowels from the severe constipation she supposed came from lack of exercise. The pain in her kidneys from the medications they had her on. The pain when she did attempt mild exercise. The fearful effort of doing anything whatsoever, from putting on a Velcro-fastened sweater to going to the bathroom. The shock when she saw herself, that scrawny twisted-face hag in the mirror. The heroic effort it took to speak a coherent fragment. The total boredom of getting through each empty day and long night. The humiliation when she could not get to the toilet in time, as happened increasingly. The smell of her own body, the smell of the bed she was condemned to. All about to finish.

She felt young inside, knowing that her exit was under her own control. This was the first power she had enjoyed after months of being helpless and at the complete mercy of others. She would not wait too long. She did not want more tests, more invasion, more time in the hospital. She hated the doctors who treated her like an idiot. She would escape them all. She saw herself as the woman she had been, slender yes but shapely, with her red hair and green eyes, with her laugh and her wit and her husky voice, with her ability not only to speak like a human being but to move rooms and crowds. She saw that woman rising up from this ruined body and escaping. It did not matter that she did not believe in an afterlife. She believed that at the moment of death she would be restored to her full ability. She would die as herself.

She would do it all correctly. She would not waver. She wanted silence, she wanted peace, she wanted out. Each time Elena brought an installment of the pills, she kissed her granddaughter's hands. Every day when she wakened in the morning, instead of despair and a return of pain, she opened her eyes to hope. It would not hurt, what she read promised her. She would pass away quietly. There would be no more awakenings to a burnt-down life. She would slide into a sleep of real peace and never waken again.

Every day she asked herself if it should be today. It had to be the weekend, when the aides were gone. She could not take the chance of one of them finding her in a coma, her secret fear. She had seen a woman who had tried to kill herself but had not taken enough pills. She was brain damaged, kept alive on machines—as punishment, Beverly supposed. She would do it right. She had been bold and efficient all her life, and she would seize the opportunity the pills gave her and make an exit under her own control.

Elena came in to sit with her. It was morning. "What day?"

"Monday, Grandma."

She felt a stab of panic. Somehow the weekend had slipped past. With her new confidence in the pills, she was letting the days slide by under her. Nothing seemed as terrible now that she knew she could call a halt. But next week was the doctor's appointment. She would have to go into the hospital for tests. She had pretended deterioration too convincingly, and now she must act.

She made a simple chart on her pad of paper. 11111. She would cross out each, starting with the first one for Monday, so she did not forget again what day it was. She must do it Friday night or Saturday night. "El . . ."

"Yes, Grandma. Do you need something?"

"Fri . . . Sat . . . Time."

She thought Elena could not possibly understand what she meant. To make it clearer, she jerked her head toward the shelf where the pills were hidden inside a nightgown. "This coming Friday or Saturday night?" Elena asked. "Or just some Friday or Saturday night?"

"Coming."

"Are you sure you want to?"

"Sure."

"I'll have to go to work anyhow, Grandma. It would look too suspicious if I didn't."

"Suzanne . . . be here."

"We'll have to make sure with Mother that she will be."

She would rather have Elena on hand. Maybe she could do it before Elena left for work or wait till she came home. So many practical arrangements to be made. "Give . . . book."

Elena of course knew exactly which book she was talking about. "Oh, you want the Bible."

Beverly did not think that was funny. "Not religious."

Elena grinned, handing her *Let Me Die Before I Wake*. Beverly loved to read about those peaceful deaths. They kept the book hidden with the pills. Now she waved Elena away so she could read her favorite account again. Everything had to be done right. She had made Suzanne and Elena both read several chapters. This was her final piece of work as an organizer, organizing her own death—with dignity. Under her own power.

"Grandma, I'll miss you so much. And so will Mother. I love you, Grandma."

"Miss . . . both." Of course she wouldn't. Silence and peace. The great comforting nothing. She would allow them to be a little sentimental, as long as they didn't try to stop her and as long as they didn't insist too much that she go along with the mushiness. She had always been hard-headed and wasn't about to change at the end. She had heard of death-bed conversions, but she had contempt for them. The values someone lived by should be sufficient to sustain them in dying. She had the same contempt for rational people who suddenly called for a priest or a rabbi as she did for those old fellow travelers or party members who went leaping to the other side and became as fanatical right-wingers as they had been fanatical on the left. Nobody seemed to undergo a conversion to tolerance and the understanding they didn't have every last penny of truth in their particular piggy bank. Religion had never interested her, and it didn't now. Politics and the economy as they impacted on ordinary people, justice and equality, those had been her passions, but she was past being able to have an effect. Time to let go, of everything.

"Grandma . . . are you asleep?"

"Thinking."

"About what?"

"What believe? You."

Elena was puzzled for a minute. "Do you mean you believe in me? Or are you asking what I believe in?"

"Both." She had actually meant the second possibility, but she did have faith in Elena.

Elena scrunched up her face. "You ask hard questions, don't you? Not much. I guess there's some power behind everything, but I can't imagine getting into a personal relationship with whatever it is. Sort of like thinking whether electricity likes you or not."

Beverly nodded, pleased.

"I guess I believe in trying to be good—a recent thing for me." Elena laughed self-consciously. "I mean, I haven't got much of a track record, do I?"

"Good to me."

"Well, maybe you've had an influence on me. I mean, I think it's cool how you were trying to help people all your life." Elena rose and paced. Beverly thought she looked as beautiful and swift as a panther. "You were cool and you had a good time anyhow. I want to do something right. I guess I really have to, to like myself. I've done so much damage. I've broken a lot of people's dishes."

Beverly motioned Elena near and squeezed her hand. She stared into her face. That face was one of the few things she would miss, her beautiful bold granddaughter. "Don't . . . lose . . . bold. . . . Dare." Glossy black hair worn unstylishly long. Long large eyes almost as dark as her hair. Full sensuous mouth and cheekbones like her own. A face that could be a tragic mask or a seductress, except it was too animated, too alive from within.

"Grandma, I don't think that's my problem. It's not thinking things through. Not being clear what I'm doing. Not guessing consequences but just driving over the cliff to see what happens."

She wanted so much to tell Elena how precious she was, and how she must value herself. How even if she made messes and even the occasional catastrophe, she was vital and glorious. She must not be tamed. She must not give up and become mediocre and gray. Beverly had never in her life loved anyone more than she loved Elena. "Love you . . . as . . . you are."

"I know, Grandma," Elena said, her voice breaking, "but I don't."

In that moment, Beverly decided: it would be Saturday night. It would be more convenient for Elena if she did it then. A last little gift of timing for her beloved, not to cause her any more trouble than she had to. Then, then, she would finish. She would have her own death and be done.

48

Suzanne

"Getting divorced is such a lot of work. I don't wonder I never went into that kind of law." Marta lay on her couch, her belly rising majestically above her.

"Everybody's wrong and nobody's right. But can't this stop while you have your baby? Can't you call a time-out?"

"Three weeks. She says it'll have to be a C-section."

"They do a lot more of those now. Did you get a second opinion?"

Marta sighed heavily. "Could you give me a back rub if I lie on my side? If I can still lie on my side."

"Sure. Where's the oil you like?"

"In the bedroom, on the dresser."

The green gym bag was no longer there. The room looked different with Jim's things gone. Marta had Adam move the bed against one wall, to make more room for the baby's crib and bassinet until she could make over Jim's office into the baby's room. Marta wanted to make the house over completely, but the divorce was impoverishing her, as Beverly's illness was doing to Suzanne. Neither of them had money to waste on new curtains or rugs. Suzanne found the almond massage oil and brought it back to the couch.

"Now that it's coming close to time, do you miss Jim?"

Marta shook her head. "Honestly, no. I realize how much time I spent stepping carefully around his ego. I want this baby. It may be self-indulgence, it may be middle-age folly, it may be the fastest way to total exhaustion known to woman, but I want her."

Jake's lawyer called at eight that evening. "The jury's back."

"What were their findings?"

"Guilty on all counts."

"No!" she said. "I can't believe it."

"I told you, with the judge's instructons, there was no other possible outcome." He sounded irritated.

"Can Jake call me?"

"I think he's disappointed in you. He hoped you would come out."

"My mother's in terrible condition. I can't leave her now. She's been deteriorating rapidly since her second stroke. My daughter and I are doing most of the caretaking, and I can't get away. I just can't! Try to make him understand. I don't know how much longer she can hang on." In one sense, she was telling the truth. In another, she was lying. She was gradually sinking in a mud hole of guilt, sinking like the creatures whose remains she had seen in the museum by the La Brea tar pits in LA. She had no idea why she should think of that—a place she had visited with Sam when Rachel was just four and Elena, nine. She felt guilty she was not in California for Jake; she felt guilty about her mother in all aspects, in all scenarios, at all times.

"I'll tell him, but you know, he's facing prison. They got him on all the misdemeanor charges, then on conspiracy to disrupt commerce. That's the big one. The lumber companies are the big employers up here and the big contributors and they get most of what they want—and they wanted Jake's hide."

"I understand. I'll be available for the appeal, I promise. That's what I do best."

"He's still going to be serving time, even if you start the appeal tomorrow—which I understand you can't do."

"Just get me the transcripts as soon as they're available. . . ."

Suzanne had all the instructions in front of her. The two types of pills were to be ground up together and put into a small amount of liquid. Beverly requested fresh orange juice. Elena did the grinding before she left for work, but it would be up to Suzanne to prepare the "cocktail" just before Beverly consumed it. "Saturday! Saturday!" Beverly had been saying all week: beaming as if she were looking forward to a date or a party. Suzanne kept going into her own room and weeping. Her stomach was lead. How could she really go through with it? It seemed to Suzanne that her mother and she had finally been communicating at least semi-well for the first time in decades. Why couldn't they continue? She had always wanted her mother's respect, and lately, she seemed to be getting at least a little of it. She felt the finality of death as a sentence on her as well as Beverly.

"I won't put the plastic bag on," Suzanne said to Elena. "I can't smother her. If she takes the pills and they stay down and work, that's her choice. But I won't put a plastic bag over her head."

Elena was dressed for work, all in black but for a red scarf. "If the pills don't work by early morning, I'll put the bag on."

"I'm going along with this because she wants it and that's her right. But I can't smother her and you shouldn't. If she wakes up, that's how it is."

"I'll be home by one at the latest."

"I'm going to sit up with her."

"So will I."

Suzanne had not felt as close to her older daughter since Elena had been a little girl. She could place their first bad fights around the time Elena was twelve—around the time of the divorce from Sam. Her home life had become a battleground, and she had responded by throwing herself into work. She needed the money, but more, she was happiest in court and most miserable while fighting with Elena. Oh, there had been a few nasty scenes with Sam, but only a few. Their divorce was probably as amicable as it was possible for such a cleavage in four lives to be. But life with her daughter had become hard fought, an unending screaming match and duel. She knew Elena had begun to lie to her constantly, unwaveringly, with an air of triumph. What could she do about it? Only throw herself further into work until the catastrophe arrived. Her beautiful daughter had become a hostile stranger who hated her and to whom nothing she said or pleaded or threatened had any meaning. Much of the time, she did not even know where Elena was, and if she asked, Elena boldly lied.

Now after the summer's mess, they had made a rapprochement. Suzanne did not understand why but she was too glad to question it. Elena had been more affectionate toward her than since she was a little girl, permitting Suzanne more expressions of her love. She even let herself be touched on occasion, hugged.

Suzanne sat beside Beverly's bed, holding her mother's withered hand. How much she had aged in the past year, as the strokes pinched and twisted her. Elena had been dyeing Beverly's hair, but the red coiffure looked incongruous around her wizened face. She had lost weight in spite of their best efforts to stuff her. Her muscles had slackened and shrunk. The biggest change was the fire gone from her eyes. Her eyes looked out but could not see much. The doctor had told Suzanne that Beverly had cataracts in both eyes, in addition to the blurring of her vision caused by the second stroke, but that he could not recommend an operation. Suzanne hoped they would be able to put this death over on the doctor, to persuade him it was natural. She prayed he would not probe, just simply sign the death certificate and let everything slide by. The hand in hers felt cold. Since Beverly's second stroke, medical interest in her condition had waned. Suzanne had tried to prepare the way by telling the doctor and aides how weak Beverly had become. She looked into her mother's eyes, eyes that had always seemed a clearer, harder green than her own. She must have inherited her myopia from her father, since Beverly had not worn glasses till she needed them for reading after she turned fifty. She had always loved Beverly's clear passionate gaze.

"How are you feeling?"

Beverly smiled. "Hopeful."

"What do you hope for?"

"De . . . liv . . . rance."

"Do you still want to go through with this tonight? There's plenty of time to change your mind." Suzanne could not keep the pleading from her voice.

"No!" Beverly shook her head from side to side three times. "Do . . . it."

What would it feel like to lie there in the bed Beverly was so weary of, and know that she would die in a matter of hours? Like a condemned prisoner, but Beverly was self-condemned. She did not see death as punishment or something to be feared, but as a release. Suzanne wished she could look out through her mother's eyes for just an hour to know if this was really what Beverly must have. Last night Suzanne had lain awake going through agonies of guilt, wondering if she had somehow let Beverly know indirectly how much it was taking out of all of them to care for her, what an enervating financial burden her support was, how overstretched Suzanne had been feeling. She had done her best to keep these feelings to herself, but she could never be sure she had suc-ceeded. She was so tired all the time, exhausted beyond any hope of repair in the brief hours of sleep she could steal. Perhaps she had not concealed her fatigue as well as she had imagined. She could not bear to think that.

"Want . . . first act . . . Mam . . . Butter . . ."

Suzanne rose and put on the CD. In the summer, she had put a speaker into this room so that Beverly could listen to music. That, and a little TV that could be operated from the bed. She had tried to make Beverly comfortable, she had tried. As she returned to sit by the bed in the flood of Puccini, she thought how weird it was that her mother's favorite opera should be about a submissive woman who killed herself for the love of a jerk. Suzanne did not care for opera: too rich, full-blown, overwrought for her tastes. She would rather listen to jazz or baroque music or Mozart. She had always found it out of character that Beverly should love opera. Beverly used to go to the City Opera or get cheap seats at the Met with a friend of hers who taught at City College. They would talk about tenors the way some women talked about movie stars or basketball players. Now the flood of passion seemed appropriate.

Beverly was lying back against her pillow with her eyes closed, waving her good hand languidly to the music. Mao lay curled on her belly.

"Isn't he heavy?"

"Keeps . . . warm."

When the first act had finished, Beverly motioned for her to get moving. Suzanne brought a tray with toast and broth. A light meal was supposed to prevent the stomach from rejecting the pills.

"Now we're supposed to wait half an hour."

"Play . . . second."

Suzanne put on the second act of the opera. She decided she would bury it with her mother, but then remembered that Beverly had already set up her cremation, making all her arrangements over the past two months, during the time she had been talking about wanting to die. "Want . . . tidy," she had said repeatedly. Beverly had little to leave. Her meager savings were long gone. The clothes she could no longer wear had been donated to Good Will months ago. She had given Elena her jewelry, mostly out-of-date costume jewelry except for an opal pendant and an onyx cat pin with tiny chips of emerald for eyes. To Suzanne, she left Mao. To Rachel, she bequeathed her own mother's wedding ring. She confided to Suzanne that she had worn it only when she was checking into hotels with various men. It was a wide lustrous gold band with a Hebrew inscription Suzanne could not read—but Rachel would be able to.

Laboriously Beverly printed on the pad, TELL R SORRY NOT WAIT.

"I know she'd want to say good-bye to you."

Beverly only gave her a crooked smile. "Time . . . now."

"Are you sure?"

"Sure." Beverly glared imperiously. "Bring . . . drink."

Suzanne dragged herself into the kitchen and mixed the ground-up pills into a mug of orange juice. She used a mug so that she could better mix the grainy white stuff into the juice. Finally she had it in suspension and experienced the strong impulse to wash it down the sink. Her hands were trembling. If she accidentally dropped it, that would be that. Finally she carried the mug in to Beverly, walking as slowly as she was able. She began to cry and stopped to snuffle back her tears, as she knew crying would anger Beverly. If this was going to be their very last time together, she did not want to taint it.

Beverly reached out. Suzanne slowly handed it to her. Beverly tasted it and made a face. "Ecch." However, she smiled wanly and drank it a gulp at a time. She reminded Suzanne of someone trying to cure hiccups by taking small sips of water. She took only sips but she kept at it, gagging once, pausing then for a minute. Finally she consumed the whole mug of drugged juice.

"There." She sighed. "Help me lie down."

"Do you want the music on?" Suzanne watched her mother carefully. Beverly could still throw up, and then it would be over. They could not go through getting all those drugs a second time. Her body might well reject the poison she was feeding it, and then Beverly would have to give this up.

"Let it . . ."

She took her mother's hand and held it. Their hands were exactly the same size, the same shape. She might never see or touch her mother's hand again. For a while, it seemed as if the pills would have no effect, and Suzanne had half an hour of hope that it was not going to happen. Perhaps Elena had mistaken the chemicals or the dosages. Beverly hummed occasionally along with the opera. She nodded to Suzanne and then freed her hand and petted Mao, who had moved to a position against her side. Her eyes fluttered shut, opened again, looked around once and again, then slowly the lids slid down. Her breathing grew more regular and deeper. Suzanne stared, wondering how she could tell the difference between normal sleep, for she often saw Beverly dozing open-mouthed in the daytime, and a mortal sleep. Suzanne would have liked to turn off the opera, but she did not want to wake Beverly by moving around the room. It felt as if it continued for an hour, but it was only twenty minutes. Then the conclusion came and silence arrived. She took Beverly's slack hand in her own. It felt a little cooler than normal and she chafed it gently. A shapely hand, still. Beverly had always been vain about her hands but never had a manicure in her life, never wore polish.

More or less silence. It was Saturday night and cars were careening up the hill and down again, local kids. A dog was barking hysterically. Someone was walking along the street calling a cat. "Max! Max!" Mournful appeal. She imagined calling after her mother, "Beverly! Beverly! Come back." It did not seem possible, what was happening, that she should be sitting here holding her mother's hand as her mother was leaving her, steadily, gradually, moving beyond the sound of her voice and the touch of her hand. She gazed at Beverly's gaunt face and felt she had never loved her as much. It could not end like this. The slight curve in her mother's nose, the way one eyebrow was more arched than the other, the softness of her unpierced earlobes, her high, fine cheekbones—all to be lost? She could not bear it. She had not spent enough time looking at Beverly, not enough time.

Beverly was breathing more deeply. She began to snore. Suzanne rose and paced into the living room and back, into the kitchen and back. She had eaten nothing for supper except the same toast and broth Beverly had consumed. She was not hungry, just anxious and exhausted. Coffee was what she wanted, but she was too wired already and could not make herself stand at the stove and make it. She kept wanting to shake Beverly by the shoulder and bring her back to consciousness, to demand a response. How could she let her mother slip away like this, further and further from her?

She decided she could run upstairs briefly to check on Marta, see if she needed anything. Marta did not know what they were doing; it was better if she didn't. Why implicate her, if anything went wrong? But Marta would think it strange if she did not appear. She was sitting at the kitchen table with her feet propped up. Suzanne remarked, "Your ankles look swollen."

"They are. All of me feels swollen." She patted her belly. "I keep thinking at least it's almost over, it's almost time. I'd forgotten how long the last month is—twice the normal length. Obviously I'm not having any more children after this. I just want to deliver her safely. I trust Helen. She's been my gynecologist for twenty-two years."

"I should get back. I just wanted to check in with you. Beverly's having a bad night."

"Don't leave. Stay. Let's just hang for a while."

"Not too long. Beverly isn't well. She has an appointment this week, Tuesday. The doctor wants to check if she had another ministroke, perhaps without us realizing it." She felt awkward and miserable lying to Marta, but she had to protect Marta and herself—and Elena. The fiction must be built up. "I have to get back down there. I don't like her being alone when she's so weak."

When she returned downstairs, Beverly was still snoring. Her breathing seemed slower. Mao raised his head to look at her. She imagined he was reproaching her. She very gently touched her mother's cool, slightly moist hand. Her mother's hands had always been dry and comfortingly warm—like Jake's, she thought suddenly—but since Beverly's stroke, they were often cold. She resumed her seat beside the bed. She was exhausted but did not want to take her gaze off Beverly's face. She still somehow hoped that Beverly would open her eyes, no matter how angry and disappointed she would be if the pills did not work. It was just after eleven. Suzanne wondered again if there were anything she could have said or promised or offered that would have kept Beverly with her.

Beverly's breathing grew shallower and less frequent. Her mouth had fallen open. Suzanne no longer hesitated to get up and move around the room, for she doubted anything she did was likely to wake her mother now. The only question was whether Beverly would slip into a coma, which in itself would simply send her to the hospital where they would discover the residue of the pills in her, or whether she would, as she had begged them, die at last. She hoped Elena had gotten the amounts and the drug mixture right. She should have checked it. Sitting there beside the unconscious Beverly, she could not believe that she had not checked out Elena's results. She had simply, blindly accepted them, because the act they were committing was too painful for her to deal with in the detail required to confirm Elena's conclusions. She was ashamed. Again she sat beside the bed and held Beverly's inert hand in her own, hoping that on some level her mother could feel her presence and be comforted by it. She spoke now and then, "Mother, it's me. I'm here with you. It's Suzanne." She spoke just in case Beverly could sense her presence or the affection she was trying to project. She sat holding the limp hand and weeping, slow tears flowing down until her face was swollen and her blouse, wet on the bodice, more tears than she thought her body could hold. The tears seeped out and out.

When Elena arrived, just after twelve-thirty, Beverly's breathing was slower, shallower, but ongoing. "I'll take over," Elena said. "Just let me change out of my work clothes and I'll sit with her."

"I think I should stay."

"You look exhausted. At least get undressed and lie down for half an hour. I'll wake you if anything seems to be happening. I'd like to be alone with her for a while."

Reluctantly and eagerly at the same time, Suzanne backed out of the room and went to undress and lie down. She did not intend to sleep. But she did.

49

Elena

Elena looked in on her mother. Suzanne had put on the flannel night-gown with little red posies Rachel had given her and was lying on her bed with a law journal open under her loosened hand. She had, as Elena hoped, dozed off.

It was a quarter after one. Now or never, she thought. She took her promise to her grandmother seriously, perhaps religiously. She doubted if Rachel would understand her use of the word, but it felt sacred to her. To untether Grandma and set her free. Elena did not exactly believe in an afterlife, but she thought something of everyone remained in the room, in the wind, in the minds of those who had loved them. She loved Beverly. No one else in her life had ever cared for her as wholly, as sweetly, as nonjudgmentally as her grandmother did. There was a price for such love, and she was about to pay it.

She took a plastic freezer bag into the sickroom where Beverly had been lying since May. It always smelled of stale body odors, but she was not squeamish. Gently she lifted Beverly's head. How light she was now. Beverly was breathing hoarsely and did not wake. Elena doubted if she ever would, unless her stomach was pumped now, but she might remain like this. Dr. Kevorkian would know if Beverly was really dying, but not Suzanne and not herself. She kissed her grandma on the forehead, and then on her cheeks. She wanted to kiss her lips, but Beverly's mouth was open and slack. Then Elena fitted the plastic bag over Beverly's face and tied it under the chin, tightly. She had read that sometimes unconscious patients would instinctively paw at the bag, trying to remove it. Beverly did not. Elena hoped she had it tight enough. It moved with Beverly's breath. Elena was unsure whether she had done it correctly. If only she could ask someone, but the world was asleep, and there was no one to ask. Elena watched. It was her duty to go the last steps her mother could not take. She took her grandmother's limp hand and kissed it. Mao got up, stretched, and went to her to be petted.

"Even though she left you to Mother, I'd take you with me, if I knew where I was going, understand?" She rubbed under his chin, the way he liked best. "Roommates are always iffy, but it's time for me to move on. If I get a good place to live, I'll come get you. That's a promise."

She had thought Beverly might jerk or kick or give some sign she was suffocating, but she did not. Instead, the breathing stopped, started again with a gasp and then once again stopped.

"Grandma, go in peace. Let yourself go," she said softly, again and again, stroking the limp hand that hung out from the blanket.

The breathing stopped, started again, stopped. She touched Beverly's neck. There was no pulse. She waited, holding the limp cold hand. The breathing did not resume. She smelled urine. In the morning, she would clean up. Carefully she lifted Beverly's head again and took off the plastic bag and put it in the garbage. Then she thought better about that and instead burned it in a flame from the gas stove, holding the corner with kitchen tongs. That residue she flushed down the toilet. She did the same with the printout from the summer. *Let Me Die Before I Wake* she carried down into the basement and stuffed way into a box containing her summer clothes. She would dispose of it tomorrow. Then she washed her hands, not of the act, but out of caution.

When she came out of the bathroom, Suzanne was awake and waiting to use it. She noticed neither of them used Beverly's bathroom. "Mother, I think she died about fifteen minutes ago."

"Why didn't you get me up? I should have stayed awake."

"It happened so gradually, I was sitting beside her, and I didn't even see it. Her breathing just got shallower and shallower and slower and slower and then I realized it had stopped. I never saw it happen. I just looked at her and realized she wasn't breathing any longer."

"It was peaceful like that?"

"I didn't even see it happen."

Suzanne went into Beverly's room and bent over her. She touched Beverly's face. "She's getting cold already." She picked up Mao and carried him off to her room. "We must go to bed, so we can discover the body in the morning. We have to get rid of those bottles."

"I took them away with me when I left. I left them in a Dumpster on Beacon Hill."

"Thank you." Suzanne turned, still holding Mao, and kissed her on the cheek. "Thank you, sweetheart. I love you."

Elena wondered for a moment if her mother had guessed what she had done; she doubted it. No one would ever know. Except if she loved someone intensely and she trusted them, maybe she would tell them. But she knew and was proud of herself. She had come through for Beverly, she had come through. She was a better person than she had been, even if most of society would never think so. She was ready to leave home again and plunge back into her life. She had kept her most important promise. She had dared to keep her word to her grandmother. Two small tears ran down her face, and she brushed them away. She gazed back at Grandma lying there, the empty body, and she thought she could feel Beverly thanking her for release, for silence, for the end.

50

Suzanne: A Year Later

Suzanne placed the yahrzeit candle for her mother in the bathtub, for fear of fire. Besides, as she admitted to herself, she found it beautiful to wake in the night and go into the bathroom lit by the small flickering of the candle in its glass. She woke several times that night and lay awake from five on. Today Karla was coming with her daughter Rosella and the twins. Rosella's husband, Tyrone, couldn't take off work. They were to arrive from Brooklyn by noon, so that they could all go to the cemetery for the unveiling and be done before sundown, as it was Friday. Elena was going to meet them at the cemetery. Rachel had already arrived and was sleeping in her old room—sleeping far better than her mother, as Suzanne could tell when she checked on her. It was ridiculous to look in on Rachel as if she were a baby, but having her in the house was a precious treat, making it impossible for Suzanne to resist a glimpse of her sleeping daughter lying on her side clutching the pillow to her, as once she had clutched a stuffed rabbit.

Marta drove the van, with Rachel and Karla's entire family onboard. Suzanne held the squirming Emily on her lap. She was blond like Marta, chubby, avid, curious, and had just begun to talk, more or less. She was still crawling everywhere and in bursts she struggled to get down. She was used to being held by Suzanne, so that was no problem, but all the people excited her. Rachel began making faces at her till she was wildly giggling. "Cool it a little, if you can," Marta said over her shoulder.

Karla, sitting up front with Marta, turned to beam at the baby. "Such a darling girl! How lucky you are. I was forty when I adopted my first little girl. I wish she could be here today."

"You know Suwanda can't be coming east all the time, Mama," Rosella said, leaning on the back of Suzanne's seat. "She's paying off her condo, and San Diego is plenty expensive. She thought the world of Aunt Beverly, so she'd come if she could."

Suzanne began to wish she had driven her own car, but then she would have had half the relatives in it anyhow. She just wanted to be quiet and find her core, not to lose this odd ritual connection with Beverly. Rachel was looking at her and understood.

"People, I think we should start to get into the mood. We should be thinking about Grandma. This is a memorial for her. To show respect for the dead and to remember her and thus keep her alive in our lives." It was Rachel's rabbi voice, fuller, more commanding than her normal speaking voice. Suzanne was just getting used to the change that would come over Rachel when she was being official, when she was on duty. Suzanne was grateful to lapse into silence. "Rosella," Rachel turned around. "Would you like to hold Emily for a while and give my mother a rest?"

Suzanne thanked Rachel with her eyes and handed Emily to Rosella. The twins set up a clamor, but Suzanne was able to close her eyes and concentrate. A year and a day since Beverly had left them. The pain of that night had never healed. It was still raw within her, but she could not believe Elena and she had done the wrong thing. Beverly would never have acquiesced in continuing. It would have been a long quarrel, not good for any of them. But the raw wound persisted and the guilt. It would never leave her.

A year ago, she had buried her mother. At least the cemetery was not far. She had been back twenty times to the grave. Now came the unveiling of the monument. As they drove in under the metal archway, Suzanne stirred herself to give directions. A car was already there— Elena's. Suzanne admitted to herself she had expected Elena to be late, but she understood when she saw Jaime and Elena together at the grave site. Jaime was never late. Under his charge, Elena made appointments even with her mother and kept them.

Suzanne had found it hard to take when Elena had moved in with him, but she had gradually got used to it. At least she liked and trusted Jaime, which was more than she could say for most of Elena's past choices. He was wearing a suit, a dark suit in which he was radiant. Elena was also in a suit. She had several styles now: her former flash at the restaurant, drab student outfits for her classes, and lately a new conservative wardrobe Jaime must have picked out. She suspected those outfits had to do with Elena's image of herself as a therapist—and the need to accompany Jaime to various functions.

Elena was standing over the grave talking to Beverly about Mao, when Suzanne came up. Elena had her grandmother's cat. As always Suzanne was a little dazzled by her own daughter. She and Jaime were a striking and gorgeous couple. Suzanne sighed. Jaime had his law degree and was clerking for a justice of the Supreme Judicial Court. That was a year's gig, and then what? She could not tell if Elena was seriously interested in him, nor could she ask her, nor could she guess from Elena's attitude. She opened her hands mentally and let the matter drop. Elena and she had a warmer relationship these days, but she could never presume on their new cordiality to pry.

As they all shuffled up to the site where a bit of canvas still hung over the stone she had ordered, Rachel took charge. Suzanne remembered meeting her when she returned from Israel deeply, darkly tanned, leaner and more defined. Her eyes looked bigger and greener against her dark skin. Her hair was cropped short to a halo of curls. That assurance, that hardening Suzanne had noticed from the moment Rachel got off the plane was still with her. The daughter Suzanne had sent off was not the daughter she got back, but one who was at once less and more than she had been.

"Judaism gives us great leeway in what we think happens after death. We are not required to believe in an afterlife or reincarnation or heaven or hell or anything in between. We are required to respect and remember the dead. We are here to share our loss of Beverly, our grandmother, our mother, our sister, our aunt, our friend. When I look at this family, I see a legacy she left us. We are a multicultural, multiracial family, and a monument to the risks she took and the bravery she demonstrated in her civil rights work and in her organizing for those who needed her. She sought justice, and to go on seeking justice is her bequest to all of us. Justice in the courts, justice in our religion, justice on the job, justice in the streets and in the legislatures of our land. Justice for everyone, not just the privileged or the fortunate. That is Beverly's legacy to us. We have lost someone dear and precious. *Ha-makom yenahem otcha v'otach.* May the Eternal One comfort you and may being in this place together today bring comfort to all of us." She pulled the cloth from the stone, black marble engraved with Peh Nun, Here Lies, Beverly's Hebrew name, Batsheva bat Shimone v'Ranit, her English name, Beverly Blume, and her dates in both calendars.

Rachel was reciting the Twenty-third Psalm in Hebrew, printed phonetically on the sheets she had handed out. Then she launched into the *El Malay Rachamim*, while they more or less joined in. Suzanne still remembered it from the funeral. Compassion. They—she and Elena—had tried to demonstrate compassion to Beverly. She would never rest quite easy in her mind that they had done the right thing, but at least they had done what Beverly had asked of them, however difficult. *Rachamim* was such a beautiful word, but so hard sometimes to act upon. Compassion, pity. It seemed larger than those English words. There had been no inquest. Beverly's primary stroke doctor had signed the death certificate after a few perfunctory questions, as Elena and she stood holding hands in the rigor of fear. They had buried Beverly the next day.

Now together they recited the Mourners' Kaddish, which Suzanne had memorized during the last year. She had managed to get to the nearest acceptable synagogue once a week to say it as it was supposed to be recited, in a minyan, but all other days, she had said it in her bedroom upon rising, and that was the best she could do. Respect and remembrance. That she had given, freely. Her eyes flooded briefly with tears and she snuffled them back.

Rachel had brought a bag of stones so that those who had not thought of it could each have a stone to place on Beverly's grave. "Here at the *bet ha-olam*, the permanent place, we place a remembrance on the *matzevah* to show we have come and paid our respect." Flowers were never used. A stone lasted. Besides, Beverly had not been a flower sort of person. She had never planted a garden or tended one in her life, and she was not the sort of woman to whom men brought flowers or who would ever buy them for herself. Men had taken her out to dinner and on an occasional trip; had brought her bottles of wine and schnapps; had given her scarves and costume jewelry. And one child. But never flowers.

She only wished, looking over to Jaime and Elena standing with less than an inch between them, that she had Jake with her. She had argued his appeal and he was out while it was decided. Still, he had not completely forgiven her for failing him, as he saw it. He had come out of prison wan and haggard. She had told him the truth about Beverly's death, and perhaps that made some difference. He was still dealing with what had happened to him. On spring break she would fly out to see him, and then they would resume being lovers or they would not. She tried to avoid thinking about it but did not succeed. She needed him now, but she had not been with him when he needed her. They would begin tentatively and then they would see what had survived between them. She put the stone she had brought with her on the top of the black marble marker. "Good-bye," she said softly. "Good-bye, Mother."

She waited until Rachel stood alone again and then she went up to her younger daughter and kissed her on the mouth. "Thank you."

Rachel looked mildly surprised. "You liked the little service? I wanted to keep it simple."

"I want to thank you for putting it together for me, what I never saw before. That I'm actually doing the same thing my mother was, in a different context. Justice. Thank you, Rachel. That was healing."

Rachel took her hand. "That's good to hear. This year, I do more and more services, but sometimes I feel like a fraud. I'm pretending to be a rabbi, 'cause I'm still a student and I know how much I don't know yet. But you make me feel as if I'm real."

"Oh, you're real, sweetheart." Suzanne looked at her family straggling toward the van and the car. "We're all real and we try."

"A sixteenth-century rabbi said that keeping the precepts of our parents is more important than saying Kaddish for them."

Suzanne smiled for the first time that day. "I don't care what some sixteenth-century rabbi said, Rachel. I care what you say. And you've given me some meaning in this. A sense of continuity with her. I can promise her, we will remember." She took Rachel's hand and pulled her along to catch up with Elena, whose arm she took, so that they left together, her between her daughters as Karla walked with her own little family. Away they went slowly from the place where she had left what remained of her mother, except for memories and the quest for justice. Maxine's appeal was going forward even as she wasted away in Framingham Prison, and Jake was free at last. Suzanne would win that appeal. The trial transcript revealed that the judge had been wildly biased. She would go on teaching and seeking justice, no matter how flawed and partial. Justice in the world, but for each other in intimacy, mercy and as much kindness as she could muster.

The very best of Piatkus fiction is now available in paperback as well as hardcover. Piatkus paperbacks, where *every* book is special.

The prices shown above were correct at the time of going to press. However, Piatkus Books reserve the right to show new retail prices on covers which may differ from those previously advertised in the text or elsewhere.

Piatkus Books will be available from your bookshop or newsagent, or can be ordered from the following address:

Piatkus Paperbacks, PO Box 11, Falmouth, TR10 9EN

Alternatively you can fax your order to this address on 01326 374 888 or e-mail us at books@barni.avel.co.uk

Payments can be made as follows: Sterling cheque, Eurocheque, postal order (payable to Piatkus Books) or by credit card, Visa/Mastercard. Do not send cash or currency. UK and B.F.P.O. customers should allow £1.00 postage and packing for the first book, 50p for the second and 30p for each additional book ordered to a maximum of £3.00 (7 books plus).

Overseas customers, including Eire, allow £2.00 for postage and packing for the first book, plus £1.00 for the second and 50p for each subsequent title ordered.

NAME (block letters)_____

ADDRESS _____

_____

I enclose my remittance for £_____

I wish to pay by Visa/Mastercard   Expiry Date _____
